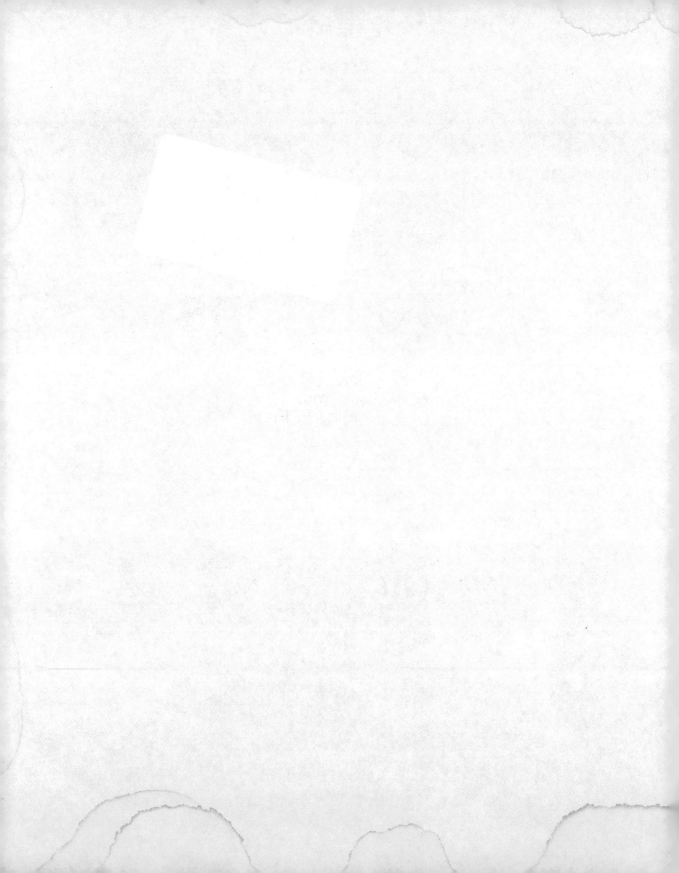

PC *Excel* Business Solutions

Elna R. Tymes
with
Charles E. Prael

COMPUTE! Books
Greensboro, North Carolina
Radnor, Pennsylvania

Cover design: Anthony Jacobson

Printed in the United States of America

10 9 8 7 6 5 4 3 2 1

Library of Congress Cataloging-in-Publication Data
Tymes, Elna.
    PC Excel business solutions / Elna R. Tymes, with Charles E.
Prael.
        p.   cm.
    Includes index.
    ISBN 0-87455-159-5
    1. Microsoft Excel (Computer program)   2. Microcomputers—
Programming.   3. Business—Data processing.   I. Prael, Charles E.
II. Title
HF5548.4.M523T94   1988
650'.028'55369—dc19
                                              88-39929
                                              CIP

COMPUTE! Books, Post Office Box 5406, Greensboro, North Carolina 27403, (919) 275-9809, is a Capital Cities/ABC, Inc. company and is not associated with any manufacturer of personal computers. IBM, IBM PC, PC-XT, PC-AT, and PS/2 are registered trademarks of International Business Machines Corporation. Lotus 1-2-3 is a registered trademark of Lotus Development Corporation. *Excel* is a registered trademark of Microsoft Corporation.

Contents

Foreword

Looking to take full advantage of the power of *Excel* but just haven't mastered the efficient use of functions and macros? Or perhaps you're already a power user of *Excel* but are looking for an easy-to-use guide to business applications. For the solutions to these and many other problems, you'll find *PC Excel Business Solutions* a powerful resource.

PC Excel Business Solutions explains, in plain English, all the functions available for constructing *Microsoft Excel* spreadsheets and macros. It then goes even further by leading you through the creation of important business applications for spreadsheets that will ease the day-to-day headaches of managing your business and investing your money. Assuming a familiarity with the *Excel* environment and spreadsheets in general, it's written for the all *Excel* user with specific business needs.

Chapters 1 and 2 offer a brief look at the program, providing ideas for using the spreadsheet and getting you going with a discussion of *Excel* and its hardware requirements. These two chapters also tell you how to use *Excel* with extended memory, *Windows*, a math coprocessor, and networks. You'll learn about working with linked files, workspaces, and importing files from other spreadsheets.

The second section of this book is a handy reference to the huge array of spreadsheet and macro functions available with *Excel*. These include:

Macro Functions

Dialog Box Functions
Action Equivalent Functions
Customizing Functions
Control Functions
Value-Returning Functions

Spreadsheet Functions

Date and Time Functions
Logical Functions
Mathematical Functions
Trigonometric Functions
Statistical Functions
Financial Functions
Information Functions
Lookup Functions
Text Functions
Database Functions
Matrix Functions

Each function is accompanied by a thorough explanation. Where further explanation would be useful, you'll find clear, helpful examples to show how the function might look entered in a spreadsheet, along with the value it would return and a suggestion or two for using the function.

The last part of the book puts everything together by building spreadsheets from the functions and macros available— spreadsheets to meet the daily needs of busy managers in any kind of environment.

Business owner and consultant Elna R. Tymes and author Charles E. Prael share their thorough knowledge of computers and business using everyday language and realistic examples. When you're finished with this book you'll be an *Excel* pro.

Acknowledgments

No book is ever written in a vacuum. We wish to thank:

Bill Gladstone, Waterside Productions, Superagent.

Stephen Levy, Editor, COMPUTE! Books, for more than a small amount of long-distance hand-holding.

Rob Bixby for all the right editorial questions.

Peter Willis and Bruce Brand for persistence, eagerness, and patience about late-night and Sunday meetings while we tried to debug the macros.

Bob Fry and Angie Jones for all-purpose encouragement.

ELNA R. TYMES
CHARLES E. PRAEL

Part 1
Introduction to *Excel*

Chapter 1

What Is *Excel?*

Microsoft Excel is a spreadsheet program that incorporates a graphics program, database features, and a number of other features that allow you to share data with other programs. Built into the spreadsheet are a large number of powerful functions and macro programming commands, allowing you to develop more complex and automated spreadsheets as you get used to the program.

Excel's database features let you create and modify records, sort your data, and query it with criteria you specify.

A full-function spreadsheet such as *Excel* lets you construct a spreadsheet with formulas and built-in functions so you can play "what if?" with your data as frequently as you need, letting the program display the results for each new set of assumptions.

Excel's power lets you run multiple-year analyses of real estate portfolios, statistical analyses of several years' worth of population changes, monthly budget forecasts broken down by department, or sensitivity analysis on market share data. Then, when you've got a set of data you want to show someone else, you can present it as a worksheet, share it with one or more other files, or turn it into any of seven different kinds of charts, formatted to best suit your needs. Or, if you prefer, you can enter your data directly into a graph.

Because number-crunching usually means your results can be used by others, you can share your spreadsheet files with a co-worker, perhaps one who doesn't even use *Excel.* So long as the destination program can recognize one of the types of files that *Excel* is capable of producing, your spreadsheet file can be given to your co-worker on a floppy disk, or sent electronically, and used in his or her office. You can also excerpt data from your current worksheet and use it with other worksheets.

What You Get with the Package

When you opened the *Microsoft Excel* package, you found several disks and several books. The disks were designed for the type of computer on which *Excel* can run: either an IBM PS/2 Series, an IBM PC-AT, a Compaq Deskpro 386, or a computer compatible with one of these models. Your package will include 3½-inch disks and/or 5½-inch floppy disks in a density that works with one of these machines. *Excel* can't work on an IBM PC-XT unless you have Extended Memory, and even then it works very slowly. It is not recommended that you try to run *Excel* on an IBM PC-XT.

Once you install *Excel,* you'll discover that Microsoft took an approach similar to many other software manufacturers, and provided a built-in tutorial with the software. You can get to the tutorial any time you want by selecting the Help menu, and choosing the Tutorial.

Figure 1-1. *Excel's* Initial Tutorial Screen

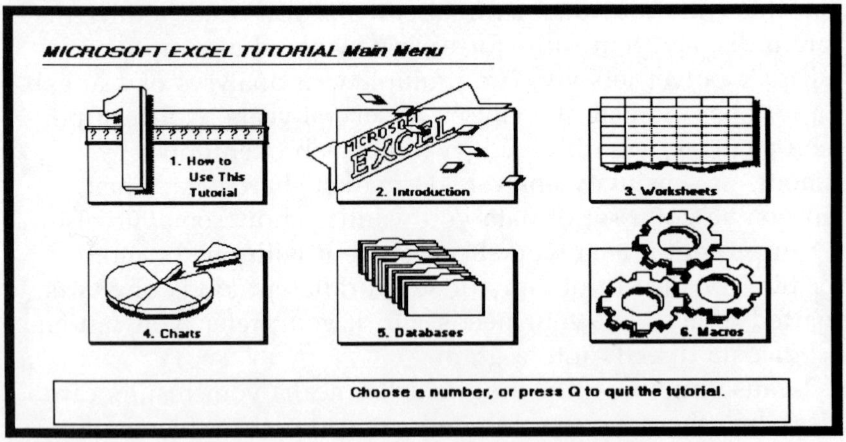

The tutorial is usually stored on disk when you install *Excel,* which means you can get to it any time you need a refresher on some point. As the initial screen (Figure 1-1) depicts, the tutorial has six general parts. You can choose any of them and see lessons on how to use *Excel.* The lessons offer several alternatives for learning as well, including several screens of information, some exercises, and even some hints on what to do if you can't figure something out by yourself. Generally, you can skip from topic to topic as the need arises.

The Feature Guide (Figure 1-2), also available from the Help menu, gives you more data arranged differently from the Tutorial. With it, you can get instant information about how to state a command, how to use a feature, and other data.

Figure 1-2. Feature Guide Initial Screen

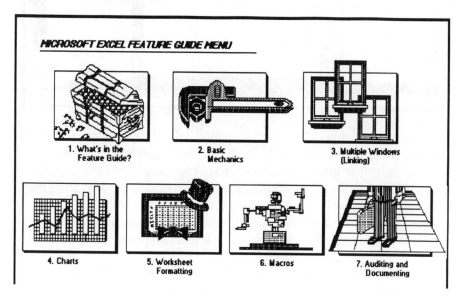

Generally, each section has a quick introduction, a demonstration of how to use the features discussed, a "side trip" showing some of the options and procedures, and some hands-on examples.

And if that's not enough, press F1 to see an alphabetically arranged index of help topics (Figure 1-3).

Figure 1-3. Help Topic Index

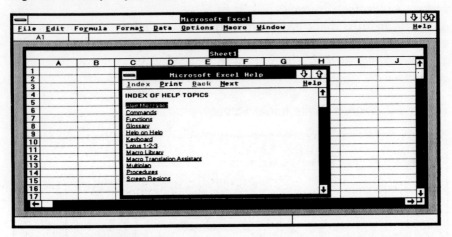

Then, of course, there are the manuals. The reference manual is arranged alphabetically by topic, with a complete discussion of the topic and any options that may apply. There are also cross-references to other topics that may provide related information. The Functions and Macros manual is basically a reference manual, listing each of the functions and showing how to use them, plus several chapters about the macro functions available within *Excel* and how to use macros.

Additionally, there are two other manuals. You'll use Getting Started and Quick Reference when you begin the Tutorial and then later when you want a quick reminder about how to do things within *Excel*. The Sampler and Idea Book provides some examples of how to use *Excel* for reporting, financial analysis, tracking data, planning and forecasting, scientific equations, and automating work.

You can also sign up for ongoing support, by calling the Microsoft Customer Support number, at (206) 882-8089 in Washington and Alaska, or at (800) 426-9400. However, to be eligible for the support program, you must register your copy of *Excel*, using the Registration Card that comes with the package.

What Can You Do with a Spreadsheet?

Suppose, for a moment, you have an annual budget with monthly income and expense portions. You'd like to know whether your monthly actual income and expense figures are on track. Can you use a spreadsheet for that?

Figure 1-4 is one small company's answer. Notice that the figures taken from the annual budget (which is stored in a different file) include those in the columns marked June Budget, YTD Budgeted, and Annual Budget. For the month of June, we've added figures for June Real, and computed the deviation from the budgeted amount, as well as the YTD Actual figures.

Figure 1-4. Budgeted Versus Actual Figures

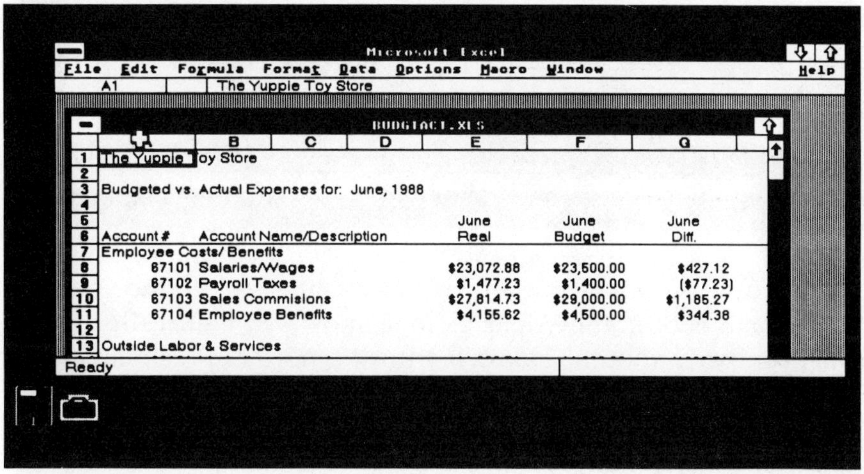

Suppose you're trying to weigh various investment strategies for some of your clients. You can do it with an ordinary *Excel* worksheet created in minutes. With it, you could make some basic recommendations to a client, and use the same figures for a year-end performance summary. As market conditions change, it's simple to change the percentages to reflect the new projections.

Or, consider the schedule in Figure 1-5, created with *Excel*. It shows different job requirements, when they're needed, and who's going to fill them. The schedule was created with *Excel*.

Figure 1-5. Stage Crew Schedule

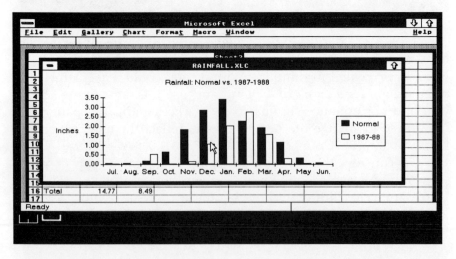

	A	B	C	D	E	F	G	H	I
1	Dotty White Dance Studio								
2				Show		Aft. & Eve.	Eve.		
3			Tech Setup	Preset	Rehearsal	Show	Show		
4			6/3/88	6/12/88	6/12/88	6/14/88	6/15/88		
5									
6	Stage Manager		Jeff S.	Jeff S.	Jeff S.	Jeff S.	Jeff S.		
7	Master Elec.	Glen B.	Glen B.	Glen B.	Glen B.	Glen B.	Glen B.		
8	Elec.		none	Rachel C.	Rachel C.	Rachel C.	Rachel C.		
9	Elec.		none	Jeremy	Jeremy	Jeremy	Jeremy		
10	Elec.		none	Jon B.	Jon B.	Jon B.	Jon B.		
11	Grips		none	Bruce M.	Bruce M.	Bruce M.	Bruce M.		
12	Sound		none	Ron C.	Ron C.	Ron C.	Ron C.		
13	House Manager		none	none	none	Brian M.	Brian M.		
14	Usher		none	none	none	Melinda	Gene H.		
15									
16									
17									

You can use data from an *Excel* worksheet to produce many different kinds of graphs, like the one shown in Figure 1-6, which compares monthly rainfall with the normal precipitation.

Figure 1-6. Rainfall Chart

What about financial analysis? How can *Excel* help you do that? One of the very best applications of a sophisticated spreadsheet is in its ability to do "What if?" analyses on numbers. One such application helps you see the results of different financial options.

Suppose you're setting up a small business. You need some idea of what kind of capital you'll need to invest before the business can stand on its own feet, and you'll also need ongoing help in the form of billing and invoicing statements for individual customers, monthly income statements, statements of accounts receivable and accounts payable, salary and tax worksheets, and a host of accounting and finance forms. Can a spreadsheet help you there?

Absolutely. We'll show you, through models in the back of this book, some sample worksheets you can adapt to your own situation and use with *Excel* in a business. With *Excel,* you can easily set up these worksheets to "talk" with one another, sharing data and updating figures whenever needed.

Here's an example of a spreadsheet that utilizes this unique communication feature, taken from the models included with the *Excel* disks. In this example, divisions from four separate countries are reporting figures to the main office. Each of the country reports includes figures in dollars, which must be updated to the current currency conversion factors in order to be accurate. Then all the divisional reports must be integrated into one final report.

The four quarterly reports from Australia, Great Britain, Japan, and West Germany can be used on the same screen, using *Excel's* windowing capabilities. Here's what they look like initially.

Figure 1-7. Four Divisional Reports

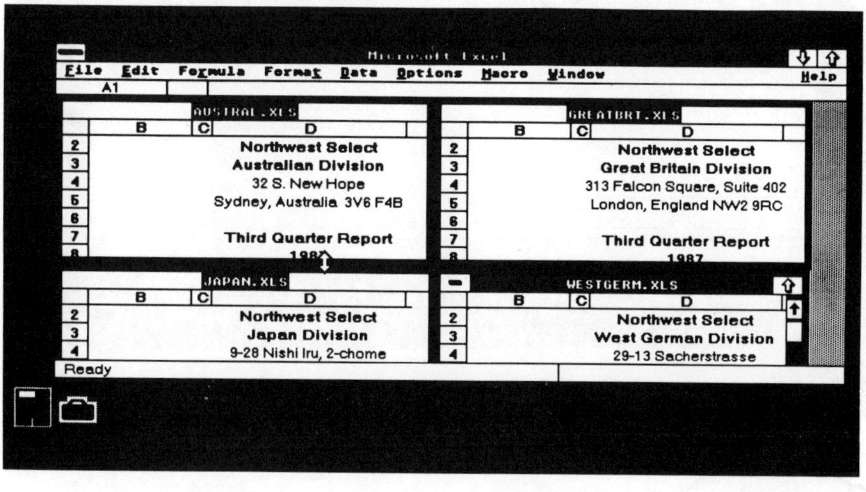

Microsoft included a currency conversion macro that helps you convert a foreign currency into U.S. dollars:

Figure 1-8. Currency Conversion Macro

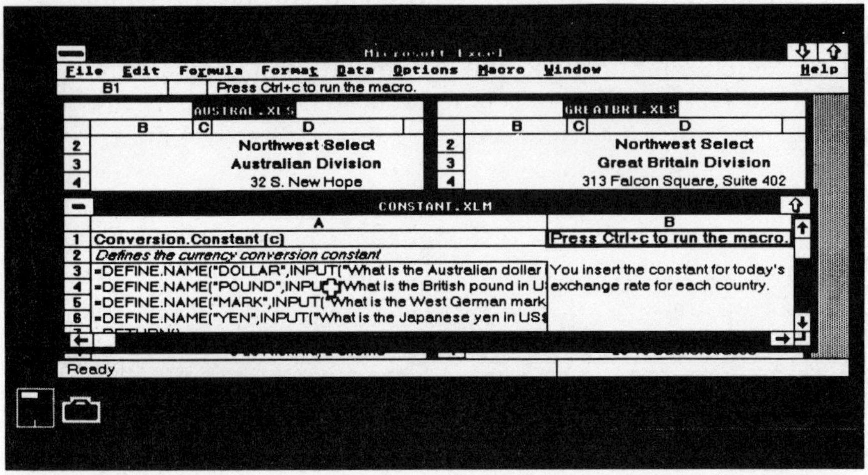

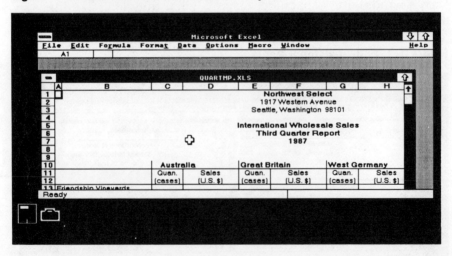

Once the figures have been correctly stated, you simply use them in a consolidated income statement, as Northwest Select did for its wine sales in the report in Figure 1-9.

Figure 1-9. Consolidated Third Quarter Report

And if you want, you can compare how the divisions are doing on sales of a particular product by charting the figures:

Figure 1-10. Chart of Chardonnay Sales

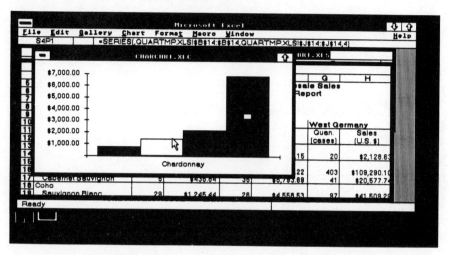

There's a lot more you can do with *Excel*. With some exploration of the program and a little practice, you can turn out reports like these with just a few minutes' work.

What's in This Book

This is an intermediate-level book about *Microsoft Excel*. It assumes you've already learned the basics about using *Excel* to produce a worksheet, so it doesn't go into any great detail about the commands. However, Chapters 3 and 4 give a complete listing of the worksheet functions and the macro commands and functions. Chapters 5 through 10 are devoted to business examples with worksheets, charts, and macros, and suggestions on how you can use *Excel* in similar situations.

Summary

This introductory chapter has given you a brief overview of some of the things you can do with *Excel,* and how to learn from things included in the package. We've shown you some examples of the kind of worksheets and other reports you can produce with *Excel.*

Chapter 2

Getting Started with *Excel*

Hardware Requirements

Microsoft Excel requires the following equipment:

Personal Computer
IBM Personal System/2, Models 25, 30, 50, 60 or 80, or compatible
IBM AT or compatible
IBM XT or compatible (with accelerator card)
Compaq 386 Deskpro or compatible
Compaq Portable II or III
AT&T Personal Computer
Tandy Model 1000

Graphics Card
IBM VGA or compatible
IBM EGA or compatible
MCGA or CGA
Hercules Graphics card or compatible with high resolution monochrome display
Compaq Portable II or III plasma display
AT&T color or monochrome display
Tandy 1000 monochrome display

Note: The quality and speed of the display will vary with the type of graphics card used.

Hard Disk
Hard disk with at least 5Mb of available space

Memory
640K

Operating System
DOS 3.0 or higher, 3.3 recommended

Note: MS-DOS versions higher than 3.0 may be needed for applications where *Excel* is running on a network, or for certain models of computers.

Recommended Optional Equipment

Printers and Plotters
Laser printers
Hewlett-Packard Laserjet and compatibles
IBM Personal Pageprinter
Apple LaserWriter and compatibles
PostScript-compatible devices
Other printers
IBM Proprinter
IBM Graphics printer and compatibles
Epson MX80, FX80 and compatibles
Any printer compatible with *Microsoft Windows* version 2.0 or higher
Plotters
Hewlett-Packard plotters such as 7470A and compatibles

Note: The number of fonts and typestyles built into *Excel* let you take advantage of a laser printer's high resolution and variable-size printing. While laser-printed output is ideal for presentation-quality graphics, *Excel* will also print spreadsheets, text, and charts on any of a number of dot-matrix printers, but at a lower resolution.

Mouse
Microsoft Mouse
IBM Personal System/2 Mouse
AT&T Mouse
Mouse Systems Mouse connected to either COM1 or COM2
VisiOn Mouse connected to either COM1 or COM2

Note: *Microsoft Excel* supports any pointing device compatible with *Microsoft Windows,* version 2.0 or higher. The setup menu lists drivers for the pointing devices listed above.

Extended Memory

Extended memory refers to memory beyond the normal 640K of resident random access memory (RAM) in your computer. This extra memory allows you to use the standard memory in your computer more efficiently when you have a portion of the program plus one or more large models in use.

While the maximum recommended size for *Excel* models is 100K, you can build considerably larger and more complex models if you have the memory to hold them. Most models will run faster anyway with an extended memory board, because some of the data that would otherwise occupy the regular RAM can be stored in the extended memory section. This in turn allows more of the *Excel* program to be stored in regular RAM, and thus allows the program to run faster than if it had to fetch portions from disk, as it normally does. Finally, if you're planning on running other large applications while running *Excel,* an extended memory card is a must.

You can get instructions on installing an extended memory card from your dealer when you buy one. You'll also need to consult the special section in the Setup program that deals with Extended Memory.

If you're planning on running several large applications simultaneously, you'll also need to run *Excel* under *Microsoft Windows* version 2.0 or higher, and use an expanded memory board that supports the Lotus/Intel/Microsoft specification, version 4.0.

Microsoft Windows

Microsoft recommends that you run *Excel* under *Microsoft Windows,* version 2.0 or higher. *Excel* can run by itself but it doesn't have the ability without *Microsoft Windows* to let you run two or more applications at once, transfer data between programs, or have as quick and easy access to the DOS commands. If you're thinking of making use of *Excel's* file transfer abilities between different programs, *Microsoft Windows* is probably a good idea.

On computers that use the Intel 80386 processor, you can use *Microsoft Windows/386,* which allows *Excel* to use the special features and memory management built into the Intel 80386 chip.

Math Coprocessor

You may want to install a math coprocessor on your computer, since its installation makes *Excel* run faster when it's performing multiplication, division, exponentiation, or trigonometric functions. Math coprocessors supported by *Excel* include the Intel 8087, 80287, and 80387.

Your computer may already have one of these coprocessors installed. Consult your dealer. If you want to install one yourself, follow the coprocessor manufacturer's instructions. *Excel* needs no special instructions to work with a math coprocessor.

Networks

You can use *Excel* on a network, provided it's one of those listed here, or it supports the formats used by the networks listed, or it's compatible with *Microsoft Windows*, version 2.0 or higher.

IBM PC Network
IBM Token Ring Network
AT&T Starlan
Ungermann-Bass/One
3Com 3+
3Com EtherSeries
Novell Netware

If you want to use *Excel* in a network environment, you'll need to install it in a network directory. This will require that you have read/write access to the network's file directory. The Setup program guides you through installation on a network if you choose this mode of operation. However, be sure your network's file access capabilities are compatible with *Windows* and *Excel* before you start.

If you want to run *Excel* from a network but still maintain your custom screen colors, fonts, menus, printers, and other default settings, you'll need to create a special WIN.INI file. *Excel* checks this file whenever it's started and uses the settings it finds there.

When *Excel* is installed on a network, the network file directory uses the version of WIN.INI that pertains to the entire network. You'll need to copy this to your personal directory, and then tailor it to your preferences. For a more complete discussion of how to do this, see the section called *Networks with Microsoft Excel* in the *Excel Reference Guide*.

Be aware, however, that if you're using *Excel* on a network, others may have access to your files, just as you'll have access to some of theirs. You can control this by specifying the mode in which a file is opened; you may allow others read/write access, or read-only access. These are controlled through the Read Only check box when you use the File Open command.

You may also create links between your *Excel* document and a document that's shared on the network. When you do this, your document is updated whenever the shared document is updated. We'll look at linking in more detail in Chapter 11.

Probably the most common use of a network is to share printers between several users. You'll want to use the File Printer Setup command to select the printer you want when you're ready to print, once the printers have been installed on *Excel* (meaning that *Excel* recognizes they're available). See Chapter 7, Printing, for more information on using printers with *Excel* in a network environment.

What's on the Screen?

When you start *Excel*, a blank worksheet appears on your computer screen, looking like Figure 2-1.

Figure 2-1. Blank Spreadsheet

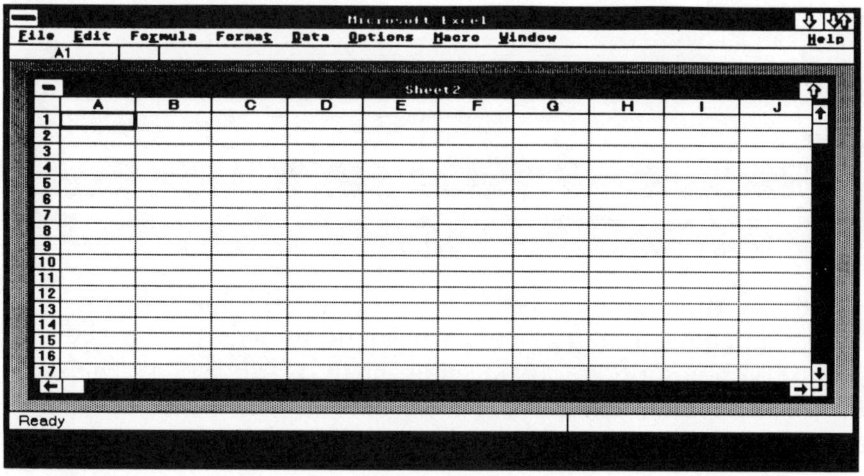

The lines at the top and the bottom of the screen contain information that will vary, depending on what you're doing. Your data goes in the middle part: the one with columns labeled A through J and rows from 1 to 17. (You don't immediately see the other rows and columns available to you, but there are 16,384 rows and columns A through IV.)

The bars at the top and bottom of the screen contain several different types of data, sometimes showing what you've done, sometimes showing options available, and sometimes giving status or error messages.

The menu bar contains the words File, Edit, Formula, Format, Data, Options, Macro, Window, and Help. When you choose any of these words, a pull-down menu appears on the screen. Figure 2-2 shows what happens if you choose the Edit menu.

Figure 2-2. Edit Menu

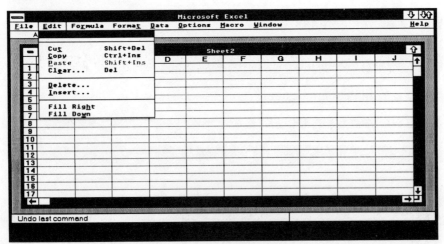

Below the menu bar is the reference area, which shows information about the active cell, what kind of activity you can perform (entering data or canceling what you've typed), the contents of the active cell if you have data or a formula entered in it, and where you are in your current typing of data.

The dark bar below the reference area shows the title of the current spreadsheet file. If several worksheet, macro, or chart files are active at once, you may see their titles, as if the files were pages stacked one on top of another, as shown in Figure 2-3.

Figure 2-3. Several Open Files

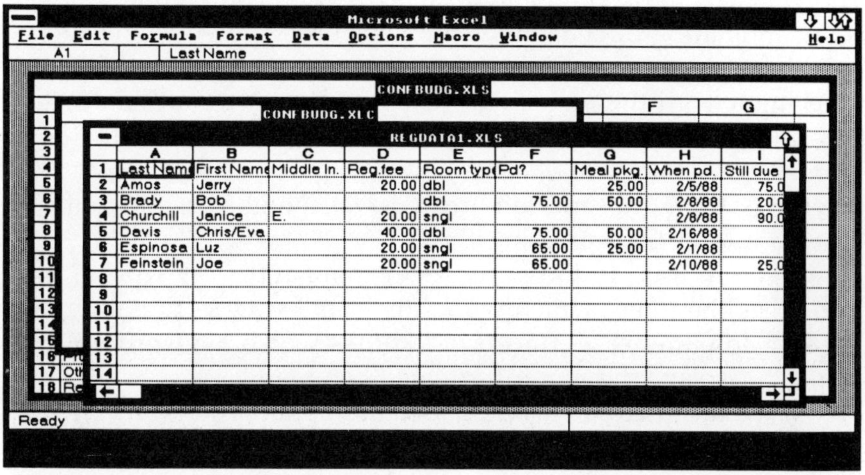

On the right side of the worksheet is the *scroll bar,* which lets you move backward and forward through your file. The shaded bar below the screen is another type of scroll bar that lets you move to the right or left within your worksheet. Both are especially useful if you have a mouse installed on your computer.

At the bottom of your screen is the *status bar,* which shows information about the currently selected command, and the current state of your workspace within *Excel.* The left side of it is the message area, which displays information about commands, dialog boxes, and processing information. You may see messages here about the current mode, what *Excel* is doing behind the scenes, or warnings about non-default settings you have chosen, as well as other information.

The right side of the status bar shows if you've selected some key with a special function, such as Caps Lock, Num Lock, or the Overtype key (Ins).

The arrows and angle at the bottom right corner of the screen are concerned with the size of the worksheet area on your screen, and its placement relative to the center of the screen. You control this with the Control menus that are accessed by pressing Alt and either the Hyphen or Spacebar.

Commands, Menus, and Dialog Boxes

You get *Excel* to do things for you by issuing commands. These commands are grouped under the keywords shown at the top of the screen, in the *menu bar*. You invoke the keyword by either touching it with the mouse pointer and dragging it down, or by pressing the Alt key and typing the underlined letter in the keyword. You can also invoke the keyword by pressing the Alt key and using the right- and left-arrow keys to highlight the word you want, and then pressing Enter.

If you're used to the Lotus *1-2-3* command style, you can also press the / key, which works the same way as pressing the Alt key. In either case, once *Excel* knows which keyword you want, it displays the menu of related commands.

Move the shaded bar to choose the option you want. The status bar at the bottom indicates what action will be taken if that command is selected (Figure 2-4, bottom).

Figure 2-4. Menu Choice Echoed at Bottom of Screen

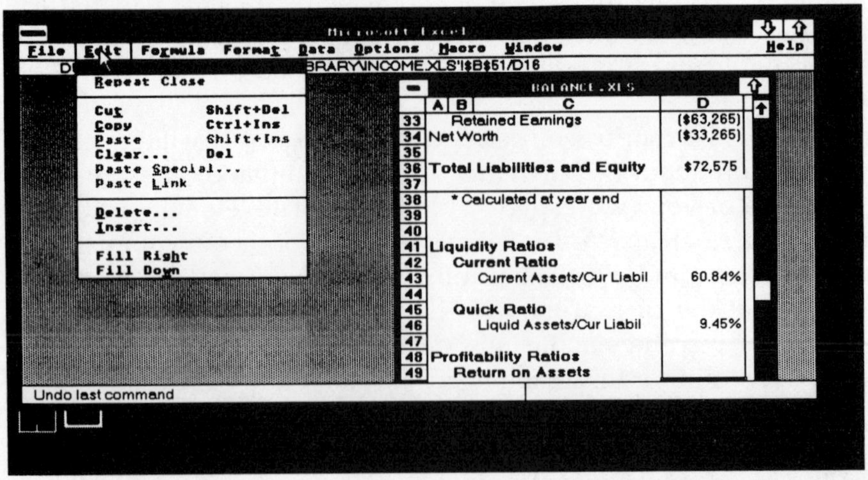

Initially, the shaded bar is over the top item, but you can use the mouse pointer or the arrow keys to move the shaded bar to any of the other commands shown. When you press the Enter key, or release the mouse pointer, the command indicated by the shaded bar is the one *Excel* acts upon.

The shortcut way to execute the command you want is to type the underlined letter denoting the command. You don't even have to press the Enter key; the command is immediately executed.

What happens next depends on the command. The commands with ellipses following them (such as Clear . . .) call up dialog boxes that prompt you for further information. We'll look at dialog boxes in a moment.

Some commands are shown in lighter characters, such as Paste, Paste Special . . ., and Paste Link in the example shown in Figure 2-4, above. The lighter typeface means these options aren't available to you at the moment, usually because some other action or condition needs to occur first. In the example in Figure 2-4, the Paste function is not available and is shown in lighter typeface, since nothing has been selected for moving or copying.

If you press the Enter key while one of the lighter-shaded commands is highlighted, *Excel* will warn you with a beep.

Each command either takes an action or presents a dialog box. If you select an action command, your current spreadsheet is acted upon and it reappears on your screen in its new form.

Dialog Boxes

When you choose a command that has several options, a dialog box appears on your screen, overlaying your current work. The options for this command are listed, allowing you to make some very specific choices about how something is to work.

For instance, if you choose the Find . . . command on the Formula menu, you'll see the dialog box depicted in Figure 2-5.

Figure 2-5. The Find . . . Dialog Box

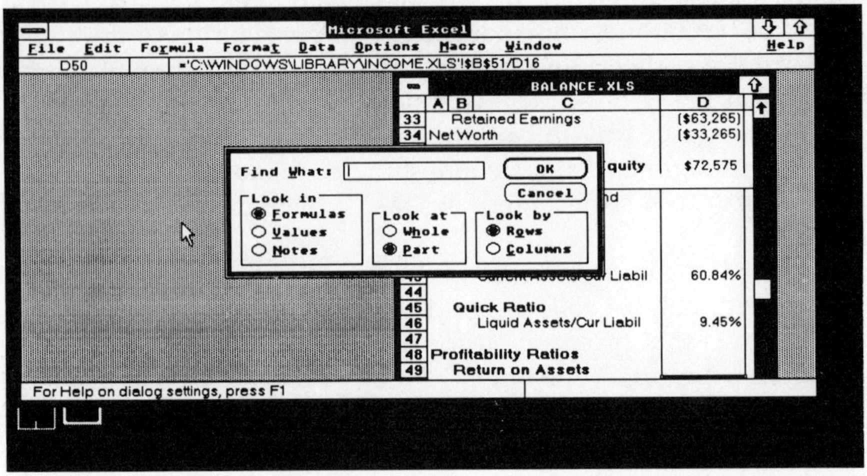

The Find What box asks you to specify what you want to find and how *Excel* will search for it. You make a choice by turning on one of the buttons or checking a box next to the option you want. When the options are configured the way you want, choose the OK bar; if you change your mind and want to exit the dialog box, choose the Cancel bar.

Excel's dialog boxes vary, depending on the options available for a given command. But generally they work like the Find box.

File Concepts

Since this is not a book for newcomers to *Excel* or spreadsheets, you won't see a great deal of detail about how to open, close, or save files in this book. However, *Excel* offers some interesting capabilities for working with more than one file at a time, and for using files from other programs; these are covered in this book.

Some Basic Concepts about Linking

If you're familiar with programming and using a link-editor to link separately compiled subroutines into a main program, you can understand how linking works within *Excel*. If not, look at the diagram in Figure 2-6.

Figure 2-6. Example of Linked Files

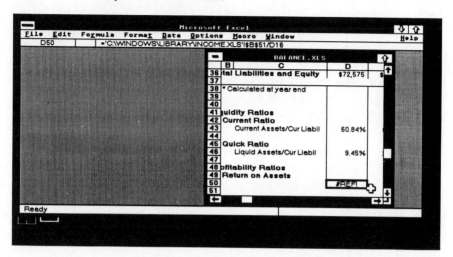

Linking may involve more than just linking to other files in the current directory or application. You can also specify a link to a file in a different application, such as other worksheet or database programs. We'll look at that process later in this chapter.

Linking involves specifying the reference containing the data or formula you want to use on another worksheet or macro sheet, just as if you were referring to another area on the active worksheet. However, linking to another file requires that you use a special notation, including both the filename and the reference of the cell or cell range you want to use, separated by an exclamation point:

Filename.WKS!Profits

or

Filename.WKS!$D$3:$M$3

Worksheets are linked in *Excel* through formulas; the current worksheet makes an external reference to a value found in another worksheet. The exclamation mark tells *Excel* the formula is to be found in an *Excel* file other than the current one. To make an external reference, the formula in your current file should look something like this:

AUSTRAL.XLS!F14*DOLLAR

23

The first part of the formula, AUSTRAL.XLS, tells *Excel* to look for another file in the current directory and names the file. The part of the formula after the exclamation mark tells *Excel* which cells or values in the external file are involved, and what to do with them. In this case, the external reference formula tells *Excel* to multiply what's in F14 on AUSTRAL.XLS by the named value DOLLAR. (DOLLAR happens to be a value that's set by another external file, one that's also linked to the active file.)

When you get used to linking files, however, you may have trouble keeping the links established if you move or change references in one file. You may also lose the link if you move a file from one directory to another. You'll have to recreate the link with the Links command.

If you follow some basic rules, you'll keep problems to a minimum:

1. If you're going to use a value or a formula in more than one file, name it. That way, if you move the cell's contents, or change it in any way, the name will let *Excel* keep track of it. *Excel* doesn't use the same method to adjust external references as it does with normal references. When you move supporting cells, external references in dependent formulas are not adjusted to reflect the new location of the supporting cells. However, the names used for these supporting cells are updated to reflect their new locations. Hence any link from the dependent file to the supporting file will be through the list of names, and location of the supporting cells won't matter.

2. Keep external reference formulas simple. *Excel* can update values for simple external references without opening the supporting worksheets. More complex ones require that the supporting files be open, thus requiring more memory and slowing performance.

3. Name the results of calculation in a supporting file; then use the name when you need to make an external reference. For instance:

NORTH.XLS!TotSales

is simpler to reference than

SUM(NORTH.XLS!$F$3:$F$15)

Creating a Link Between Worksheets

You create a link between worksheets when you use a value
from a previously created worksheet in the current worksheet.
To do that:

1. Open the worksheets you want to link, and activate the supporting worksheet window. Be sure the supporting file is
   open, or *Excel* will display an error message when you try to
   copy the cell reference over to the dependent file.
2. Select the cell or range you want to use in the dependent
   worksheet.
3. Choose Copy from the Edit menu. A dotted line appears
   around the cell or cells you've selected.
4. Activate the dependent worksheet window.
5. Position the active cell where you want the supporting cell to
   go, or where the upper left corner of the supporting range
   should be.
6. Choose Edit Paste Link. You'll see the external reference formula appear in the formula bar, and the appropriate value in
   the active cell and any other cells involved.

   Note: *Excel* automatically creates external reference formulas
using absolute cell references unless names have already been
given. If you want to type the formula, you can.
   When you open a worksheet that's linked to dependent
files, or if you decide to leave some dependent files closed to
save memory, you may see a message asking if you want to update references to unopened documents. These refer to external
reference formulas. If you want *Excel* to update the simple external reference formulas, choose the Yes bar. If you want to use
the last values in them, choose the No bar.

If the external reference formulas are more complex, and you choose the Yes bar, the values in cells containing more complex external reference formulas will be replaced by the error value #REF!, which will stay there until the supporting files are opened. If you choose the No bar, the last values will be used.

Figure 2-7. Linked Worksheet with Unopened Supporting Files

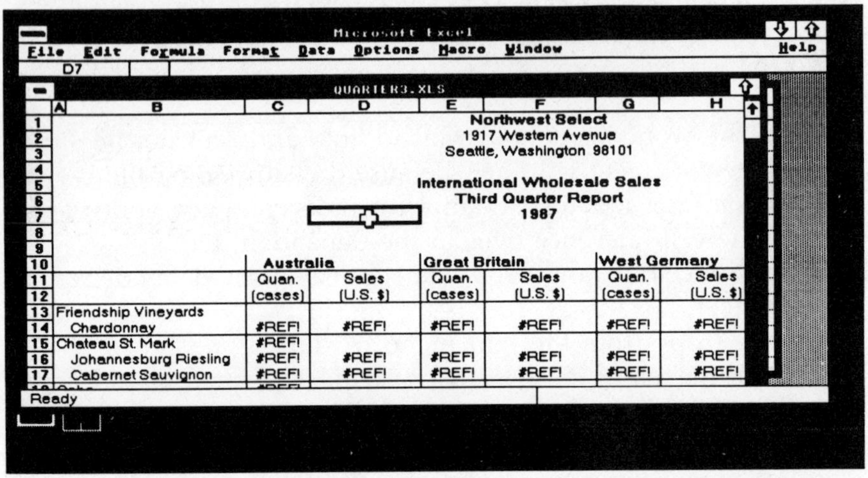

In the example in Figure 2-7, two of the supporting files have been opened, along with a summary file. The message about unopened documents was answered Yes. Notice that the cells requiring data from the unopened West German supporting file now contain the error value #REF!. As soon as the West German file is opened, these error values are automatically changed to the corresponding values.

The formulas in cells containing references to values in unopened files look different in the formula bar. In the example below, the same set of opened files was used as above. However, one of the supporting files is still closed. When the active cell is moved to a cell containing a reference to a value in the unopened file, the formula bar shows the full path name, as it does for cell D14 as shown below:

Figure 2-8. Figure Cell Reference to Unopened File

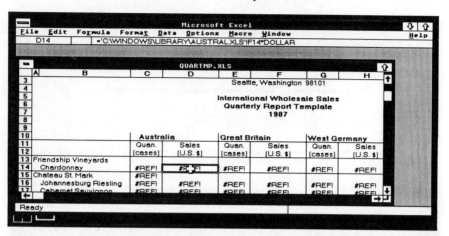

Cell references to values in opened files use just the filename convention we described earlier.

Opening Linked Files

Use the File Links command to open files that are linked to the currently active file.

The Link . . . command is used when you're opening several linked files, and don't know what should be open. When you choose the Link . . . command, *Excel* displays a dialog box showing you the names of the supporting files in the current directory. If one of those files is still closed, the entire path name is shown (see Figure 2-9).

Figure 2-9. File Link Dialog Box

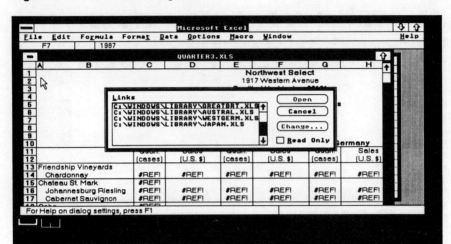

Notice in the illustration that the reference for WEST-GERM.XLS is different from the others. That's because this file was still closed when the File Link command was issued. Notice that the filename for WESTGERM.XLS includes the complete path name, including drive and directory.

If you want to open one of the files listed that's still closed, you can do it through this dialog box. Make sure the path name is highlighted, and choose the Open bar. If you want to open more than one of the linked files shown, select as many as you want. Use the arrow keys to select a single file, the Shift and arrow keys to select several that are together, or the Ctrl and arrow keys plus the space bar to select several files that aren't together. When the Links box shows what you want to open, choose the Open bar.

Whether to use Links command to open multiple linked files or to use the File Save Workspace command to create a file listing a group of files that will be opened all at once is a matter of personal preference.

If you'll be using the same group of files again and again, it makes sense to save them as a workspace and open them all at once.

If you'll be selecting from a group of linked files, not always needing to have the same files opened, use the Link command to open only those you need at the time.

The Links dialog box also shows you another option: the
Change . . . bar. This lets you change the list of supporting files
used by external references in the currently active file. To change
a link, select the new supporting files in the Links list, and
choose the Change . . . bar. For each link you want to change,
Excel shows a new dialog box (Figure 2-10).

Figure 2-10. Links Change Dialog Box

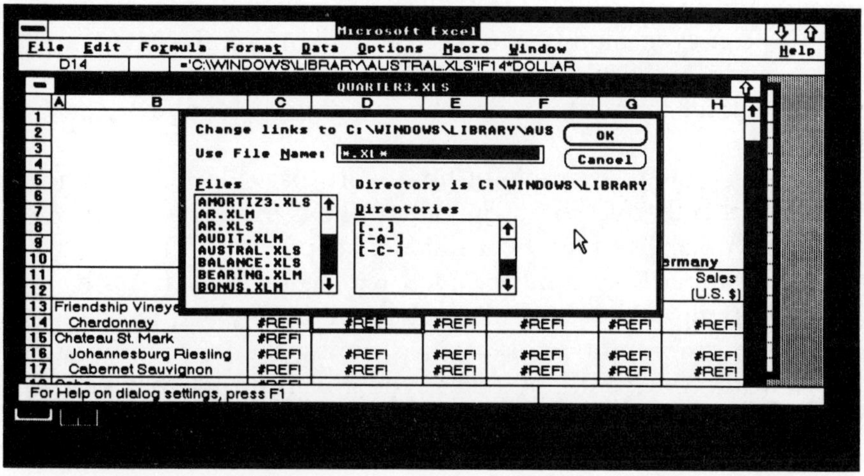

The Use File Name bar shows the type of files displayed in
the Files list box by extent. As you move the highlight bar down
the list of files shown, the name will appear here. You can also
type the name of a file you want to use as a new supporting file.
If you want to change the drive or directory, select what you want
in the Directories box, and choose the OK bar; then come back
and use the Links command again to choose the file you want.

Workspaces

If you have several linked files, and use them on more than an
occasional basis, you may find the concept of a workspace useful. A workspace is *Excel*'s way of keeping track of a specific
group of related files. You can open, close, and save a workspace just as you would any other file. The workspace file contains the names of the windows and documents open at the
time. When you open a workspace file, you are prompted to
open the listed files; opening the workspace file doesn't automatically open the other files.

Once you get used to the idea of using a workspace to hold several open files simultaneously, you may decide to use it regularly.

You can set up a special AUTOEXEC.BAT file that will automatically open a workspace whenever you open a certain worksheet or macro file.

You can use the concept of a workspace to set up related files while you work on a budget, inventory control, or accounting problem.

You can even modify the file used when you first start up *Excel*. The WIN.INI file contains all your default settings including the default format for currency and time, column size, and other settings.

To give you an example of how workspaces look and function (and also to give you a preview of how *Excel* lets you link separate worksheets into a consolidated report), let's use a set of sample files that Microsoft provided with your *Excel* disks. If you're working with a hard disk, they were provided in the LIBRARY directory, and were installed during the Setup process. If you're working with floppy disks, you'll want to use the Library disk.

This example will show you how to use separate sales reports from different divisions (even using different currencies) and consolidate them into a single consolidated report, with amounts shown in current U.S. dollars.

This exercise requires you to open six files:

AUSTRAL.XLS   WESTGERM.XLS
GREATBRT.XLS   CONSTANT.XLM
JAPAN.XLS   QUARTMP.XLS

The first four are the divisional sales reports. CONSTANT.XLM is a macro file you use to update currency conversion rates. QUARTMP.XLS is the quarterly report template.

With *Excel* open, and a blank worksheet on your screen (make sure all your other files have been closed, since you'll have several open by the time you finish this exercise), use the File Open command to change directories. With the File Open box on your screen, use the Tab key and Down-arrow key to highlight the LIBRARY directory, and press the Enter key to choose it, or use your mouse to double-click the LIBRARY directory entry. (When you're done with this project, return to the normal WINDOWS directory by choosing the . . (dot-dot) directory. The dot-dot directory is the directory one step closer to the root directory. It's the directory of which the current directory is a subdirectory.)

Once you're in the LIBRARY directory, open the four divisional sales reports, one at a time. Each appears in its own window, occupying one quarter of the screen. When all four have been opened, your screen will look like Figure 2-11.

Figure 2-11. Four Sales Reports

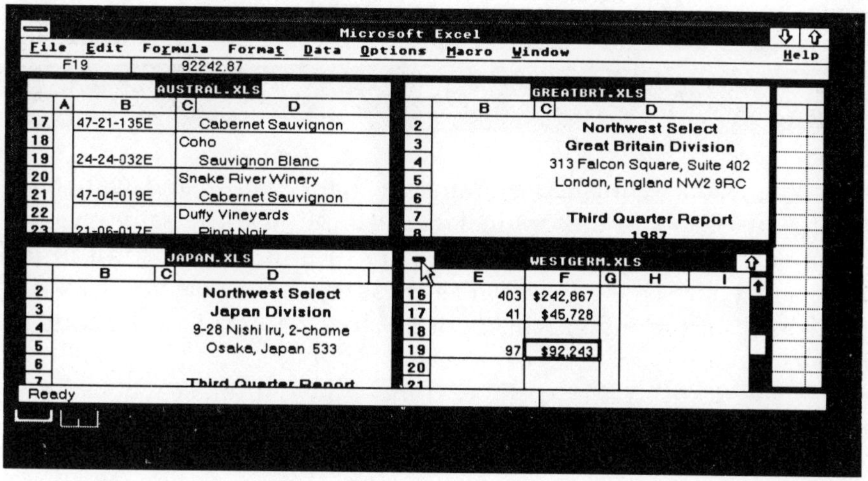

Since each is a window, you can move from report to report by selecting it on the Window menu. If you want the window to be larger, use the Control menu (press Ctrl-hyphen or click on the hyphen in the upper left corner of the window you want to enlarge, choose the Size command, and move the arrows in the direction(s) you want to enlarge).

For instance, if you wanted to do some more work on the West German sales report, you could enlarge it with the Size command on the Control menu, so it looks something like Figure 2-12.

Figure 2-12. Enlarge Sales Report in Window

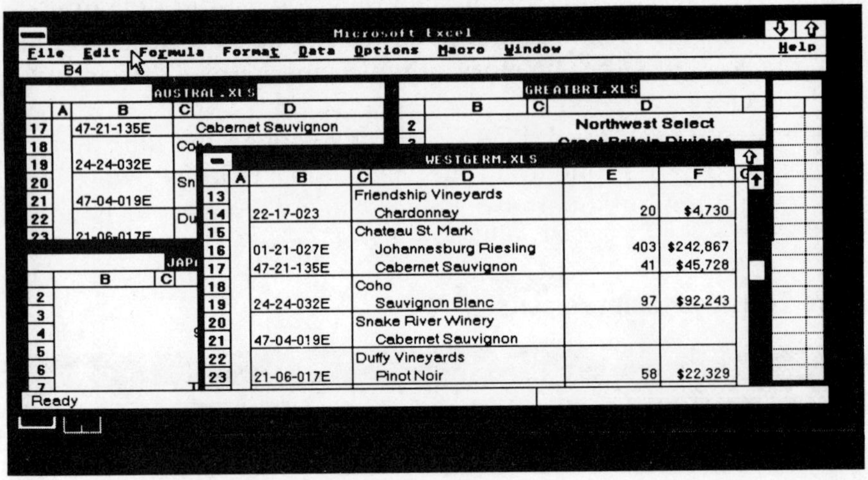

When you're finished working in that window and want to return the report to the original size, simply use the same Size command on the Control menu and reduce the report to fit in its corner of your screen. This isn't necessary, however; you can make each of the individual reports whatever size is most comfortable.

If you want to accept the currency rates in effect when the developers at Microsoft wrote the example, you don't have to open CONSTANT.XLM. If you'd like to update the currency rates, open this macro file and be sure you have up-to-date currency rates at hand. (You can get them from the Foreign Exchange rates table in the business section of your newspaper. Use the most current value in the columns headed *Foreign Currency in dollars*.)

To run the macro, press Ctrl-C, and enter the appropriate values in response to the prompts that will appear.

When the currency values are correct, open the quarterly report template. You may be asked if you want to update the values. Choose Yes if this question appears. The template overlays the four divisional reports on your screen, and looks like Figure 2-13.

Figure 2-13. Consolidated Quarterly Report

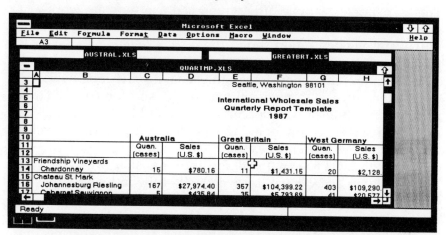

Note that there are several non-default values present in this worksheet. For starters, the fonts have been changed, making the material easier to read. Notice also that the Format Borders command has been used to leave some grid lines in and take others out.

If you move the active cell around, you'll notice that the formula bar shows that the contents of the cells where numbers appear is actually a formula. For instance, you updated your currency values with the CONSTANT.XLM macro, so the sales of Friendship Vineyards Chardonnay in Australia were reported as $780.16 in U.S. dollars. Note that with D14 as the active cell (on the QUARTMP.XLS worksheet), the formula bar shows the contents to be

AUSTRAL.XLS!F14*DOLLAR

This is the way *Excel* refers to the contents of cells in other currently active worksheets. In this case, the formula refers to the worksheet file (AUSTRAL.XLS!) and cell within that file (F14), and multiplies that value by the dollar conversion value for Australia, which is stored as the named variable DOLLAR. (In the case of Great Britain, the equivalent conversion value is stored as POUND.)

If you move the active cell around the consolidated report, you'll find that most of the values shown are taken from the component divisional sales reports, and that the only calculations done on the summary sheets are the totals in columns K and L. This is a simple example of how you can use separate worksheets to do calculations, and by linking the separate worksheets to the consolidated report, bring the results together in a composite worksheet.

The entire environment—all the separate divisional worksheets, the currency conversion macro file, and the consolidated report—constitutes a workspace. You can add and delete files from your worksheet by opening and closing them individually. Or you can save the entire set of files as a workspace, perhaps calling it QUARTER. (*Excel* will add the extension .XLW for you.) However, you'll also have to save or close the individual files. Once saved or closed, you can retrieve the whole set of files again when you open the workspace file.

This concept of saving associated files as a workspace is one of *Excel*'s unique features. It makes it far easier to work on linked files, saving them on an interim basis as your work gets interrupted, and retrieving them all as they were when you had to leave.

Let's go back to the example. Once you've loaded the individual reports with data and have it reported on the consolidated report, save the consolidated report with a name other than QUARTMP.XLS. Your LIBRARY directory includes one such example: QUARTER3.XLS, which produces the report in Figure 2-14.

Figure 2-14. Consolidated Third Quarter Report

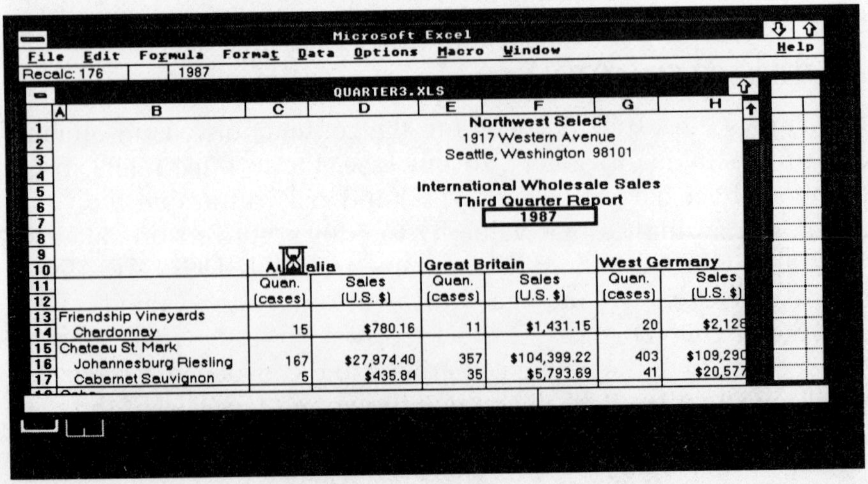

The workspace example shown here is but one application of this feature. You'll soon grow accustomed to saving and retrieving groups of associated files and working on them individually. It's easy to save as a workspace all the spreadsheet and database files associated with a list of accounts receivable or payable, or a spreadsheet and its associated charts showing sales by region and product.

Using the Save Workspace command allows you to stop safely in the middle of a complex project to attend a meeting or go to lunch, or even go home for the evening. This allows you to reopen all the files you were working on with everything where it was when you left it. However, each of the files must have been saved on disk at least once before. If you haven't saved a file before, you won't be able to reopen it.

You can work on any individual file in a workspace file. When the workspace file is loaded, the updated version of the file will be retrieved. Also, any changes you make to its window size and position will be reflected the next time you open the file as part of a workspace.

The Already Existing File

Excel can open a file that's in any of the following formats:

Source	Extension
Excel	.XLS
	.XLC
	.XLM
	.XLW
An ASCII text file	Any extension
A CSV file	.CSV
1-2-3, Symphony	.WKS, .WK1 or compatible
A SLK file	Any extension
A DIF file	Any extension
A DBF2 or DBF3 file	Appropriate extensions

When you choose the File Open . . . command, the dialog box assumes you're interested only in *Excel* files, and displays a list of the files in the current directory that have the characters .XL and another character as their extension. That's what is shown in the filename box. This allows you to choose from a list of files that includes all the .XLS, .XLC, .XLM, and .XLW files.

If the file you want to open doesn't fit that description, you can type in the filename and extension, or use some combination of characters and asterisks to indicate the set of files you'd like to inspect. For instance, if your current directory includes some Lotus *1-2-3* files that you'd like to use under *Excel*, type the file specification

.WK

in the File Name box to see a list of all the Lotus *1-2-3* files in the current directory. *Excel* will show you a list of each file in the current directory that has the letters WK as the first two letters of its extension.

However, this assumes the file you're after is in the current directory, which is shown following the phrase

Directory is C:\WINDOWS

Below that line, in the Directories box, is a list of all the other disk drives installed under *Excel's* setup program, and the names of any other subdirectories on drive C: that use the WINDOWS directory. If you choose another drive, *Excel* will show you the directories available on that drive. The directory immediately above the one you're using is referred to by two periods (. . , also called *dot-dot*). If you want to change directories on the current drive, choose it in the Directories list and press the OK bar. *Excel* will then show you the list of files from that directory.

The Read Only check box is particularly useful on a network where access to your files is not controlled. If you open a file with the Read Only box turned on, others on the network can also open this file at the same time. They may change the file you're examining, and you may be unaware of the changes until the next time you open it. You'll be unable to change the file if you opened it with the Read Only box turned on.

If you open the file with the Read Only box turned off, you can change the file. Others who open the file while you're looking at it will be able to look at the file, but will be unable to change it.

You can use files from other programs with *Excel,* either completely, or as individual cell values. If your other program operates under Windows, you can establish automatic links from files created with that program to your current worksheet. However, you can also use data from another program even if it doesn't operate under *Windows.*

You can link a current worksheet to a file created by another program running under Windows, provided both applications are running under *Microsoft Windows,* Version 2.0 or higher. The program doesn't necessarily have to be from Microsoft, but it must meet the *Windows* environment requirements; most programs that do so will state this in the documentation.

Installing other programs under *Windows* will not be described here in detail. The basic concepts of windowing are covered in the *Excel Reference Guide* under the topic *Windows.* The purpose of having the other programs installed under *Windows* is so they can share the Clipboard and other utilities, and so the file access method is one *Excel* can share.

One method by which *Windows* applications share data is called *Dynamic Data Exchange* (DDE). It's covered in detail in the *Excel Reference Guide.*

The other method of sharing data is by using the Clipboard, an electronic facility in *Windows* where data is temporarily stored while it's being moved or copied from one application to another.

To use data from another program running under *Windows,* it must ultimately become data that can be stored meaningfully in a cell. If it's numeric data, it has to be in a form that can become data that *Excel* can work with. This may require that you use one or more of *Excel's* functions or the Data Parse command to manipulate it.

For instance, if there's a date buried in a text string in your incoming data, you may want to use the text-processing functions to strip the other data away, leaving just the date, and if necessary use one of the date functions to store the date in a format *Excel* can use.

Generally, however, most numeric data is likely to be stored in a cell-like format that *Excel* can use, so you can directly link to the location of the supporting data.

When linking to a file created with a non-*Excel* program, but one running under *Windows,* the procedure is similar to linking to another *Excel* file:

1. Open both the dependent worksheet and the non-*Excel* file to which you wish to link.
2. Activate the supporting document window.
3. Select the cell, range, value, or field of the data you want to use, and choose Edit Copy.
4. Activate the dependent worksheet window.
5. Position the active cell where you want the incoming data to go.
6. Choose Edit Paste Link

Excel establishes the link with a formula that follows specific conventions, in the form:

= *'APPLICATION__NAME'* | *'DOCUMENT__NAME'* ! *reference*

Each portion of the formula tells *Excel* how to find the data you want.

APPLICATION__NAME — Must be immediately preceded by an equals sign (=) and immediately followed by a vertical bar (|). The application name must either be a legal *Excel* name or be enclosed in single quotes. In the example above, APPLICATION__NAME was enclosed in quotes to make it acceptable to *Excel.*

| — A vertical bar must separate the application name and the document name. It's used to tell *Excel* that what follows is not just a different *Excel* directory.

DOCUMENT__NAME — Must be the name of the file in the other application. (Some applications, particularly some network servers, consider documents to be *topics;* use the topic name here, in that case.) This name can be up to 255 characters long, and may include the full path name, the name of a terminal, and any opening parameters necessary for *Excel* to use to get to the document you want. If there is any question about *Excel* being able to understand the document name (perhaps because of the presence of some characters required at the other end that *Excel* considers illegal), enclose the document name in single quotes.

! 　　　　Separates the document name from the cell reference or value.

reference 　　　　Reference stands for the cell, range, name, value, or field of data you want to use. What goes here can be a cell or range address, the name of the cell or range, the value you want to use, or the reference to the datafield (in a database, for instance) containing the information you want to use. Cell referencing methods were discussed in an earlier chapter. They'll be examined in greater detail with reference to getting data from a database in Chapters 8 and 11. If the name of the data looks like a cell reference (for instance, AT50, which could be taken to be the cell on row 50 in column AT, or may be the name of a value derived when some condition reaches 50), enclose it in single quotes.

The procedure for opening and updating a worksheet linked to another application is very similar to that used in opening and updating another linked *Excel* worksheet. When you open a worksheet containing remote references to another application, *Excel* asks if you want to re-establish links to that other application. Answer Yes if you want the links; answer No if you want to use the last values received from that application.

If *Excel* tries to establish a link and fails (the supporting application isn't running, or can't be accessed), it then asks if you want to start the application. If you agree, *Excel* tries to start the application; if it can't, the cells with external references to this application display the #REF! error value.

Converting Data from Another Program into an *Excel* File

The formats mentioned earlier are accepted by *Excel* as valid file formats. In some cases you may need further conversion (using the Macro Translation Assistant for Lotus *1-2-3* macros, for instance), but generally, if it's a spreadsheet or database file in one of the formats listed, you can use the data directly in *Excel*.

The method for using one of these files is simply to open it. *Excel* may ask you how you want to use it. If you receive this prompt, specify whether it's a worksheet file or a chart file, depending on what kind of information it contains.

You can also use *Excel* files in other applications. To do so, simply use the File Save As command and use the correct file-name extension. Note, however, that *Excel* charts won't correctly convert to Lotus *1-2-3* charts.

When *Excel* opens a file with one of the non-*Excel* formats, it tries to convert the formulas. If it can't, you'll see a message giving the cell references involved. Note these on a piece of scratch paper, so you can go back and modify them later. The same message will ask if you want to see the next formula that can't be converted. Answer Yes and you'll see all the places where *Excel* couldn't convert the formula. If you answer No to the prompt, or in either case when *Excel* is finished with the conversion, *Excel* will tell you how many formulas it didn't convert. This gives you the number of formulas you'll have to fix. When a formula doesn't convert, *Excel* preserves the value of the formula.

You can also convert files from *Excel* for the Macintosh to files using the MS-DOS version of *Excel*. Worksheet files coming from the Macintosh must have been saved as SLK files (also known as *Sylk* files). Cell attributes (formulas, values, formatting, protection status), names, calculation settings, and display settings (displaying or hiding gridlines, row and column headings) are converted. Window characteristics, such as window size, position, split, the location of the current cell, and the position of scroll bars, and printing formats such as margins, headers and footers, don't convert.

SLK worksheet files coming from *Multiplan* can also be used directly by *Excel*. As with Macintosh *Excel*, the cell attributes and names are converted, but window and some printing characteristics are not. If some of the formulas can't be converted, you'll see messages indicating the location of these cells.

If you copy or cut data from an existing worksheet and display the Clipboard (press Alt-space bar for the Control menu, then choose the Run command, and on the dialog box choose Clipboard), you'll see a list of terms, such as Picture, Printer__ Picture, Bitmap, and so on, followed by an R1C1-style description of the cell or cells that have been selected. The list of terms is a list of file formats that *Excel* can use to send whatever has been put on the Clipboard to another application. You can send your data in any of these formats, or even send it in more than one format.

To send data from *Excel* to another application running under *Microsoft Windows*, open the window you want and select the cells involved; then choose Copy or Cut as appropriate. If you display the Clipboard at that point, you'll see the selected cells indicated by address. Next, open the receiving application and use the appropriate commands to retrieve the cells from the Clipboard.

Summary

This chapter has given you an overview of hardware requirements to run *Excel* and some tips about advanced file concepts, including linking to other *Excel* files, using a workspace, windows, and non-*Excel* files.

Part 2
The Building Blocks
of *Excel*

Chapter 3

The Functions

A *function* is a shortcut for typing a more complex formula. Before discussing functions, let's review some basic concepts about formulas in *Excel*.

Formulas

A spreadsheet lets you use formulas to manipulate and reference values by location or name. You can set up a formula to reference values by specific cell references (G3 + H6) or by name (SALES – COMMISSIONS), and have the spreadsheet perform the calculation every time, regardless of what values you've put in G3 or COMMISSIONS or any of the other references.

    Excel recognizes a string of characters as a formula if they start with an equal sign (=). Once you put = as the first character in a cell, *Excel* will try to evaluate the remainder of that entry as a mathematical expression that may include values, operators, cell references, names, and/or functions. If *Excel* can evaluate these characters successfully, the result of the calculation appears in the cell. Otherwise, you'll see an error message.

    There are four types of operators used in formulas: arithmetic, text, comparison, and reference.

Arithmetic

+	Addition
−	Subtraction or negation
*	Multiplication
/	Division
%	Percentage
^	Exponentiation

Text

&	The ampersand is the only text operator. It joins two or more text values, creating a new text value.

Comparison

=	Equal
<	Less than
< =	Less than or equal to
>	Greater than
> =	Greater than or equal to
< >	Not equal to

A comparison operator compares values on either side of the operator and produces the logical value TRUE or FALSE. Don't try to use comparison operators in the Find What text box. They're not recognized as comparison operators there.

Reference

:   The colon is the *range* operator. Range allows one reference to include all the cells from the cell specified to the left of the colon through the cell to the right of the colon.

space   The space is the *intersection* operator. Using the intersection operator results in one reference to the cells common to the two references. If there are no cells in common, the #NULL error value is returned.

,   The comma is the *union* operator. A union results in one reference that includes all the cells in both references.

Reference operators allow you to combine absolute references, relative references, and named areas. The range reference operator lets you refer to entire columns (B:B refers to all cells in column B), entire rows (3:3 refers to all cells in row 3), all rows in a range (5:9 refers to all cells in rows 5 through 9), or the entire spreadsheet (A:IV).

Excel evaluates the operators in a formula according to the following priorities:

−	Negation, highest priority
%	Percent
^	Exponentiation
* and /	Multiplication and division
+ and −	Addition and subtraction

                               Text operator

= < > <= => <>   Comparison operators, lowest priority

To change this order, enclose values in parentheses. *Excel* evaluates the formula in the parentheses first, then uses those values to calculate the rest of the formula.

You can use absolute or relative cell reference. $D$5 is an example of an absolute reference to cell D5 (note the dollar signs). G11 is an example of a relative reference that will change if move, insert, or delete operations change the location of the cell it references.

What's a Function?

Functions are formula shortcuts. *Microsoft Excel* comes with 129 different built-in formulas, or functions, that can be used if you also supply the necessary data in the required format. They'll be discussed later in this chapter.

A word of warning about functions: Since they start with a text string, such as DATE or GROWTH, be careful to not use the name of a function as the name of a cell or cell range.

Some of the functions supplied with *Excel*, such as SUM, AVERAGE, and PMT, are standard forms of a mathematical formula you could type. However, there are other functions, such as IF, CHOOSE, and LOOKUP that would be difficult, if not impossible, to type in a single cell since they involve some programming or multiple steps. Some, such as IRR, involve many iterations of a test calculation—something that's impossible to do in a single cell.

Function Syntax

Functions have a particular syntax, which means you have to enter the name of the function and the data that goes with it in a particular order, punctuated properly. Most of *Excel*'s functions enclose the associated data in parentheses, like this:

=SUM(C5:D11)

The left parenthesis must immediately follow the function name. If you put a space (or any other inappropriate character) between the function name and the left parenthesis, *Excel* will display an error message. There must be a corresponding right parenthesis at the end of the arguments, or *Excel* will display another error message.

Inside the parentheses are *arguments*. Most of the functions have one or more arguments. They tell *Excel* which cells or values the function is to act upon. When using arguments with *Excel* functions, use a comma to separate the arguments.

Some functions let you use more than one kind of value as arguments. The SUM function lets you also use numbers or even text as arguments. Here's an example using numbers:

= **SUM(5,10,15,20,25)**

Excel adds the numbers indicated and displays the result, 75, in the cell where you typed the function. In this particular function, you can combine cell addresses and numbers, as well as other values, and get a numeric total. Later in this chapter you'll see what kind of arguments are used with each function.

When typing the functions and their arguments, you can use uppercase or lowercase letters, or mix them. *Excel* doesn't distinguish case in functions.

It's important to type the correct number of arguments for any function you use. If a function requires three arguments, for example, and you only supply two, *Excel* will either substitute what it thinks is an appropriate value (usually 0, FALSE, or " ", the empty text value) or return an error message.

If in the explanations later in this chapter you see an argument followed by an ellipse (. . .), this means you can have more than one argument of the previous data type. For instance:

= **MIN(number1,number2,. . .)**

means you can have several numbers as arguments, like this:

= **MIN(100,520,C25,E48)**

You may need to use as an argument a reference that uses a comma to indicate union. For example, = AREAS(B5,D4) might appear legitimate to you as another way of indicating a range, but *Excel* interprets B5 and D4 as separate arguments and, since AREAS requires only one reference, it will return an error message. In such a case, use parentheses to enclose the values on either side of the comma: = AREAS((B5,D4)).

Pasting Functions

Excel makes typing a function name easier by giving you the Formula Paste Function command. When you select the cell or cells where you want a particular formula to go, and choose the Formula Paste Function command from the Formula menu, *Excel* shows you a list of all the built-in functions, along with any other custom functions you may have created with function macros. Select the one you want. If you want *Excel* to remind you what arguments are needed for the function, turn on the Paste Arguments check box.

Next, choose the OK button, and type or edit the arguments, separating them with commas. When the formula appears as it should, complete with arguments, press the Enter key. The formula is then stored in the cell or cells you selected.

List of Functions

In each of the function explanations in the remainder of this chapter, you'll find the function name along with the arguments it needs, a brief definition, and an explanation that includes some examples of how to use the function.

Functions are grouped by category. A list of all the functions can be found in the Quick Reference Guide in Appendix A.

Date and Time Functions

Excel stores date and time values as numbers. Date is stored as an integer from 1 to 65380, representing the dates in sequence from January 1, 1900 through December 31, 2078. Time is stored as a decimal fraction from 0 through 0.9999, representing each second from 0:00:00 (midnight) to 23:59:59 (one second before midnight). Date and time calculations are performed on this serial number, much as if it were any other integer or decimal number. What you see in a cell, however, depends on what function you used and how the cell is formatted.

DATE(*year,month,day*)

Serial number of date specified.

When you specify the date in the format shown, *Excel* stores the serial number corresponding to that date in the cell. For example, if you specify =DATE(88,1,1), *Excel* returns the serial number 32143. What you see in the cell, however, depends on the format of the cell. You may see 01/01/88, or 01-Jan-1988 or the serial number, depending on the format.

Year, month, and *day* must be numeric values: *Year* must be from 0 to 199, *month* must be from 1 to 12, and *day* must be from 1 to 31.

Examples

= DATE(88,06,01) = 32295

= DATE(100,01,01) = 36526

DATEVALUE(*datetext*)

Serial number of *datetext*.

DATEVALUE differs from DATE in that you enter text rather than numbers as the argument. Like DATE, DATEVALUE needs a date from January 1, 1900 to December 31, 2078. You can use any of *Excel*'s date formats, such as 12/31/87 or 31-Dec-87.

If you omit the year portion of the argument for DATE-VALUE, *Excel* uses the current year from your computer's built-in clock. Any information about time of day entered as part of the argument will be ignored.

Be sure the 1904 Date System check box in the Options Calculation box has been turned off, unless you want to have the date serial number begin with January 2, 1904. If you've imported a file from *Microsoft Excel* for the Macintosh, the 1904 Date System box has been turned on automatically.

Examples

= DATEVALUE("01/01/88") = 32143

= DATEVALUE("Apr-04") = 1553

DAY(*serialnumber*)

The day of the month equivalent to *serialnumber*.

DAY converts the serial number you give into a date, paring off the month and year information and returning only the number representing the day.

You can also enter *serialnumber* as a text value, such as "4-15-1988" or "15-Apr-1988." With this function, *Excel* converts a date entered in recognizable text form to a serial number.

As with DATEVALUE, the description assumes the 1904 Date System check box in the Options Calculation dialog box has been turned off.

Examples

=DAY(5)=5

=DAY(32237)=4

=DAY("15-Apr")=15

HOUR(*serialnumber*)

The hour of the day equivalent to *serialnumber*.

HOUR converts the time serial number you give into the hour of the day, paring off any information about minutes and seconds. The hour is in a 24-hour clock format, ranging from 0 (midnight) to 23 (11 p.m.).

You can also enter the argument as text, such as "15:45:00" or "3:45:00 PM" or one of the other acceptable time formats.

You may also wish to use TIMEVALUE within the HOUR function to get the hour portion of a string that's in one of the time formats.

Examples

=HOUR(.5)=12

=HOUR(1357.13579)=3

=HOUR(TIMEVALUE("9:15"))=9

MINUTE(*serialnumber*)

The minute of the hour equivalent to *serialnumber*.

MINUTE converts the time serial number you give into the minute of the hour involved, paring off any information about hours and seconds.

You can also enter the argument as text, such as "20:15:00" or "8:15:00 PM" or one of the other acceptable time formats.

Examples

=MINUTE(1.5)=0

=MINUTE(0.01)=14

=MINUTE("2:35:52 PM")=35

MONTH(*serialnumber*)

The month of the year equivalent to *serialnumber*.

MONTH converts the serial number you give into the number corresponding to the equivalent month of the year (1–12). As with the previous date and time functions, *Excel* assumes the 1904 Date System check box has been turned off.

You can also enter the argument as text, such as "4-15-1988" or "15-Apr-1988."

Examples

= MONTH(12345) = 10

= MONTH(.7531) = 1

= MONTH("01-Jan-1988") = 1

NOW( )

Serial number of the current date and time.

NOW lets you insert the current date and time into your worksheet. *Excel* reports the serial number for both date and time, in the form 11111.11111. To use the serial number in one of the time or date formats, format the cell appropriately.

If you want just the current date, use the INT function with NOW; if you want just the current time, use the MOD function (see the examples below).

Note that the parentheses are required, even though they contain no arguments.

Examples

= NOW( ) = 32203.59

= INT(NOW( )) = 32203

= MOD(NOW( ),1) = 0.59

SECOND(*serialnumber*)

The equivalent in seconds of *serialnumber*.

SECOND converts the time serial number you give into the second of the hour involved, paring off any information about hours and minutes.

You can also enter the argument as text, such as "20:15:00" or "8:15:00 PM" or one of the other acceptable time formats.

Examples

= SECOND(.007) = 5

= SECOND(32445.007) = 5

= SECOND("1:52:27 PM") = 27

TIME(*hour,minute,second*)

The serial number of the time specified.

    The TIME function translates the time you enter into the corresponding time serial number. The time entered can be positive or negative, so long as the resulting serial number is positive. You can also enter time as text, provided it's surrounded by quotation marks.

Examples

= TIME(12,0,0) = 0.5

= TIME(19,45,15) = 0.82309

= TIME(16,48,0) – TIME(12,0,0) = 0.2

TIMEVALUE(*timetext*)

The serial number of *timetext*.

    Like DATEVALUE, TIMEVALUE translates the value specified in *timetext* into an equivalent time serial number. The value in timetext can be in any of the *Excel* time formats.

Examples

= TIMEVALUE("2:24 AM") = 0.1

= TIMEVALUE("7:15:45 PM") = 0.802604

WEEKDAY(*serialnumber*)

The day of the week equivalent to *serialnumber*.

    WEEKDAY translates the serial number given into an integer corresponding to the equivalent day of the week. The integer ranges from 1 (Sunday) to 7 (Saturday).

    You can also enter the argument as text, in an acceptable date format.

Examples

= WEEKDAY("6/1/88") = 4

= WEEKDAY(32143) = 6

YEAR(*serialnumber*)

The year equivalent to *serialnumber*.

YEAR converts the serial number you give into the number corresponding to the equivalent year, from 1900 to 2078. As with the previous date and time functions, *Excel* assumes the 1904 Date System check box has been turned off.

You can also enter the argument as text, such as "4-15-1988" or "15-Apr-1988."

Examples

= YEAR(29747) = 1981

= YEAR("15-Apr-1988") = 1988

Logical Functions

Logical functions compare items specified as arguments, and generally returns the values TRUE or FALSE.

AND(*logical1,logical2,. . .*)

Returns the value TRUE if every argument is true, otherwise returns FALSE.

AND can have up to 14 arguments, which can be local values, arrays, or references containing logical values. If any array or reference argument contains text or empty cells, those values are ignored. If any argument contains a numeric value of 0 or 1, those are evaluated as logical false and logical true, respectively.

If there are no logical values in the range specified, the error message #VALUE is returned.

Examples

= AND(TRUE,FALSE) = FALSE

= AND(TRUE,TRUE) = TRUE

= AND(C4,D6,E8,F10) = TRUE (if each of the cells mentioned can be evaluated as TRUE)

FALSE( )

Returns logical value FALSE.

FALSE is frequently used in IF or conditional formulas, where it's important to recognize that a false condition is one of the potential results. The logical zero it returns is the same as a numeric zero.

Note that the parentheses are required, even if they contain no argument.

Examples

=FALSE( )= FALSE or 0

IF(*logicaltest, truevalue, falsevalue*)

Tests *logicaltest*; returns TRUE if *logicaltest* is true and returns FALSE if it's false.

IF is used to make conditional tests of cell values and formulas. If *logicaltest* is evaluated as true, the next argument is used; if *logicaltest* is evaluated as false, *falsevalue* is used.

Truevalue and *falsevalue* can be numbers, text, more tests or other formulas, or even macro instructions dictating where the cursor is to be positioned next.

Up to seven IF functions can be nested as *truevalue* and *falsevalue* arguments, permitting you to construct some fairly elaborate conditional tests.

If any of the arguments are arrays, every argument is evaluated when the IF statement is executed. If some of the arguments are action-taking functions, all the actions are taken.

Example

=IF(B5>C8,"Over Limit","OK") = "Over Limit" (if B5 is greater than C8)

NOT(*logical*)

Returns TRUE if *logical* is false, returns FALSE if *logical* is true.

NOT reverses the value of whatever is given in the argument. If the argument can be evaluated as TRUE, the NOT function is evaluated as FALSE.

Examples

=NOT(TRUE)=FALSE

=NOT(2+2=4)=FALSE

OR(*logical1, logical2,. . .*)

Returns TRUE if any of the arguments are true, otherwise returns FALSE.

OR can have up to 14 arguments. Each one is evaluated, and if any of them are TRUE, the result is TRUE. Arguments can be logical values, numbers, or text versions of logical values. Arguments that are empty cells, error values, or text that can't be translated into logical values will result in an error message. If any of the arguments are arrays or references, only the logical values within them are evaluated.

Examples

= OR(TRUE,FALSE) = TRUE

= OR(2 + 2 = 4,5*2 = 9) = TRUE

= OR(A25,C47,F35) = FALSE (if each of the cells mentioned contains conditional expressions that are evaluated as FALSE)

TRUE( )

Returns logical value TRUE.

TRUE, like FALSE, is frequently used in IF or conditional formulas, where it's important to recognize that a true condition is one of the potential results. The logical one it returns is the same as a numeric one.

Note that the parentheses are required, even if they contain no argument.

Example

= TRUE( ) = TRUE

Mathematical Functions

Mathematical functions are concerned with numerical evaluation of arguments.

ABS(*number*)

Absolute value of *number*.

The absolute value of a number is the value of a number without its sign.

Examples

= ABS(4) = 4   = ABS(−4) = 4

EXP(*number*)

The constant e ($e = 2.718$ . . .) to the power of *number*.

The constant e, 2.71828182845904, is the base of the natural logarithm. The EXP function calculates e raised to the power of the number you specify. (To calculate powers of other bases, use the ^ to indicate exponentiation.)

EXP is the inverse of LN, the natural log of *number*.

Examples

= EXP(1) = 2.718281828   = EXP(LN(2)) = 2

FACT(*number*)

Factorial of *number*.

The factorial of a number is equivalent to:

(number)*(number − 1)*(number − 2)*. . .*(number − n)

where (*number − n*) = 1. *Number* should be an integer, or the non-integer part is truncated.

Examples

= FACT(1) = 1
= FACT(2.5) = 2
= FACT(4) = 24

INT(*number*)

Number rounded down to the nearest integer.

INT shaves off the decimal or fractional part of *number,* and leaves the integer part. It rounds the number to the nearest integer.

Examples

= INT(3.14159) = 3   = INT(4*B55) = 2 **(the integer portion of the result of multiplying .51, the contents of cell B55, times 4)**

LN(*number*)

Natural logarithm of *number*.

LN returns the natural logarithm of the number you specify, using the mathematical constant *e* as a base. The number you give as an argument must be positive.
LN is the inverse of the EXP function.

Examples

= LN((100) = 4.60517

= LN(2.7182818) = 1

= LN(EXP(4)) = 4

LOG(*number,base*)

Returns the logarithm of *number*. LOG10(*number*) returns the base 10 logarithm of number.

Both LOG and LOG10 return the logarithm of the number you specify. If you omit base with the LOG function, *Excel* assumes it to be 10, and the result is the same as if you had used the LOG10 function.

Examples

= LOG(10) = 1

= LOG10(10) = 1

= LOG(86,2.7182828) = 5.721434

MOD(*number,divisor*)

Remainder of *number* divided by *divisor*.

MOD evaluates the formula *number/divisor*, where *divisor* is any number other than 0, and returns the remainder (modulus). The result has the same sign as *divisor*. If *divisor* is 0, *Excel* displays an error message (#DIV/0!).

Examples

= MOD(8,2) = 0 (8/2 has no remainder)

= MOD(7,2) = 1

= MOD(3, − 2) = − 1

= MOD(− 3,2) = 1

PI( )

Value of pi.

Returns the number 3.14159265358979, rounded to the format used in that cell. The parentheses are required.

Examples

=PI( )=3.14159

=PI( )/2=1.57079

=PI( )*5=15.70795 (the circumference of a circle with a diameter of 5)

Trigonometric Functions

Trigonometric functions are concerned with the numerical evaluation of sides and angles of plane and spherical triangles.

ACOS(*number*)

Arc cosine of *number*.

The arc cosine of a number is the angle in radians whose cosine is the number. The number you specify must be between −1 and 1. If you want to convert from radians to degrees, multiply the result by 180/PI( ).

Examples

=ACOS(−0.5)=2.094

=ACOS(1)=0

=ACOS(0)=1.570796

ASIN(*number*)

Arc sine of *number*.

The arc sine of a number is the angle in radians whose sine is the number. The number you specify must be between −1 and 1. If you want to convert from radians to degrees, multiply the result by 180/PI( ).

Examples

=ASIN(0)=0

=ASIN(1)=1.570796

=ASIN(−.05)*180/PI( )= −30 (degrees)

ATAN(*number*)

Arc tangent of *number*

    The arc tangent of an angle is the angle in radians whose tangent is the number given.

Examples

=ATAN(1)=0.785398

=ATAN(1)*180/PI( )=45 (degrees)

ATAN2(*xnumber,ynumber*)

Arc tangent of point defined by *xnumber* and *ynumber*.

    ATAN2 determines the arc tangent of the angle between the *x* axis and a line drawn from the point of coordinates *xnumber* and *ynumber* to the zero point on both axes. The result is an angle in radians. A positive result is a counterclockwise angle from the *x* axis; a negative result is a clockwise angle.

Examples

=ATAN2(1,2)=1.107149

=ATAN2(5,10)=2.034444

=ATAN2(1,1)*180/PI( )=135 (degrees)

COS(*radians*)

Cosine of *radians*.

    Returns the cosine of the value you specify in *radians*, where *radians* is an angle.

Examples

=COS(1)=0.540302

=COS(0)=1

=COS(60*PI( )/180)=.5

SIN(*radians*)

Sine of *radians*.

    Returns the sine of the value you specify in *radians*, where *radians* is an angle.

Examples

=SIN(0.5)=0.47942554

=SIN(1)=0.84147098

=SIN(PI( )/2)=1

TAN(*radians*)

Tangent of *radians*.

Returns the tangent of the value you specify in *radians*, where *radians* is an angle.

Examples

=TAN(4) = 1.157821

=TAN(0) = 0

=TAN(45*PI( )/180) = 1 (the tangent of 45 degrees)

Statistical Functions

Statistical functions are concerned with collections of data.

AVERAGE(*number1,number2,. . .*)

Average of numbers given as arguments.

Calculates the average of the values specified as *number1, number2,* and so on. You can have as many as 14 arguments, each of which can be numbers, arrays, or references that contain numbers. Arguments containing text, logical values, or empty cells result in those values being ignored.

Examples

=AVERAGE(2,6,10) = 6

=AVERAGE(A4:A8) = 15 (if cells A4 through A8 contain the values 11, 13, 15, 17, and 19)

COUNT(*value1,value2, . . .*)

Counts the numbers in *value1,value2, . . .*

COUNT determines how many numbers are in cells referenced by value1, value2, and so on. You can specify up to 14 arguments. Arguments can be arrays, references, numbers, empty cells, logical values, or text representation of numbers. However, if an array or reference contains empty cells, logical values, text, or error messages, those values are ignored.

Examples

=COUNT(D5:D6) = 2 (assuming D5 and D6 contain numbers)

=COUNT(D1,D5:D7) = 4 (assuming all four cells contain acceptable values)

=COUNT(0.5,FALSE,"six",25,3.14159,#DIV/0!) = 4

COUNTA(*value1,value2, . . .*)

Counts the values in *value1,value2, . . .*

COUNTA determines how many values there are in the list of arguments. If an argument is an array or reference, empty cells within the array or reference are ignored. Like COUNT, COUNTA can have up to 14 arguments.

Note that COUNTA determines values, but COUNT determines numbers.

Examples

= COUNTA(E48:E49) = 2 (if E48 and E49 contain values)

= COUNTA(4,,8) = 3

= COUNTA(E48:E49,TRUE,25) = 4

GROWTH(*knowny's,knownx's,newx's*)

Values on an exponential trendline.

GROWTH fits an exponential curve to the data *knownx's* and *knowny's*. It then returns the *y* values along that curve for the array of *newx's* you specify.

The array *knownx's* can include one or more sets of variables. If only one variable is used, *knowny's* and *knownx's* can be ranges of any shape as long as they have the same dimension. If more than one variable is used, *knowny's* must be a range with a height or width of 1.

If the array *knowny's* is in a single row, each row of *knownx's* is considered to be a separate variable.

If you include *newx's*, one dimension of that array must be the same as *knownx's*. If *knowny's* are in a single column or a single row, *knownx's* and *newx's* must have the same number of columns or rows as each other.

If you omit *newx's*, they're assumed to be the same as *knownx's*. If you omit both *knownx's* and *newx's*, they are assumed to be the array {1,2,3, . . .}, and the same size as *knowny's*. If any of the numbers in *knowny's* are negative, you'll get the error message #NUM!.

Formulas that return arrays must be entered as array formulas, with the Ctrl-Shift-Return keys. This is a complex operation, and you're advised to look at the section on Arrays in the *Microsoft Excel Reference Guide*.

Example

Figure 3-1. Sample Spreadsheet

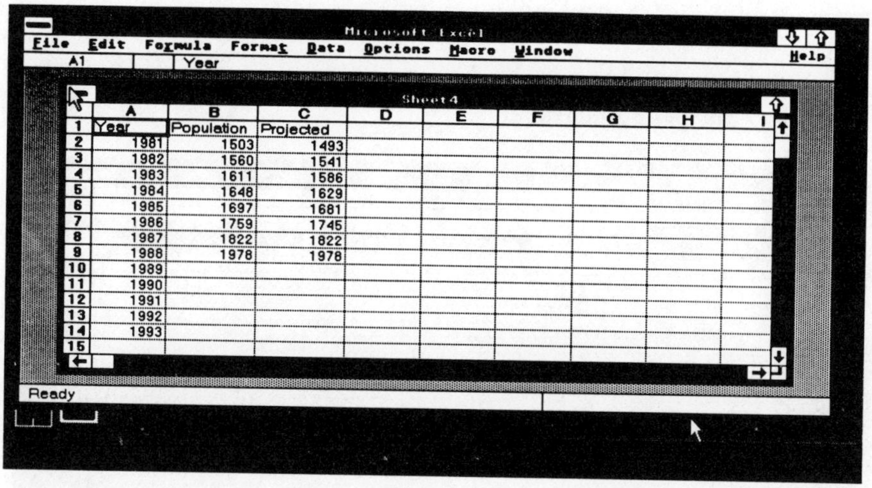

In the above example, you can calculate the growth in population for the subsequent five years, based on data for the previous eight. The formula

=GROWTH(B2:B9,A2:A9,A10:A14)

values in B10:B14 will contain projected values. You can also get values along the calculated exponential curve for the known eight years with the formula

=GROWTH(B2:B9)

which shows those values in C2:C9.

LINEST(*knowny's,knownx's*)

Parameters of linear trend.

LINEST calculates a straight line that fits your data, and produces an array that describes that line. A linear projection with a single variable is usually written as a series of data points solving the equation

$$y = ax + b$$

where *a* is the slope of the line, and *b* is value of *y* at the point at which the line crosses the *y* axis. Once you know the values of *a* and *b,* you can calculate any point on the line by inserting *x* or *y* values.

Not all data fits a smoothly sloping line, however. LINEST makes an estimate of what this smooth slope would be, allowing for each data point to have the smallest possible deviations from the line. Figure 3-2 is an example of some property values over a period of years.

Figure 3-2. Sample Spreadsheet

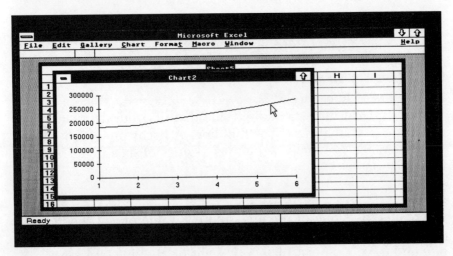

Figure 3-3 is one attempt to make that data fit a smooth line.

Figure 3-3. Linear Graph

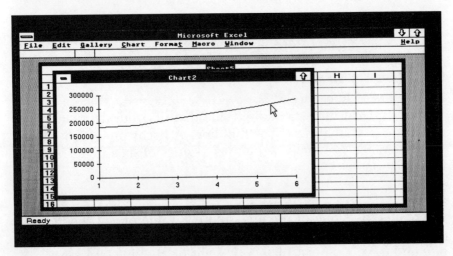

The LINEST function to find *a* and *b* in this case is:

=LINEST(C2:C7)

In this case, they're *X* and *Y*. Because the x-axis is a sequential progression (Year1, Year2, Year3, . . . which is equivalent to the array {1,2,3, . . .}) you can omit the *knownx's*.

Other factors being equal, you could use this set of data and the linear formula it produced to project where property values will go in the next few years. A word of warning, however: Other factors are rarely equal. While linear projections are a useful tool in making estimates, be sure to take into account the "other factors" that could influence results.

LOGEST(*knowny's, knownx's*)

Parameters of exponential trend.

Like LINEST, LOGEST attempts to fit your data contained in the arrays in *knowny's* and *knownx's,* to a curve. However, while LINEST attempts to produce a linear projection, LOGEST attempts to produce an exponential curve.

The same conventions about data that were described in LINEST apply also to LOGEST. The same formula,

y = ax + b

applies to exponential curves.

Example

Business school students frequently run into case studies where an optimistic entrepreneur has forecast growth with a "hockey stick" curve. The projected growth curve looks like Figure 3-4.

Figure 3-4. Hockey Stick Growth Curve (Broken Line)

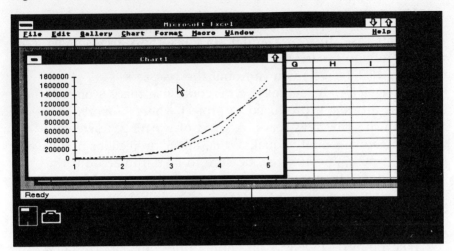

Assuming some of the assumptions about sales and marketing and product development and support are correct, it's still more reasonable to assume that growth won't be along straight lines, but along a curve.

If we were to go along with our entrepreneur's optimism, we'd be more likely to get projected sales data using the LOGEST function like Figure 3-5 (row 5).

Figure 3-5. Sample Spreadsheet

	A	B	C	D	E	F	G	H	I
1	Annual Cash Flow Projection								
2		Month	Month	Month	Month	Month			
3		1	2	3	4	5			
4	Sales	20000	40000	150000	750000	1500000			
5	Log Sales	16651	52936	168293	535031	1700950			
6									
7	Op. Exp.	3000	5000	30000	45000	60000			
8	Marketing	1250	15000	30000	50000	80000			
9	Mfrg.	1100	3000	12500	40000	65000			
10	R & D	10000	12000	30000	60000	90000			
11									
12	Tot. Exp.	15350	35000	102500	195000	295000			
13									

An exponential growth curve, using this data, would look more like the dotted line in Figure 3-4.

MAX(*number1,number2,. . .*)

Largest number in series given.

MAX gives you the largest numeric value in the list of arguments. You can specify up to 14 arguments, which can be numbers, empty cells, logical values, or text representations of numbers. If an argument is an array or reference, only numbers in that array or reference are used.

Examples

=MAX(15,2,19,8,11)=19

=MAX(C5:C9,22,B4:B8)=35 (if B4:B8 contains the series 31, 31, 33, 34, and 35 and C5:C9 contains the series 5, 10, 15, 20, and 25)

MIN(*number1,number2,. . .*)

Smallest number in series given.

MIN gives you the smallest numeric value in the list of arguments. The same limitations about arguments that were true for MAX also apply to MIN.

Examples

=MIN(15,2,19,8,11)=2

=MIN(C5:C9,22,B4:B8)=5 (if B4:B8 contains the series 31, 31, 33, 34, and 35 and C5:C9 contains the series 5, 10, 15, 20, and 25)

STDEV(*number1,number2,. . .*)

Estimate of standard deviation of a population, given sample specified in arguments.

A standard deviation of a list of values is the square root of the variance of all those values from the average. STD is used to test the reliability of that average as representative. The more the individual values vary from that average, the higher the value returned by STDEV. Conversely, the less the individual values vary from that average, the lower the STDEV value and hence the more reliable the mean is likely to be.

In a normally distributed population, 68 percent of all data points fall within one standard deviation from the mean (plus one standard deviation and minus one standard deviation, where the single largest number of values is assumed to be at the mean). Normal distribution also assumes that about 95 percent of the data points fall within two standard deviations.

The values given in the arguments should be numbers. Text, logical values, or empty cell values cause errors.

Use STDEV if the numbers you're using as arguments represent a sample of the population. STDEV uses the *non-biased* or *n1* method. If the numbers represent the entire population, use STDEVP. STDEVP uses the *biased* or *n2* method.

Examples

Suppose you have cell values as follows:

	A	B	C	D	E
47	241	198	203	247	225

= STDEV(A47:E47) = 21.959

STDEVP(*number1,number2, . . .*)

Standard deviation of a population based on the entire population given in arguments.

STDEVP calculates the standard deviation of a population, given the entire population as arguments. Like STDEV, STDEVP can have up to 14 arguments. If any of the included data contains text, logical data, or empty cell values, this will cause an error.

Example

Assume you have the following data that represents a complete population (or all the data points there are for this calculation):

	A	B	C	D	E
32	141	150	137	153	145

= STDEVP(141,150,137,153,145) = 5.810

SUM(*number1,number2, . . .*)

Sum of numbers.

SUM adds up all the values either shown or referenced. You can have up to 14 arguments with SUM, and arguments that are numbers, empty cells, logical values, or text representations of numbers are considered. If an argument is an array or a reference, only numbers in that array or reference are used; empty cells, logical values, text, or error values in the array or reference are ignored.

Examples

= SUM(A5:A15) = 55 (the total of all values in cells A5 through A15)

= SUM(25,B9:D11,"three") = 192 (the total of the values 25 plus the contents of B9 through D11 plus 3)

TREND(*knowny's,knownx's,newx's*)

Values on linear trend.

TREND, like LINEST, calculates a straight line that fits your data. It then returns the *y*-values along that line for the array of *newx's* you supply.

A linear projection with a single variable is usually written as a series of data points solving the equation

$$y = ax + b$$

where *a* is the slope of the line, and *b* is value of *y* at the point at which the line crosses the *y* axis. Given the known *x* and *y* values, *Excel* calculates the *a* and *b* values, and then uses the resulting formula to determine further points on the line described by the values you give as *newx's*.

TREND, like LINEST, is useful in making linear estimates of growth, but is subject to the same limitations.

You can use TREND for polynomial curve fitting by using the same variable raised to different powers and declaring the range containing the values of the different powers as the knownx's. See the discussion on TREND in the *Microsoft Excel Functions and Macros* manual for an example involving polynomials.

Example

Suppose you had the data shown below as sales data for the first four months of the year, and you wanted to project what the next four would be like (see Figure 3-6).

Figure 3-6. Sample Spreadsheet

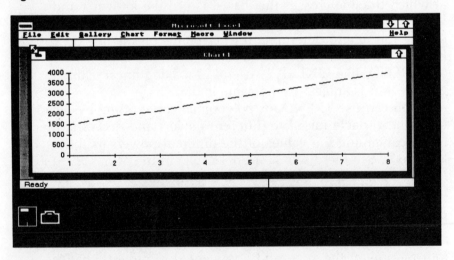

$=\text{TREND(B4:B7,,\{5,6,7,8\})} = 2889$

for month 5 and produce a trendline as shown in Figure 3-7.

Figure 3-7. Trendline for Sales Projection

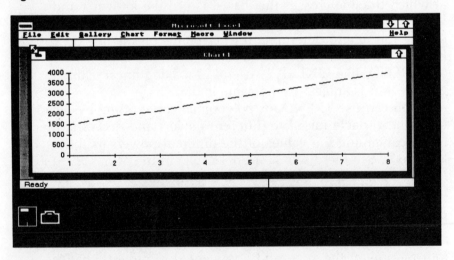

VAR(*number1,number2, . . .*)

Estimate of variance of a population based on sample given in arguments.

VARP(*number1,number2, . . .*)

Variance of a population based on the entire population.

Variance is another of the standard measures of reliability of a set of data. It's the square of the standard deviation from the mean, and measures how much data points vary from the mean value. The higher the figure, the more nearly random the sample is likely to be. (See the discussion about deviation from the mean under STDEV.)

VAR and VARP can each have up to 14 arguments. All text, logical values, or empty cell values cause errors. VAR assumes its arguments are a sample of the population. If your data represents the entire population, use VARP.

Example

Suppose you have student test scores as shown in Figure 3-8.

Figure 3-8. Sample Test Scores

	A	B	C	D	E	F	G	H
1	Student		Test A	Test B	Test C	Final Exam		Weighted Average
2			20%	20%	20%	40%		
3	Austine, S.		78	86	82	88		84
4	Blues, B.		68	77	84	85		80
5	Cala, C.		98	90	91	87		91
6	Dowden, T.		90	100	91	94		94
7	Edwards, S.		83	87	89	88		87
8	Fry, B.		69	76	78	72		73
9	Giguette, A.		93	92	97	99		96
10	Hardy, J.		57	68	67	72		67
11	Inders, D.		86	81	84	89		86
12	Johnson, J.		[illegible]	90	93	100		95
13								
14								
15								

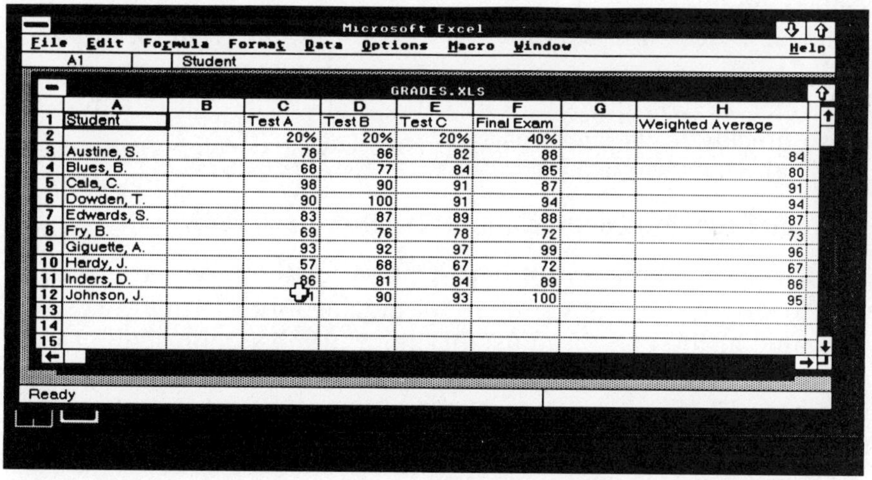

You'd like to know if the test was of reasonable difficulty and you're willing to say it was reasonable if the test scores follow a normal distribution. A normal distribution would mean that about ⅔ of the test scores will be grouped within plus and minus one standard deviation from the mean.

A large standard deviation, and hence a large variance, means scores are widely scattered. A smaller standard deviation and a smaller variance means scores are closer together; this is what you want if the test was a valid test of what students had learned, other things being equal.

The function =VAR(D3:D12) lets you determine whether the test scores for Test B fell into a normal pattern. VAR, remember, works on a sample of the population, not the population as a whole. The result, 86.45555556, indicates the test might not have been so reasonable.

The function =VARP(C3:F12) gives you a look at the distribution for the entire population. The result, 100.2875, indicates that your tests may not have been appropriate for this class.

Financial Functions

The financial functions included in *Excel* are standard ones used in financial calculations in real estate, banking, and investing.

DDB(*cost,salvage,life,period*)

Calculates the depreciation of an asset using the double-declining balance method.

Double-declining balance is a method of determining the depreciation of an asset. It's most often used when you want to depreciate an item quickly in its early years of useful life, and not so quickly in its later years.

DDB uses the formula

((cost total previous depreciation)*2) / life

to determine the amount of depreciation for the a period. You need to supply as arguments the original *cost* of the item, its *salvage* value at the end of its useful life, a number representing its useful *life,* and the *period* for which you want to know DDB depreciation. The numbers specified for *life* and *period* must be in the same unit: years, months, weeks, and so on. All four arguments must be positive numbers.

Example

You've bought a new copier for your business. You paid $1800, and you expect it to last four years, at which time you think you might be able to get $150 for it. The double-declining balance method produces the following depreciation figures for it:

=DDB(1800,150,4,1)=900 (depreciation for the 1st year)

=DDB(1800,150,4,2)=450 (depreciation for the 2nd year)

= DDB(1800,150,4,3) = 225 (depreciation for the 3rd year)

= DDB(1800,150,4,4) = 75 (depreciation for the 4th year)

= DDB(1800,150,48,1) = 75 (depreciation for the 1st month)

= DDB(1800,150,48,2) = 71.87 (depreciation for the 2nd month)

= DDB(1800,150,208,1) = 17.31 (depreciation for the 1st week)

FV(*rate,#periods,pmt,pv,type*)

Future value of an investment.

FV is one of the five *Excel* functions concerned with *annuities*. An annuity is a term referring to a series of constant cash flows made over a continuous period of time.

FV lets you determine the net amount you'll get at the end of a specified number of periods if you make regular payments into an account, at a fixed rate of interest.

The arguments *rate, #periods,* and *pmt* are required; *pv* (present value) and *type* are optional.

Rate is the interest rate per period. It's entered as a number with a decimal fraction (if any), with a percent sign: 8%, or 6.5%, for instance.

#periods is the total number of payment periods. In a 30-year loan with monthly payments, *#periods* would be 360.

Pmt is the amount of the payment each period. It doesn't change from period to period, and in a fully amortized loan contains principle and interest payments. However, though the amount stays the same, the percentage of each payment that reflects principle and interest changes from period to period. *Excel*'s convention is that if you pay it out, *pmt* is a negative number; if you receive it, *pmt* is a positive number.

Pv is present value, or the net amount you could get for the projected series of cash flow.

Type indicates when payments are due: 0 if they come at the end of each period, and 1 if they come at the beginning of each period. If omitted, type is assumed to be 0.

Example

Suppose you were trying to save enough money to take time off and go to Fiji for several months. You couldn't plunk down several thousand dollars right now, but you figured you could squirrel away $200 a month for three years, in an investment that safely paid 11 percent per year. How much would your nest egg be worth at the end of three years?

The FV function to tell you what you'd have to work with is:

$$= FV(11\%/12,36,200) = 8484.62$$

You could get quite a suntan with that.

IPMT(*rate,per,#periods,pv,fv,type*)

Interest payment for an investment.

IPMT returns the interest payment for a given series of cash flows, over a specified period of time, and at a constant interest rate.

IPMT is useful for calculating how much of any given payment on a loan is interest. If you know the full payment amount, you can then also determine how much of the payment is principal.

Rate, #periods, pv, fv, and *type* were discussed under the FV function. (*Fv* and *type* are optional; if omitted, they're assumed to be 0.) *Per* is the number of the period for which you want to determine the amount of interest. If you start making monthly payments in January, the September payment will be payment 9.

Example

You have a 4-year, $5000 loan at 10 percent interest on which you began making payments in December. You know you can deduct the interest portion of that month's payment on your tax return, so you use the IPMT function to figure it out.

$$= IPMT(10\%/12,1,48,5000) = 41.67$$

The PPMT function works in a similar way, but it determines the amount of principal in a payment.

IRR(*values,guess*)

Internal rate of return for series of cash flows in values. IRR gives you an investment rate for a series of cash flows you specify as arrays or references. Unlike an annuity, which would require equal cash flows, IRR can handle unequal amounts, and both income (positive) and payments (negative). If the payments are monthly, the rate you'll get will be a monthly rate.

Guess is optional and represents your estimate of what the

IRR will be. Since IRR is an iterative calculation, guess narrows the field by giving *Excel* a place to start. *Excel* tries a number of values until it gets a result that's accurate to within .00001 percent, but gives up (with a #NUM! error message) if it hasn't found an accurate answer within 20 tries. If you omit *guess*, it is assumed to be 0.1 (10 percent). If the answer seems odd, or if you get the #NUM! error message, try a different value for *guess*.

IRR computes the discount rate that equates the present value of future cash flows to the cost of the investment. In other words, what would be the interest rate at which the cost of this investment could be placed that would generate the present value of the cash flows you specify?

The cells you specify in values must contain numbers; at least one must be negative and at least one must be positive.

Example

You want to purchase a small fourplex and fix it up, and plan to sell it after 18 months. Your projected cash flows are shown below:

Figure 3-9. Real Estate Cash Flows

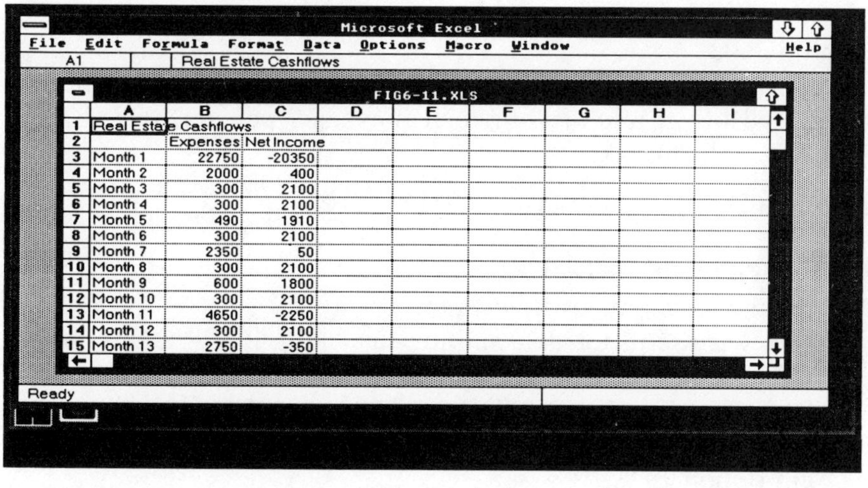

To calculate the rate of return at the end of the investment period, the IRR function is:

=IRR(C3:C20,12%) = 0.096257

MIRR(*values, financerate, reinvestrate*)

Modified internal rate of return.

A modified internal rate of return takes into account both the cost of the investment, in financerate, and the interest received in reinvestment of cash, in *reinvestrate.* Like IRR, the cash flows are in the array or range specified in values. *Financerate* applies to the first value, which ordinarily would be the purchase cost of the investment, and *reinvestrate* applies to any subsequent cash flows.

Example

Take the example shown above under IRR. When you purchased the fourplex, you had to get the money from some other account, which was probably paying interest. The rate at which that down payment was earning interest is what you specify as financerate.

The cash flows are assumed to go directly into an account that also earns interest, such as a money market fund, and the rate at which those cash flows earn interest is what you specify as reinvestrate.

Since you've already specified a reinvestment rate, along with a rate at which your down payment was also earning interest, it's not necessary to give a guess as to the internal rate of return.

If your down payment had been earning 9.5 percent, and the reinvestment rate of your cash flows is 9 percent, the MIRR function looks like this:

= MIRR(C3:C20,9.5%,9%) = 0.094115

NPER(*rate, pmt, pv, fv, type*)

Number of payments of investment.

NPER is useful for determining how long it will take you to pay off a loan.

It assumes payments will be regular, and the interest rate is constant. The values *rate, pmt,* and *pv* must be specified; *fv* and *type* are optional.

Example

You've loaned a cousin $1000, at seven percent interest, with $75 monthly payments. How long will it take for the loan to be paid off? The NPER function shows you:

$$= \text{NPER}(7\%, 75, 1000) = 14$$

NPV(*rate, value1, value2, . . .*)

Net present value of the amounts you specify in values.

Net present value calculates the current worth of a series of future payments (negative values) and income (positive values), discounted at a rate you specify.

The net present value of an investment is today's value of a series of future cash flows, both positive and negative. It assumes the rate you specify is what you might have received for a competing investment, or for the rate of inflation. This is not the same as an interest rate, which compounds growth on a regular basis.

Net present value lets you compare dissimilar investments that provide future cash flows, taking into account factors that could influence what you might otherwise earn over equivalent periods.

In the computation of net present value, the interest is removed from a future amount to arrive at the initial amount invested. The process of reducing future values to present values is called discounting, and for that reason, net present value is sometimes called a discounted value. The interest to be subtracted is called the discount, and the rate of interest is called the discount rate. It's this discount rate you specify in a net present value function.

Example

You have an investment that requires a $10,000 investment in a year, but will pay annual cash flows to you over the subsequent three years in the amounts of $3000, $4200, and $6800. Assume that between the rate of inflation and the rate you could get for the money used for your down payment, you will use a discount rate of 10 percent. What would be the net present value of this investment?

$$= \text{NPV}(10\%, -10000, 3000, 4200, 6800) = \$1188$$

The cash flows are discounted at the rate indicated to come

up with a current value for the income stream. Then the down payment is subtracted from this to produce the net present value for the entire investment.

PMT(*rate,#periods,pv,fv,type*)

Periodic payment on investment.

PMT calculates the periodic, regular payment for an investment at a constant interest rate.

Rate is the periodic interest rate. If you use an annual interest rate but want monthly payments, specify the annual rate divided by 12 (for instance, 8 percent divided by 12 would provide the monthly rate for an annual percentage rate of eight percent).

Specify the number of periods for the life of the investment. If you'll be making monthly payments, multiply the number of years by 12 to get the number of monthly payments.

The value given for *pv* represents the amount of the investment, or principal.

The *fv* (future value) and *type* arguments are optional, and assumed to be 0 if omitted. They were discussed under the FV function.

Example

You're buying a car with an $8500 loan at 12.5 percent interest for five years. What will your monthly payments be? Using the PMT function:

$$= PMT(12.5\%/12,60,8500) = -191.23$$

PV(*rate,#periods,pmt,fv,type*)

Present value of investment.

PV determines the present value of an annuity, or regular series or cash flows, at a constant rate of interest over a specified number of periods. The values *rate, #periods*, and *pmt* are required; *fv* and *type* are optional.

Example

You're approached by a broker who is offering you a limited partnership interest that will pay you $500 a month for 5 years. You can invest these payments and get 8 percent on your money. The cost of the partnership interest is $20,000. Should you buy an interest?

The PV function tells you:

=PV(.08/12,5*12,500)= −24659.22

The negative result means money you'd pay out now to get the annuity specified. Since the broker is asking $20,000 as the price, it sounds like a good deal.

RATE(*#periods,pmt,pv,fv,type,guess*)

Rate returned on an investment.

Rate is similar to IRR and MIRR in that it returns an interest rate. It differs in that IRR and MIRR can work with uneven cash flows, but RATE needs the constant payments of an annuity.

The values *#periods, pmt,* and *pv* are required for RATE; *fv,type,* and *guess* are optional.

Like IRR, RATE is an iterative calculation. *Excel* tries up to 20 guesses at a solution; if they don't converge to within 0.0000001 after 20 tries, you'll get a #NUM! error message.

Example

You've borrowed $15000 from your parents to complete the down payment for a house. You've promised to pay it back at $200 a month for 10 years. What implicit rate of interest have you agreed to? The RATE function tells you:

=RATE(10*12, −200,15000)=0.008511 (the monthly interest rate)

Multiply the monthly rate by 12 to convert to an annual rate. In this example, the effective annual interest rate is 10.21 percent.

SLN(*cost,salvage,life*)

Straight line depreciation for an asset.

Straight line depreciation is the simplest and most commonly used form of depreciation. It assumes an item depreciates in linear fashion, with equal amounts of value lost each year of its useful life.

Suppose you own a rental property, and you've purchased a new washer and dryer for it. Because it's considered "business equipment" for tax purposes, you can depreciate it and deduct the depreciation when you compute your taxes. To make things easier, you decide to use straight line depreciation. The appliances cost you $780, and you expect them to last five years, after which time you can probably get $100 for them when you trade them in on newer models.

The SLN function to tell you how much you'll be able to deduct for them each year is:

= SLN(780,100,5) = 136

SYD(*cost, salvage, life, period*)

Sum-of-the-years'-digits depreciation for an asset.

SYD is a form of depreciation that results in more depreciation in the earlier years of an item's useful life, and less toward the end.

Each period's depreciation will differ, so SYD has you specify the period for which you want to determine the amount of depreciation. If you're looking for an annual amount, specify the year number of the item's life. (Be sure to use the same unit for both life and period.)

Example

You've bought a truck for $15,000 that has a useful life of 10 years, and you estimate a salvage value of $1000. Using the SYD method, how much depreciation can you take in the first year?

= SYD(15000,1000,10,1) = 2545.45

Note: When preparing to calculate tax deductions that involve depreciation, it's wise to compare what the different methods will produce for you. For instance, compare the depreciation amounts for the same truck if you use the double-declining balance method and the straight line methods:

= DDB(15000,1000,10,1) = 3000

= SLN(15000,1000,10) = 1400

In this case, you'll get more depreciation the first year using the double declining balance method. However, you may want to weigh your decision in terms of how much depreciation you'll get in subsequent years.

Information Functions

The information functions are generally used to return data about cell location, status, and type of contents.

AREAS(*reference*)

Number of areas in *reference*.

AREAS counts the number of separate groupings of cells in the range specified in *reference*. It's an especially useful function in a macro where you want to test if a reference is a multiple selection.

Examples

= AREAS(C2:C20) = 1

= AREAS(POPULATION) = 3 (if the range named POPULATION refers to C2:C20, D2:D16, and D17:D20)

CELL(*infotype,reference*)

Information about formatting, location, or contents of reference.

CELL returns data about the upper left cell in the range identified in *reference*. If *reference* is omitted, *Excel* assumes it's the current cell. If *reference* is a multiple reference (such as POPULATION in the AREAS example above), *Excel* returns the error value #VALUE!.

Infotype must be a text value that specifies the type of cell information you want, and should be one of the values in the table below:

Infotype	Result
"width"	Column width of cell, as an integer.
"row"	Equals the row number in reference.
"col"	Equals the column number in reference.
"protect"	Lock status: 0 if cell is not locked, 1 if it is.
"address"	Coordinates of the first cell in reference, as text.
"contents"	The value currently in reference.
"prefix"	A text value corresponding to the label prefix of the cell:
	`" ' "` Left-aligned
	`" " "` Right-aligned
	`" "` Centered
	`" "` Anything else

Infotype	Result
"type"	A text value corresponding to the data in the cell: "b" blank, empty cell "l" label, text "v" value or anything else
"format"	A text value corresponding to the format in the cell:

Text Value Returned	Format
"G"	General
"F0"	0 or #,##0
"F2"	0.00 or #,##0.00
"C0"	$#,##0 ($#,##0)
"P0"	0%
"P2"	0.00%
"S2"	0.00E+00
"D4"	m/d/yy or m/d/yy h:mm
"D1"	d-mmm-yy
"D2"	d-mmm
"D3"	mmm-yy
"D7"	h:mm AM/PM
"D6"	h:mm:ss AM/PM
"D9"	h:mm
"D8"	h:mm:ss

Note: if you need to use cell information in a macro, use the GET.CELL macro command.

Examples

=CELL("row",D15:G15)=15

=CELL("format",D15)="P2" (if cell D15 has been formatted to display percentages as 0.00%)

COLUMN(*reference*)

Number of columns in *reference*.

COLUMN returns the number of columns in the area specified. If *reference* is a range, COLUMN returns the column numbers as a horizontal array. *Reference* cannot refer to multiple areas, such as those contained in POPULATION in the example under AREA.

Examples

=COLUMN(D5)=1

=COLUMN(D5:G20)={1,2,3,4}

COLUMNS(*array*)

Number of columns in *array*.

COLUMNS returns the number of columns in the *array* specified. The *array* must be entered in proper form.

Examples

=COLUMNS(D5:G20)=4

=COLUMNS{1,2,3;4,5,6}=3

INDIRECT(*text, type*)

Contents of the cell from its reference.

INDIRECT is one way of getting the contents of a cell. Do this by specifying the name of the cell or its address in either A1 style or R1C1 style. If you use the name of a cell, enclose it in double quotes.

Examples

Assume cell D5 contains the text "F22" and cell F22 contains the value $542.35. The function

=INDIRECT(D5)=542.35

Assume cell A1 contains the text "R2C2." Then the function

=INT(INDIRECT(R1C1,FALSE))=1

ISBLANK(*value*)

Returns TRUE if *value* is blank.

ISBLANK tests a cell to see whether it's blank. If it finds an empty cell, it returns TRUE; otherwise it returns FALSE.

Examples

=ISBLANK(C5)=FALSE (if C5 contains 0)

=ISBLANK(C5)=FALSE (if C5 contains "TRUE")

=ISBLANK(C5)=TRUE (if C5 is blank)

ISERR(*value*)

Returns TRUE if *value* is any error value except #N/A.

ISERROR(*value*)

Returns TRUE if *value* is any error value.

These two functions test for the presence of error messages. ISERR tests for any error value except #N/A. ISERROR tests for any of the *Excel* error values:

#N/A
#VALUE!
#REF!
#DIV/0!
#NUM!
#NAME?
#NULL!

If anything other than the specified contents are found, it returns FALSE.

Example

ISERR and ISERROR are particularly useful in formulas and macros where you want to find errors or unusable values in a calculation. For instance, suppose you wanted to average the numbers in cells C50:C55, but you wanted to be sure there were numbers in each of those cells before you started because if all of the cells are blank it will result in an error (you'd get the error message #DIV/0!). If you were to use the formula

=IF(ISERROR(AVERAGE(C50:C55)),
"Blanks",AVERAGE(C50:C55))

you'd receive the message *"Blanks"* in the current cell if *Excel* found any of the cells in C50:C55 to be blank, but would compute the average if some of them contained numbers.

ISLOGICAL(*value*)

Returns TRUE if *value* is a logical value.

ISLOGICAL tests for the presence of TRUE or FALSE, or a value that can be interpreted as TRUE or FALSE.

Example

=ISLOGICAL(A14)=TRUE (if A14 contains the value TRUE)

=ISLOGICAL(A14)=FALSE (if A14 contains $243.75)

ISNA(*value*)

Returns TRUE if *value* is the error value #N/A.

ISNA looks specifically for the error value #N/A. This is useful when checking for errors as a result of earlier calculations.

Example

=ISNA(D42)=FALSE (if D42 contains the error value #NUM! or the values $750 or TRUE)

ISNONTEXT(*value*)

Returns TRUE if *value* is not text.

ISNONTEXT checks for the presence of anything other than text, and returns a TRUE if it is anything other than text, or a FALSE if it finds text.

Example

=ISNONTEXT(E18)=TRUE (if E18 contains a number or a logical value)

=ISNONTEXT(E18)=FALSE (if E18 contains "Name")

ISNUMBER(*value*)

Returns TRUE if *value* is a number.

ISNUMBER checks for the presence of a number, and returns TRUE if it is a number, or FALSE if it finds anything else.

Example

=ISNUMBER(B35)=TRUE (if B35 contains a number)

=ISNUMBER(B35)=FALSE (if B35 contains TRUE)

ISREF(*value*)

Returns TRUE if *value* is a reference.

ISREF checks *value* for a reference, and returns TRUE if it is a reference, or FALSE if it finds anything else.

Example

=ISREF(Salary)=TRUE (if Salary is a range name)

ISTEXT(*value*)

Returns TRUE if *value* is text.

ISTEXT checks *value* for the presence of text, and returns a TRUE if it finds text, or a FALSE if it finds anything else.

Example

=ISTEXT(F12)=TRUE (if F12 contains "Mary Smith")

N(*value*)

Translates *value* into a number.

The function N evaluates whatever you specify, and translates what it finds into a number.

If you enter or refer to a number as the argument, N returns that number. If the argument is or refers to TRUE, N returns the value 1. If the argument is or refers to anything else, N returns a 0.

Generally, *Excel* translates values as indicated above, regardless of the presence of the N function. It's provided here to make *Excel* compatible with other spreadsheet programs.

Examples

=N("4/15/88")=0 (because "4/15/88" is text)

=N(5)=5 =N(C5)=1 (if C5 contains TRUE)

NA( )

Error value #N/A.

The NA function is usually used to mark empty cells. If a calculation includes cells that should contain values but don't, the error message #N/A! will flag the situation. This situation commonly occurs when you don't have all the data you need to complete a spreadsheet.

The NA function inserts the value #N/A wherever you enter it. You can also type the value #N/A directly into the cell.

If you use the NA function, you must include the parentheses or *Excel* will report a syntax error.

Example

Suppose you have values as follows:

	L	M	N	O
33	15	25	35	45
34	247	134	105	
35	101	#N/A	125	117

AVERAGE(L33:O33) = 30

AVERAGE(L34:O34) = 162

AVERAGE(L35:O35) = #N/A!

ROW(*reference*)

Returns number of rows in *reference*.

ROW returns the number of rows in the area specified. If *reference* is a range, ROW returns the row numbers as a horizontal array. *Reference* cannot refer to multiple areas, such as those contained in POPULATION in the example under AREA.

Examples

= ROW(D5) = 5 = ROW(D1:G4) = {1,2,3,4}

ROWS(*array*)

Returns number of rows in *array*.

ROWS returns the number of rows in the array specified. The array must be entered in proper form.

Examples

= ROWS(D1:G4) = 4 = ROWS{1,2,3;4,5,6} = 2

T(*value*)

Translates *value* into text.

If it encounters text, T returns whatever was specified as *value*. Otherwise, T returns " ", as empty text.

Generally, *Excel* translates values as indicated above, regardless of the presence of the T function. It's provided here to make *Excel* compatible with other spreadsheet programs.

Examples

=T(B48)="TRUE" (if B48 contained the text value "TRUE")

=T(TRUE)=" "

TYPE(*value*)

Returns type of *value*.

TYPE returns a number indicating the data type of *value*. Numbers returned are as follows:

Value	TYPE Returns
Number	1
Text	2
Logical value	4
Error value	16
Array	64

Examples

=TYPE(A5)=1 (if A5 contains 365)

=TYPE(D1)=2 (if D1 contains "March")

Lookup Functions

The lookup functions are used when you want to find data within a table. Generally, the functions use an index value to tell *Excel* to look within the table for data.

CHOOSE(*indexnumber,value1,value2, . . .*)

Uses *indexnumber* to select a value from values.

CHOOSE works a little like the IF function: It returns results based on values you specify. It differs from IF in that you can have a number of items to consider rather than a single item for a TRUE condition and one item for a FALSE condition.

It also bears some resemblance to the LOOKUP functions (which follow), but CHOOSE works with any of the values referenced in the argument list, rather than just those arranged in table form.

The arguments for CHOOSE can be range references as well as individual values. This allows you some interesting possibilities for calculations:

=SUM(CHOOSE(Offset,C5:C9,D5:D9,E5:E9))

This formula lets you sum the results of any of the three ranges shown, depending on whether the named cell Offset contains a 1, 2, or 3.

You can also use CHOOSE in a macro with GOTOs as the value arguments. For instance, you could use the following functions in a macro:

=CHOOSE(Counter,GOTO(First),GOTO(Second),GOTO(Third))

Examples

=CHOOSE(A5,"Pass","Fail","Conditional")="Pass" (if cell A5 contains 1)

=SUM(D23:CHOOSE(F2,D32,D36,D40))=SUM(D23:D40) (if F2 contains 3)

HLOOKUP(*lookupvalue, table, rownumber*)

Finds a value in *rownumber* of *table* selected by *lookupvalue.*

The functions HLOOKUP and VLOOKUP let *Excel* find values from a table in much the same way you scan a table. HLOOKUP assumes the values are stored in ascending order from left to right in two or more rows; VLOOKUP assumes the values are stored in ascending order from top to bottom in two or more columns.

With HLOOKUP, *Excel* scans the top row of table, looking for the last value that doesn't exceed *lookupvalue.* Having found that, it drops down the number of rows indicated in *rownumber,* and returns the value it finds there.

Example

HLOOKUP lends itself nicely to dealing with tax tables. For instance, suppose you wanted to determine the amount of straight-line depreciation for property, using a table that shows the percentages for properties with various standard useful lives. Below is such a tax table:

Depreciation rate for recovery period, by years

	AA	AB	AC	AD	AE	AF	AG
10		3	5	7	10	15	20
11	1	33.33%	20.00%	14.29%	10.00%	5.00%	3.75%
12	2	44.45%	32.00%	24.49%	18.00%	9.50%	7.219%
13	3	14.81%	19.20%	17.49%	14.40%	8.55%	6.677%

Rows 11 through 13 are for years 1, 2, and 3 in each category. If you wanted to determine the depreciation for an item with a 7-year life, in its third year, the HLOOKUP function would look like this:

= HLOOKUP(7,AB10:AG13,3) = 17.49%

Depreciation for the second year of an item with a 15-year life would look like this:

= HLOOKUP(15,AB10:AG13,2) = 9.50%

INDEX(*ref,rownumber,columnnumber,areanumber*)

INDEX(*array,rownumber,columnnumber*)

Reference in *ref* or *value* in array selected by index values.

The INDEX function has two forms, one that works with cell references and one that works with arrays. The former uses a reference to one or more cell ranges in an argument called *ref*. If *ref* contains more than one range, use the optional argument, *areanumber,* to indicate which range is to be considered. The array reference form uses a reference to an array constant, and returns a value or array of values.

Both forms use numbers to refer to rows and columns within the range(s) specified: 1 is the first row within the range, regardless of its actual row number, 2 is the second row, and so on. The same principle is used to number columns within a range.

Example

Suppose you have the following table, listing among other things, various types of lettuce seeds for your nursery. It's keyed to a stock number as follows:

	A	B	C
35	Simpson	1.85	B-59535
36	Bibb	2.10	B-58982
37	Buttercrunch	1.95	B-59543
38	Great Lakes	1.95	B-59550
40	White Cos	1.95	B-59014
41	Ruby	1.95	B-59048
42	Tango	2.10	B-59600

To obtain the stock number of Buttercrunch seeds, the INDEX function would look like this:

= INDEX(A35:C42,3,3) = "B-59543"

In array form, an array must be entered instead of a reference to a range or set of ranges. For instance,

= INDEX({2,4,6;20,40,60},2,2) = 20

The value of 20 is the result of the formula because the arguments 2,2 point to the second value in the second part of the array (the second element in the second range).

If the array or cell reference only contains one row or column, only one argument needs to be provided.

LOOKUP(*lookupvalue,lookupvector,resultvector*)

LOOKUP(*lookupvalue,array*)

Value in a table selected by *lookupvalue*.

The LOOKUP function has two forms. One form works with vectors, and the other works with arrays.

A vector is an array that contains only one row or one column. The vector form of LOOKUP inspects *lookupvector* for *lookupvalue* or the largest value that doesn't exceed *lookupvalue*. It also moves to the corresponding position in *resultvector* and returns the value it finds there.

The array form of LOOKUP looks for *lookupvalue* in the first row or column of array, moves down or across to the last cell, and gives the value of that cell.

The array form of LOOKUP is very similar to HLOOKUP and VLOOKUP in that all three search tables. However, HLOOKUP inspects the first row, VLOOKUP inspects the first column, but LOOKUP searches according to the dimensions of the array. If the array has the same number of columns as rows, or more columns than rows, LOOKUP inspects the first row; if the array has more rows than columns, LOOKUP inspects the first column.

Additionally, HLOOKUP and VLOOKUP let you index within the table; LOOKUP always returns the last value in the row or column.

Example

	A	B	C	D	E	F
1	1	2	3	4	5	6
2	red	orange	yellow	green	blue	violet

In the table above,

LOOKUP(5,A1:F1,A2:F2) = "blue"

LOOKUP(3.5,A1:F1,A2:F2) = "yellow"

LOOKUP(2.999,A1:F1,A2:F2) = "orange"

The array form works a bit differently:

=LOOKUP("E",{"e","s","p","f";1,2,3,4}) = 1

=LOOKUP("Beringer",{"a",1;"b",2;"c",3}) = 2

MATCH(*lookupvalue,lookuparray,matchtype*)

Index of a value selected by *lookupvalue.*

MATCH returns the relative position of the element in *lookuparray* that satisfies *lookupvalue,* according to the value of *matchtype.* You can choose three types of matches:

Matchtype	MATCH finds	Order of Lookuparray
1, or omitted	Largest value less than or equal to *lookupvalue*	Must be in ascending order: $-2, -1, 0, 1, 2$ . . .; A–Z; FALSE, TRUE

Matchtype	MATCH finds	Order of Lookuparray
0	First value that exactly matches *lookupvalue*	Can be in any order
−1	Smallest value greater than or equal to *look-upvalue*	Must be in descending order: TRUE,FALSE; Z–A; . . . 2,1,0, − 1, − 2, . . .

MATCH gives the position of the matched value, not the value itself. If *matchtype* is 0 and *lookupvalue* is text, *lookupvalue* can contain the wildcard characters * and ?.

Examples

	A	B
1	Month	Mean Temp.
2	1	57
3	2	59
4	3	64
5	4	69
6	5	73
7	6	74
8	7	71
9	8	70
10	9	72
11	10	69
12	11	65
13	12	60

=MATCH(9,A2:A13,0)=9

=MATCH(9,A2:A9,1)=8

=MATCH(9,A2:A13, − 1)=#N/A! (because the range is incorrectly ordered for type − 1)

VLOOKUP(*lookupvalue, table, columnnumber*)

Finds a value in *columnnumber* of *table* selected by *lookupvalue*.

VLOOKUP inspects the first column of the table for a value that's less than or equal to lookupvalue. It then indexes over col-umnnumber of columns and returns the value it finds there.

Like HLOOKUP, VLOOKUP lends itself to tax table work. For instance, suppose you want the program to determine your tax based on your taxable income and status. (You actually could use *Excel* to determine tax amounts, using the current year's tax tables from the appropriate IRS document and a combination of lookup functions and mathematical operations.) A portion of a tax table might look like this:

	AZ	AA	BB	BC	BD
		Single	Mar/joint	Mar/sep.	Head hshld
10	30050	6363	4647	7054	5317
11	30100	6380	4661	7071	5331
12	30150	6398	4675	7089	5345
13	30200	6415	4689	7106	5359
14	30250	6433	4703	7124	5373
15	30300	6450	4717	7141	5387
16	30350	6468	4731	7159	5401
17	30400	6485	4745	7166	5415
18	30450	6503	4759	7194	5429
19	30500	6520	4773	7211	5443

A VLOOKUP function to determine the tax for a single tax-payer with a taxable income of $30,335 would look like this:

= VLOOKUP(30335,AZ10:BD19,1) = 6450

Text Functions

Text functions let you use character strings within labels. They aren't concerned with mathematical evaluations.

CHAR(*number*)

ASCII character corresponding to *number*.

CHAR returns the ASCII character that's equivalent to the decimal number you specify. The argument number can range from 1 to 255. See the ASCII chart in Appendix B.

Examples

= CHAR(72) = H = CHAR(52) = 4 = CHAR(35) = #

CLEAN(*text*)

Removes control characters from *text*.

Some ASCII characters are not printable. If you want *text* to include only printable characters, use CLEAN to remove non-printing characters.

Examples

Say you have a cell named Buffer in which you've placed the name *Norman Howard*, along with several nonprinting characters.

=CLEAN(Buffer)=Norman Howard (the string of characters stored in the cell minus any non-printing characters)

CODE(*text*)

ASCII code of the first character in text.

CODE is the inverse of CHAR, except it returns only the code of the first character in the text string you specify as an argument.

Example

CODE("Animal")=65 (65 is the ASCII value of the letter A)

DOLLAR(*number,decimals*)

Rounds a number and returns it as text in currency format.

DOLLAR converts the number you specify to the format $#,##0.00 or ($#,##0.00). If the number you give for decimals is positive, it specifies the number of digits to the right of the decimal point. If the number you give for *decimals* is negative, number is rounded to the left of the decimal point the specified number of spaces.

The important difference between using DOLLAR to format a number and using the currency format on it is that DOLLAR returns the value as text, while the currency format leaves it a number.

If you omit the decimals argument, *Excel* assumes it to be 2.

Examples

=DOLLAR(543.21)="$543.21"

=DOLLAR(543.21,−2)="$500"

=DOLLAR(9876543.21,3)="$9876543.210"

EXACT(*text1, text2*)

Tests to see if *text1* and *text2* are exactly the same.

EXACT returns the value TRUE if text1 and text2 are exactly the same. If they're not identical, EXACT returns the value FALSE.

The arguments *text1* and *text2* must be text values, or references to text values.

Examples

=EXACT("this","this")=TRUE

=EXACT("this","that")=FALSE

=EXACT("This","this")=FALSE

FIND(*findtext, withintext, startnumber*)

Finds *findtext* within *withintext*.

FIND allows you to search a specified set of text for a specific character string, and returns the character number within that specified text at which *findtext* first occurs. (The first character of *withintext* is character 1.) The text to be searched is specified as *withintext*, and may be the name of a cell containing text. You indicate what you want to find as *findtext*. FIND is case sensitive, and you may not use wildcard characters in *findtext*.

Startnumber is optional. It represents the character number in *withintext* at which *Excel* should start looking for *findtext*.

If *startnumber* is larger than *withintext*, or is zero or a negative value, or if findtext is not found in withintext, FIND returns the error message #VALUE!.

Examples

=FIND("A","Ampersand")=1

=FIND("a","Ampersand")=7

=FIND("and","Ampersand")=7

=FIND("and",CHAR)=7 (where the cell named CHAR contains the text "Ampersand")

FIXED(*number, decimals*)

Rounds *number* and gives it as text.

FIXED rounds a specified number to the number of digits to the right of the decimal point specified in the argument decimal.

It adds the decimal point and commas as necessary, and returns the result as text.

If the argument decimal is negative, the number is rounded to the equivalent number of digits to the left of the decimal point. If you omit the decimals argument, it's assumed to be 2.

The important difference between using FIXED to format a number and using the Format Number command is that FIXED returns the value as text, while the Format Number command leaves it as a number.

Examples

= FIXED(54321) = "54321.00"

= FIXED(543.21, − 2) = "500"

= FIXED(9876543.21,3) = "9,876,543.210"

LEFT(*text,charnumber*)

Extract first *charnumber* characters of text.

LEFT counts the characters in text, and copies the leftmost *charnumber* of them into the current cell. If *charnumber* is omitted, it's assumed to be 1.

Examples

= LEFT("Paul Gauguin",6) = "Paul G"

= LEFT("80386-inspired architecture",5) = "80386"

= LEFT(A22,7) = "FY 1987" (if A22 contained the text string "FY 1987: 3rd Quarter")

LEN(*text*)

Length of *text* in characters.

LEN measures the length of text and returns the number of characters it finds. LEN is particularly useful when preparing to insert text of uncertain length into some other cell. In some of these cases, it may be useful to increase the cell width to accommodate the full length of text string.

Examples

= LEN("Puyallup") = 8

= LEN(Name) = 25 (if the first cell of the range Name contains 25 characters of text)

LOWER(*text*)

Converts *text* to all lowercase.

LOWER is the opposite of UPPER, in that LOWER makes all characters in text lowercase, whereas UPPER capitalizes all letters in text.

Examples

= LOWER("JANUARY") = "january"

= LOWER("First Friday") = "first friday"

= LOWER(B22) = "prices" (if cell B22 contained "Prices")

MID(*text,startnumber,charnumber*)

Extracts *charnumber* of characters from *text*, starting at *startnumber*.

MID allows you to extract a specified number of characters from *text*. Specify where the extracted string should begin in the argument *startnumber*.

If *startnumber* is less than one, or if *charnumber* is negative, MID returns the error message #VALUE!. If *startnumber* is greater than the length of text, the result is " ", the empty text value. If *startnumber* plus *charnumber* takes you past the end of text, the result will be all the characters to the end of text, with no spaces or fill characters added.

MID can be useful if some other manipulation has removed all spaces from text, and you need some of the characters from within that compacted text.

Examples

= MID("Here'sasampleofcompactedtext",8,6) = "sample"

= MID("4007 Hall Blvd. NE",6,20) = "Hall Blvd. NE"

PROPER(*text*)

Converts *text* to initial capitals.

PROPER capitalizes all text strings it finds in *text*. It considers anything that follows a space or punctuation to be a text string.

Examples

= PROPER("JAN FEB MAR APR") = "Jan Feb Mar Apr"

= PROPER("It's a boy!") = "It'S A Boy!"

REPLACE(*oldtext,startnumber,charnumber,newtext*)

Replaces *charnumber* of characters in *oldtext* with *newtext*.

REPLACE allows you to selectively replace characters in text. You have to specify the number of characters from the beginning to start, and how many characters are to be replaced.

Examples

=REPLACE("Proj. Mgr: Linda Smith",12,11,"Duc Ng")="Proj. Mgr: Duc Ng"

=REPLACE("Review 12/1/87",8,7,"6/1/88")="Review 6/1/88"

REPT(*text,number*)

Repeats *text number* of times.

REPT allows you to repeat a character or set of characters the number of times specified in the argument number.

Examples

=REPT(" =*= ",4)=" =*= =*= =*= =*= "

=REPT("phth",5)="phthphthphthphthphth"

RIGHT(*text,charnumber*)

Returns rightmost *charnumber* characters in *text*.

RIGHT counts the characters in text, and copies into the current cell the number of characters specified in the argument *charnumber* from the right end of the *text*.

If *charnumber* is omitted, it's assumed to be 1.

Examples

=RIGHT("Paul Gauguin",7)="Gauguin"

=RIGHT("123WistfulVista,Tustin,CA90022",5)="90022"

SEARCH(*findtext,withintext,startnumber*)

Searches *withintext* for *findtext,* starting at *startnumber.*

SEARCH lets you pinpoint a specific text string, and returns the character number within the specified text where it was found.

Enter the text string you're looking for in the argument *findtext,* and the text you want to search through in *withintext.* If *withintext* is extensive, you can help SEARCH speed up the process by specifying an optional *startnumber.* If *startnumber* is omitted, it's assumed to be 1.

SEARCH is not case-sensitive, meaning *findtext* can be entered in any combination of upper- and lowercase letters. You may also use the wildcards * and ? within *findtext*.

If *startnum* is 0 or less, or is greater than the number of characters in *withintext*, SEARCH returns the error message #VALUE!

Examples

= SEARCH("5","11223344556677889900") = 9

= SEARCH("i","April") = 4

= SEARCH(" ","false start",2) = 6

= SEARCH("?tart","false start") = 7

SUBSTITUTE(*text, oldtext, newtext, instanceno*)

Substitutes *newtext* for *oldtext* in *text instanceno* number of times.

SUBSTITUTE works like REPLACE, except you specify the text you want to replace, whereas with REPLACE you have to specify the number of characters from the beginning of text, and how many characters are to be replaced for the operation to start.

If you specify *instanceno*, only that instance of *oldtext* is replaced and the others are left alone.

Examples

= SUBSTITUTE("data query","y","ies") = "data queries"

= SUBSTITUTE(Min.Height,"5'10","6 ft.") (substitutes the text value "6 ft." in the cell named Min.Height)

= SUBSTITUTE("hi de di","hi","ho",2) = "hi de ho"

TEXT(*value, textformat*)

Converts *value* to text using *textformat*.

TEXT lets you reformat a value, and store it as text. The major difference between formatting a value with any of the Format commands, and using TEXT to do so is that TEXT stores the result as text, while the Format command leaves the value as it was.

Examples

= TEXT("5/25/1988","mmm d, yyyy") = "May 25, 1988"

= TEXT("1234.567","00.00%") = "1234.57%"

TRIM(*text*)

Removes spaces from *text*.

TRIM compacts a text string, leaving only one space between words.

Examples

=TRIM("145 4467 9887") = "145 4467 9887"

=TRIM("125 Howard Ave.") = "125 Howard Ave."

UPPER(*text*)

Converts *text* to uppercase.

UPPER converts all the text you enter or reference as an argument to uppercase letters. It's the inverse of LOWER.

Examples

=UPPER("february") = "FEBRUARY"

=UPPER(C5) = "TOTAL AMOUNT DUE" (if C5 contained the text "Total Amount Due")

VALUE(*text*)

Converts *text* to a number.

VALUE translates a text representation of a number to its numeric value. It works on any of the number, date, or time formats recognized by *Excel*. If text is not in one of those formats, you'll get the error message #VALUE!

Generally you don't have to use VALUE to translate this form of text to a number, since *Excel* will automatically do this conversion, where appropriate. VALUE was included to make *Excel* compatible with other worksheet programs.

Examples

=VALUE("April 15, 1988") = 32248 (the serial number of April 15, 1988)

=VALUE("15:58:00") − VALUE("11:10:00") = 0.2 (the serial number equivalent to 4 hours, 48 minutes)

Database Functions

Each of the database functions use the same three arguments: database, field, and criteria.

Database is the range of cells that comprise the database. This range must be a contiguous range of cells organized into records (rows) and fields (columns). The argument given for database can be either a range name, such as Prices, or range coordinates, such as D55:G61. If you've used the Data Set Database on a selected range, *Excel* has automatically named the range Database.

Field identifies which fields, or columns are to be used within the function. Each field must have an identifying name at the top of the column, which may be used as text in the field argument ("w/Discount", "Net"). You may also use a number to indicate which field within the database is being referenced in the field argument: 1 for the first field, 2 for the second, and so on.

Criteria is the range of cells that contains the database criteria. This is the table that's been previously constructed to indicate criteria for manipulating the data in the database. The criteria argument can be entered as a range or range name. If you've used the Data Set Criteria command on the criteria table, *Excel* has already named the range Criteria, and you can simply specify Criteria as this argument.

Note: If the Data Set Database and Data Set Criteria commands have created these named ranges, don't use "Database" and "Criteria" as text surrounded by quotes.

DAVERAGE(*database,field,criteria*)

Average of numbers in specified *field* of records in *database* matching *criteria*.

Figure 3-10. Sample Database

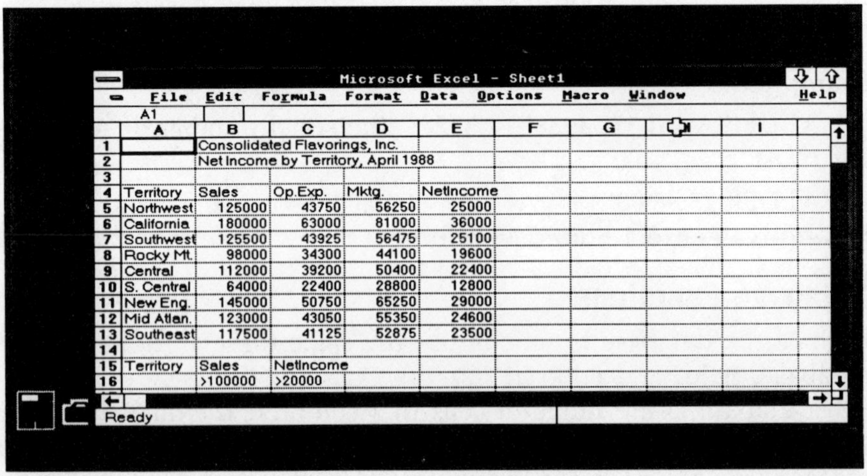

DAVERAGE looks only at the numbers in the field you've specified, and calculates the average of the numbers it finds there. In the sample database, above, are the average sales for the territories with sales over $100,000 and Net Income over $20,000.

DAVERAGE(Database,"Sales",A15:C16) = 132571.4

Here's the formula to calculate the average Net Income for the territories with the same criteria.

DAVERAGE(Database,"NetIncome",A15:C16) = 26514.29

Like the other functions, once you've typed the function into a cell, you can change the data in your database and the function will be automatically recalculated, unless you've turned off the Recalc option.

DCOUNT(*database,field,criteria*)
Count of numbers in specified *field* of records in *database* matching *criteria*.

Like COUNT, DCOUNT inspects the records (cells) in the specified field, and returns a count of the ones that contain numbers. However, the number it returns includes another screening; the cells counted also contain numbers that match the criteria specified.

In DCOUNT, the field argument is optional. If it's not specified, DCOUNT inspects all records in the database, and returns the count of the ones that contain numbers and also match the selection criteria.

DCOUNTA(*database,field,criteria*)
Count of nonempty cells in specified field of records that match the criteria entered in the argument database.

DCOUNTA counts nonempty cells, rather than cells containing numbers the way DCOUNT does. However, like DCOUNT, DCOUNTA also screens the cells in the field specified and returns only the number of nonempty cells containing data that matches criteria.

Like DCOUNT, the field argument in DCOUNTA is optional. If omitted, DCOUNTA inspects all records in the database, returning the number of nonempty cells that match the criteria specified.

DMAX(*database, field, criteria*)

Maximum of numbers in specified field of records in database matching criteria.

DMAX inspects the column specified as field, and returns the largest number that matches the criteria specified.

Example

In the database shown in Figure 3-10,

DMAX(Database,"Sales",A15:C16) = 180000

DMIN(*database, field, criteria*)

Minimum of numbers in specified *field* of records in *database* matching *criteria*.

DMIN inspects the column specified as field, and returns the smallest number that matches the criteria specified.

Example

In the database shown in Figure 3-10,

DMIN(Database,"Sales",A15:C16) = 112000

DPRODUCT(*database, field, criteria*)

Product of numbers in specified *field* of records in *database* matching *criteria*.

DPRODUCT multiplies the values in field that match the criteria specified, and returns the resulting product.

DSTDEV(*database, field, criteria*)

Estimate of standard deviation of a population, based on a sample, using numbers in specified *field* of records in *database* matching *criteria*.

DSTDEV gives the standard deviation of a sample population, cells of which are entirely located in field, and screened to match the specified criteria. DSTDEV is the database equivalent of STDEV.

DSTDEVP(*database, field, criteria*)

Standard deviation of a population, based upon the entire population, using numbers in specified *field* of records in *database* matching *criteria*.

DSTDEVP gives the standard deviation of a complete population, cells of which are entirely located in field, and screened to match the specified criteria. DSTDEVP is the database equivalent of STDEVP.

DSUM(*database, field, criteria*)

Sum of numbers in specified *field* of records in *database* matching *criteria*.

DSUM totals the numbers in field that match the criteria specified. In the example in Figure 3-10,

= DSUM(Database,"Sales",A15:C16) = 928000

DVAR(*database, field, criteria*)

Estimate of variance of a population, based on a sample, using numbers in specified *field* of records in *database* matching *criteria*.

DVAR gives the standard deviation of a sample population, cells of which are entirely located in field, and screened to match the specified criteria. DVAR is the database equivalent of VAR.

DVARP(*database, field, criteria*)

Variance of a population, based on the entire population, using numbers in specified *field* of records in *database* matching *criteria*.

DVARP gives the variance of a complete population, cells of which are entirely located in field, and screened to match the specified criteria. DVARP is the database equivalent of DVARP.

Matrix Functions

MDETERM(*array*)

Determinant of *array*.

The matrix determinant, or MDETERM, is a number derived from the values in the array you specify. It's usually used to solve systems of mathematical equations that involve several variables.

The number you specify as an array must be a numeric array with an equal number of rows and columns.

For example, in a three-column, three-row array, the determinant is found as follows:

A1*(B2*C3 − B3*C2) + A2(B3*C2 − B1*C3) + A3(B1*C2 − B2*C1)

The number specified as an array can be a cell range (A1:C3), or an array constant, such as {1,2,3;4,5,6;7,8,9}. If the array does not contain an equal number of rows and columns, or if any of the cells are empty or contain text, MDETERM returns the error message #VALUE!

Examples

Figure 3-11. Matrix in a Spreadsheet

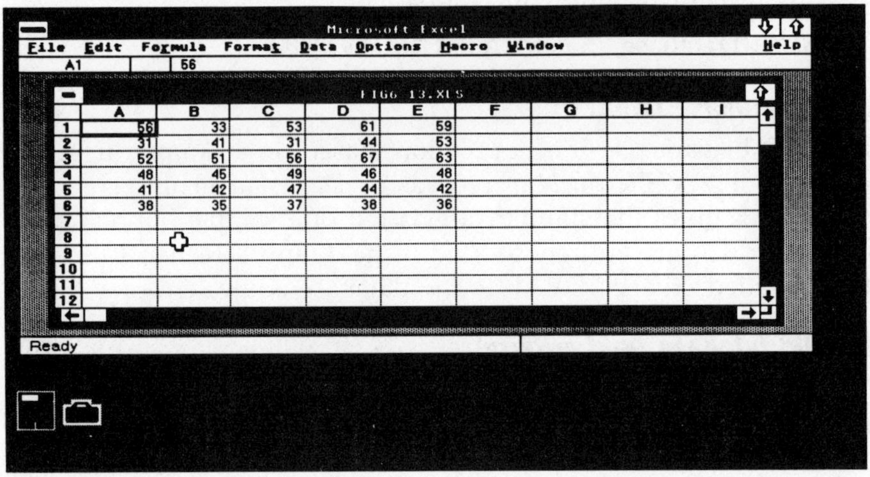

In the spreadsheet above,

=MDETERM(C4:E6)= 648

=MDETERM(A1:C3)=6745

=MDETERM(A1:E6)=#VALUE! (because there are more rows than columns in the array specified)

MINVERSE(*array*)

Inverse of *array*.

The inverse matrix is used, like the determinant, in solving equations involving several variables. The product of a matrix and its inverse is the identity matrix; the square array in which the diagonal values equal 1 and all the other values equal 0.

Formulas that return arrays must be entered as array formulas. Enter them by pressing Ctrl-Shift-Enter and then entering the formula. (If you're using a mouse, press Ctrl-Shift when you click the check box in the formula bar.

Examples

Using the sample spreadsheet shown in Figure 3-11, above

=MINVERSE(A1:E6)=#VALUE! (because it's not a square array)

MMULT(*array1,array2*)

Product of two arrays.

MMULT multiplies two arrays, given as *array1* and *array2*, and returns the product.

In the spreadsheet shown in Figure 3-11

=MMULT(A1:B2,C1:E2)=3991 =MMULT(A1:C3,D1:E3)=8419

=MMULT(A1:C3,D1:E2)=#VALUE! (because the first array has more columns (3) than the second array has rows (2)).

TRANSPOSE(*array*)

Transpose of array.

The transpose of an array rearranges array values so the first row is arranged as the first column, the second row becomes the second column, and so on.

Example

Suppose the array specified contains values as shown below:

	A	B	C	D	E
1	20	30	40	50	60
2	100	200	300	400	500

and the function is entered as follows:

=TRANSPOSE(A1:E2)={20,30,40,50,60;100,200,300,400,500}

and the returned values would look like this:

	A	B
1	20	100
2	30	200
3	40	300
4	50	400
5	60	500

Chapter 4

Using Macros

A macro is a series of commands that tell *Excel* to perform a specific set of actions, such as formatting data, performing complex calculations, printing certain blocks of cells, or prompting the user for certain kinds of input.

Macros can be very simple or very complex, or anywhere in between. Generally, they're referred to by a name you give them, and stored as a type of file.

You can create two kinds of macros with *Excel: command macros* and *function macros.*

Command macros carry out some sequence of actions, such as specifying commands, entering data, selecting cells, formatting, or selecting parts of a chart.

Function macros operate like the worksheet functions, in that they use values for input, make calculations, and return the resulting values.

Macros are created and stored on *macro sheets.* A macro sheet looks like a worksheet but differs in a few basic ways. A macro sheet normally displays formulas, whereas a worksheet normally displays values. A macro sheet also begins with wider columns, to better accommodate formulas.

When you use one of the built-in functions in constructing a macro, you'll see that while there are many macro functions equivalent to worksheet functions, there are also many more functions that work just with macros. If you use the Formula Define Name function in constructing your macro, you'll notice that the dialog box has more options to accomodate different types of macros.

Macros save time and effort. They can perform simple tasks, such as making the text in a cell boldface, or more complex tasks, such as calculating the amount of a given mortgage payment that goes to interest and principle. They can also be helpful in simplifying a large worksheet so others can follow your logic, or so you can reduce calculation time. You can also use them to create menus and dialog boxes on customized application worksheets to help people who don't normally create worksheets enter data and get calculated results. You can even use them to run other applications under *Microsoft Windows* version 2.0 or higher.

How Does a Macro Work?

On the disks that come with the *Excel* files, Microsoft provides a number of sample worksheets and macros located in two libraries called EXCELCBT and LIBRARY. Packed with the manuals is a booklet entitled *Microsoft Excel Sampler,* and in the booklet is an example of an application to create and print mailing labels from information in an *Excel* database. The files involved are CUSTOMER.XLS and LABEL.XLM, and the example starts on page 66 of the Sampler.

To get an idea of how macros work, open both the files AR.XLS and AR.XLM, and compare what you see on your screen of the Accounts Receivable file with the examples shown in the booklet.

The macro file AR.XLM contains five command macros, each of which performs a different set of actions.

The original database contains a list of invoices in invoice-number order. You can use the macros to add new invoices, enter payments on an existing account, delete entries that are paid off, prepare an aging report, and prepare reports by company.

When you open the macro file AR.XLM, you won't see it immediately; it's been hidden. To see it, use the Windows Unhide command. The first macro, Add.Invoice, looks like this:

Figure 4-1. Add.Invoice Macro

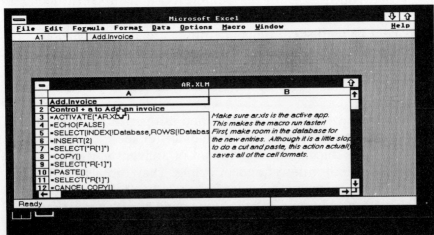

Notice that the name of the macro, Add.Invoice (A), is on the first line, and an explanatory line is on line 2. The letter in parentheses indicates that the macro has been designed so you can use it with a shortcut key: If you press Ctrl and the letter indicated, the macro will be run. The ability to run a macro with a shortcut key is one of distinguishing marks of a command macro.

The actual macro instructions start with the third line, where the commands start with an equals sign. These commands are run in logical sequence, ending with the =RETURN( ) command on the last line. Notice that the writer of this macro did something quite commendable: Each instruction is paired with a set of comments in the adjacent column. Comments are very useful in helping the user understand how a macro works, so another user can decide whether the macro is applicable in a new worksheet.

The Add.Invoice macro is run when you have the AR.XLS worksheet as the active document, and the AR.XLM macro file open. Choose the Macro Run command, choose the Add.Invoice macro, and press the Enter key to run the macro. Or you can use the shortcut key: Press Ctrl-A. Look at the example in the Sampler to see how your database will look after this step.

Next, run the macro to enter new payments. This macro, Payment.Entry, is listed on the same macro sheet. To see it, press the PgDn key or scroll down with your mouse.

This macro, like the Add.Invoice macro, can be run by using the shortcut key shown. In this case, press Ctrl-P. Like the new invoice macro, this one prompts you for information.

A third macro, Cleanup, deletes invoices that have a $0.00 balance. If you wanted to adapt this macro to your own office environment, you might want to copy the paid invoices to another file before deleting the records from your master Accounts Receivable file.

The fourth and fifth macros, Aging and Report.By.Co, sort the data in the worksheet, and present it in report format. The Aging report lets you know who's behind in their payments, and how long they've been falling behind. The Report.By.Co macro lets you inspect the receivables situation for a particular company.

You can construct command macros like these by typing the commands, or you can use Record mode, which turns your keystrokes into macro commands for you. We'll discuss the Recorder in more detail shortly.

The other form of macro is a function macro. These work much the same way as worksheet functions: You can use the Formula Paste Function to paste the general form of the function in place, and then fill in the arguments with your own data. You can also type the function yourself, starting with an equals sign, and enclosing any arguments in parentheses.

Function macros have a particular structure, and because of their complexity may take some study before you feel comfortable writing them. With a function macro, you first specify the type of data you expect as a result of the function macro (the return value). Second, you specify an argument function statement for each argument that must be provided when the macro is called. Third, you specify the formulas or actions that the macro is to perform. Fourth, you specify that the macro is to return to the instruction that called it.

Writing macros is like writing programs, and as such deserves time and attention to what you want the macro to do, and how to construct the commands logically. Macros can contain branches to other macros, If-Then statements, prompts for user action, application-specific error messages, and a host of other details that emphasize the similarity between macro construction and programming.

Once constructed, however, it's important to do two things to a macro: Test and debug it, and document it.

Testing a macro means putting the macro through its paces, using different values or cell references, running it in different ways. The end purpose is to test the macro's logic thoroughly. Most people who write macros recognize that this phase can be humbling: You run the macro deliberately looking for errors, and when you find them, you have to debug the macro and fix the logic so it does what you want.

Too many people overlook the documentation phase, thinking nobody else will need to figure out how the macro works, and that they'll always remember their own logic. Unfortunately, those are the same kind of people who think they'll always remember where they put the car keys, and who miss the first half of the football game because they're turning the house upside down trying to find them.

Adding comments to a macro helps both the writer and anyone else who needs to use the macro understand how it works, and what is needed in the way of arguments or calling sequences.

Comments in *Excel* macros don't interfere with the logic, and they take up very little extra memory.

The Recorder

Microsoft made it easy for you to construct a command macro. Simply turn on the Macro Record command, pick a name for your macro, and step through the action you want to take. The Recorder opens a macro sheet, gives it the name you've specified, and translates your actions to macro commands (sometimes changing the cell reference style). When you're through, choose Macro Stop Recorder, and *Excel* closes the macro.

Once the actions have been recorded, they're yours to edit, format, document, or change in any way you wish. Cell references will be absolute unless you specifically ask that they be relative. (You can change from absolute to relative or vice versa at any time during the recording process.)

Once your actions have been recorded, and you begin to see how recording your actions can be translated into macro commands, you may decide to modify the macro in other ways:

- You can create your own dialog boxes and menus that appear with a macro.
- You can prompt the user with ALERT and MESSAGE functions, and ask the user to type in a value with the INPUT function.
- You can suspend macro action with the WAIT function, or have it start automatically when a certain time occurs with the ON.TIME function, or when data arrives from another program, with the ON.DATA function.
- You can create loops within your macro, so certain actions are performed several times, with IF-NEXT or WHILE-NEXT functions.
- You can use information about the active worksheet, open windows, references, names within the active worksheet or any other to which you have access, and send information to other worksheets or other programs with some of the value-returning macro functions.

The point is that the Recorder gives you a simple way to translate your actions to a macro that can be used again and again, but one which can also be modified so it performs far more sophisticated actions.

The remainder of this chapter looks briefly at each of the macro functions and commands.

Macro Functions: Command Equivalent Functions

When you execute a command equivalent function in a macro, you perform the same action as if you were choosing the equivalent command from a worksheet menu. Arguments specified with a command equivalent function specify options associated with the command.

Shown below are the macro functions equivalent to worksheet commands, and the comparable worksheet command.

Macro Function	Worksheet Command Equivalent
ACTIVATE	Window (document)
ADD.ARROW	Chart Add Arrow
ADD.OVERLAY	Chart Add Overlay
ALIGNMENT	Format Alignment
APP.MAXIMIZE	Control Maximize (application)
APP.MINIMIZE	Control Minimize
APP.MOVE	Control Move (application)
APP.RESTORE	Control Restore (application)
APP.SIZE	Control Size (application)
APPLY.NAMES	Formula Apply Names
ARRANGE.ALL	Window Arrange All
ATTACH.TEXT	Chart Attach Text
AXES	Chart Axes
BORDER	Format Border
CALCULATE.DOCUMENT	Chart Calculate Document
	Options Calculate Document
CALCULATE.NOW	Chart Calculate Now
	Options Calculate Now
CALCULATION	Options Calculation
CELL.PROTECTION	Format Cell Protection
CHANGE.LINKS	File Links
CLEAR	Edit Clear
CLOSE	Control Close (document)
CLOSE.ALL	File Close All
COLUMN.WIDTH	Format Column Width
COMBINATION	Gallery Combination

Macro Function	Worksheet Command Equivalent
COPY	Edit Copy
COPY.PICTURE	Edit Copy Picture
CREATE.NAMES	Formula Create Names
CUT	Edit Cut
DATA.DELETE	Data Delete
DATA.FIND	Data Find
	Data Exit Find
DATA.FORM	Data Form
DATA.SERIES	Data Series
DEFINE.NAME	Formula Define Name
DELETE.ARROW	Chart Delete Arrow
DELETE.NAME	Formula Define Name
DELETE.OVERLAY	Chart Delete Overlay
DISPLAY	Info Cell
	Info Dependents
	Info Format
	Info Formula
	Info Names
	Info Note
	Info Precedents
	Info Protection
	Info Value
EDIT.DELETE	Edit Delete
EXTRACT	Data Extract
FILE.CLOSE	File Close
FILE.DELETE	File Delete
FILL.DOWN	Edit Fill Down
FILL.LEFT	Edit Fill Left
FILL.RIGHT	Edit Fill Right
FILL.UP	Edit Fill Up
FORMAT.FONT	Format Font
FORMAT.LEGEND	Format Legend
FORMAT.MOVE	Format Move
FORMAT.NUMBER	Format Number
FORMAT.SIZE	Format Size
FORMAT.TEXT	Format Text
FORMULA.FIND	Formula Find
FORMULA.GOTO	Formula Goto
FORMULA.REPLACE	Formula Replace
FULL	Control Maximize (document)
	Control Restore (document)
FREEZE.PANES	Options Freeze Panes
GALLERY.AREA	Gallery Area

Macro Function	Worksheet Command Equivalent
GALLERY.BAR	Gallery Bar
GALLERY.COLUMN	Gallery Column
GALLERY.LINE	Gallery Line
GALLERY.PIE	Gallery Pie
GALLERY.SCATTER	Gallery Scatter
GRIDLINES	Chart Gridlines
HIDE	Window Hide
INSERT	Edit Insert
JUSTIFY	Format Justify
LEGEND	Chart Add Legend
LIST.NAMES	Formula Paste Name
MAIN.CHART	Format Main Chart
MOVE	Control Move (document)
NEW	File New
NEW.WINDOW	Window New Window
NOTE	Formula Note
OPEN	File Open
OPEN.LINKS	File Links
OVERLAY	Format Overlay
PAGE.SETUP	File Page Setup
PARSE	Data Parse
PATTERNS	Format Patterns
PASTE	Edit Paste
PASTE.LINK	Edit Paste Link
PASTE.SPECIAL	Edit Paste Special
PRECISION	Options Calculation
PREFERRED	Gallery Preferred
PRINT	File Print
PRINTER.SETUP	File Printer Setup
PROTECT.DOCUMENT	Chart Protect Document
	Chart Unprotect Document
	Options Protect Document
QUIT	File Exit
	Control Close (application)
REMOVE.PAGE.BREAK	Options Remove Page Break
REPLACE.FONT	Format Font
ROW.HEIGHT	Format Row Height
RUN	Macro Run
SAVE	File Save
SAVE.AS	File Save As
SAVE.WORKSPACE	File Save Workspace
SCALE	Format Scale
SELECT	Chart Select Chart
	Chart Select Plot Area

Macro Function	Worksheet Command Equivalent
SELECT.SPECIAL	Formula Select Special
SET.CRITERIA	Data Set Criteria
SET.DATABASE	Data Set Database
SET.PAGE.BREAK	Options Set Page Break
SET.PREFERRED	Gallery Set Preferred
SET.PRINT.AREA	Options Set Print Area
SET.PRINT.TITLES	Options Set Print Titles
SHORT.MENUS	Options Full Menus
	Options Short Menus
	Chart Full Menus
	Chart Short Menus
SHOW.INFO	Window Show Document
	Window Show Info
SIZE	Control Size (document)
SORT	Data Sort
SPLIT	Control Split
TABLE	Data Table
UNDO	Edit Undo
UNHIDE	File Unhide Window
	Window Unhide
WORKSPACE	Options Workspace

Dialog Box Functions

Dialog box functions are available for every command that brings up a dialog box. Each dialog box function has the same name as the command equivalent function. The only difference is that the function is stated with a question mark.

For instance, the dialog box function for File Save As is SAVE.AS? The dialog box function for Edit Insert is INSERT?

Some dialog box functions don't display dialog boxes. We'll look at these individually in the sections below.

Action Equivalent Functions

The action equivalent functions listed below neither have command equivalents nor are dialog box functions. Arguments are shown in parentheses. If parentheses are shown they must be included in the function as used, even if they contain no arguments.

A1.R1C1(*r1c1*)

Displays A1 or R1C1 references.

Works the same as choosing the Options Workspace command and turning on the R1C1 check box if the *r1c1* argument is true, or turning off the R1C1 check box if the *r1c1* argument is false.

ACTIVATE(*windowtext,panenumber*)

Selects a window.

Works the same as activating a pane in a window. *Windowtext* is the name of a window and must be enclosed in double quotation marks; *panenumber* is the number of the pane to activate.

ACTIVATE.NEXT( )

Selects the next window.

Equivalent to pressing Ctrl-F6.

ACTIVATE.PREV( )

Selects the previous window.

Equivalent to pressing Ctrl-Shift-F6.

CANCEL.COPY( )

Cancels the selected cell for a copy operation.

Equivalent to canceling the marquee around a selected cell, by pressing the Esc key after you copy or cut a selection.

COPY.CHART(*number*)

Copies a picture of a chart.

The pictures shown depend on the number indicated:

1   As shown on the screen
2   As shown when printed

The COPY.CHART?(*number*) format is also acceptable; it's included for compatibility with *Microsoft Excel* for the Apple Macintosh. In *Microsoft Excel* for *Windows*, it's the same as the COPY.PICTURE macro function without the (*appearance*) argument.

DATA.FIND.NEXT( )

Finds the next matching record in a database.

DATA.FIND.PREV( )

Finds the previous matching record in a database.

These macros find the next or the previous matching record in a database. They work the same as pressing the Up- or Down-arrow keys after choosing the Data Find command. If no matching record can be found, the function returns the value False.

DELETE.FORMAT(*formattext*)

Deletes a Format Number command format.

Works the same as using the Format Number command to delete the format specified, where *formattext* is the format string and enclosed in double quotes, for instance, "#,##0".

DIRECTORY(*pathtext*)

Changes directories and returns a new path name.

Sets the current drive and directory to the path given in *pathtext*, and returns the name of the new path as text. If a drive or directory name is not included in *pathtext*, it assumes the current drive or directory.

FORMULA(*formulatext,reference*)

Enters a formula in a cell, or text on a chart.

This function works differently, depending on whether the active document is a worksheet or a chart.

If the active document is a worksheet, the function enters the formula specified by *formulatext* into the cell specified by *reference*. If no cell is specified, it uses the active cell.

The formula must be in the form it would be if you entered it in the formula bar, but must be enclosed in double quotes. It can be a formula, a number, text, or a logical value. However, any cell references in a formula must be in R1C1 form. (If you're using the Recorder, *Excel* converts any A1-style references to R1C1 style.)

If the active document is a chart, *Excel* enters text labels or SERIES functions. If formulatext can be treated as a text label, and the current selection is a text label, the selected text label is replaced with formulatext. If the current selection is not a text label, the function creates a new text label. If formulatext can be treated as a SERIES formula, and the current selection is a SERIES formula, formulatext replaces the selected SERIES formula.

119

If the current selection is not a SERIES formula, the function creates a new SERIES formula.

Examples

=FORMULA(625) (enters the value 625 in the active cell)

=FORMULA("=R6C[-1]*(1+R8C10)") (enters the formula
=F6*(1+$J$8) into the active cell if the active cell is G6)

=FORMULA("=SERIES(""Name"",,{1,2,3},1") (enters a SERIES
formula on the chart. Note that within the text value you have to
enter two sets of double quotation marks in order to represent a
single quotation mark)

FORMULA.ARRAY(*formulatext,reference*)

Enters an array formula on a document.

Works the same as entering an array formula while pressing
Ctrl-Shift-Enter. The function enters the formula specified in *formulatext* as an array formula in the range specified by *reference*, or
in the current selection if *reference* is not given.

FORMULA.FILL(*formulatext,reference*)

Fills a range with a formula.

Works the same as entering a formula while pressing Shift.
The function enters the formula specified in *formulatext* into the
area specified in *reference*, or in the current selection if *reference* is
not given.

FORMULA.FIND.NEXT( )

Finds the next cell, as described in the Formula Find dialog box.

FORMULA.FIND.PREV( )

Finds the previous cell, as described in the Formula Find dialog
box.

These two functions work the same as pressing F7, and
Shift-F7 respectively. The function finds the next or previous
matching cells on the worksheet, as defined in the Formula Find
dialog box. If no match is found, the function returns the value
False.

HLINE(*numbercols*)

Horizontally scrolls the active window by columns.

This function scrolls the worksheet a number of columns to the right or left, depending on the number given in *numbercols*. If the number is positive, the worksheet scrolls to the right that number of columns; if the number is negative, the worksheet scrolls to the left that number of columns.

HPAGE(*numberwindows*)

Horizontally scrolls the active window one full window at a time.

This function scrolls the worksheet a number of windows to the right or left, depending on the number given in *numberwindows*. If the number is positive, the worksheet scrolls to the right that number of windows; if the number is negative, the worksheet scrolls to the left that number of windows.

HSCROLL(*scroll,value*)

Horizontally scrolls a document by percentage or by column number.

HSCROLL lets you scroll to the right or left edge of your document, or anywhere in between. If *value* is TRUE, HSCROLL scrolls to the position represented by the number you specify as scroll. If *value* is FALSE or omitted, HSCROLL scrolls to the position represented by the fraction given in *scroll*. If *scroll* is 0, HSCROLL scrolls to the left edge of your document; if *scroll* is 1, it scrolls to the right edge of your document.

To scroll to a specific column, either use the form HSCROLL(*colnumber*,TRUE) or HSCROLL(*colnumber*/256).

Examples

Assuming you're starting from A1, the following uses of HSCROLL all scroll to column 64, 25 percent of the way across the worksheet:

HSCROLL(64,TRUE)

HSCROLL(25%)

HSCROLL(.25,FALSE)

HSCROLL(64/256)

SELECT(*selection,activecell*)

Selects a reference.

This is one of two forms of the SELECT function. This is the one used if the selection is on a worksheet or macro sheet. (The following version is used if the selection refers to a chart.)

This function is used to select a cell or cell range, as specified in *selection*, and to make *activecell* the active cell. Both arguments must be preceded with exclamation marks if the A1 reference style is used.

Selection must be either a reference on the active worksheet (for instance, !B23:C24, !Netsales) or an R1C1-style reference to the currently active cell (such as "R[− 1]C5:"). If you omit *selection*, SELECT doesn't change the selection.

Activecell must be within selection, and may be either a reference to a single cell on the active worksheet, such as !B23, or an R1C1-style reference to the active cell in the current selection, as in the paragraph above.

If you're recording a macro with the Macro Relative Record command and you select something, *Excel* uses R1C1-style references as text. If you're using Macro Absolute Record, *Excel* uses absolute references.

SELECT(*itemtext*)

Selects an item on a chart.

This is one of two forms of the SELECT function. This is the one used if the selection is a chart. The preceding version is used if the selection refers to a worksheet or macro sheet.

Itemtext must be enclosed in double quotes, and refers to a chart object, as follows:

Selection	Itemtext
Entire chart	"Chart"
Plot area	"Plot"
Legend	"Legend"
Main chart value axis	"Axis 1"
Main chart category axis	"Axis 2"
Overlay chart value axis	"Axis 3"
Overlay chart category axis	"Axis 4"
Chart title	"Title"
Label for main chart value axis	"Text Axis 1"
Label for main chart category axis	"Text Axis 2"
Nth floating text item	"Text n"

Selection	Itemtext
Nth arrow	"Arrow n"
Major gridlines of value axis	"Gridline 1"
Minor gridlines of value axis	"Gridline 2"
Major gridlines of category axis	"Gridline 3"
Minor gridlines of category axis	"Gridline 4"
Main chart droplines	"Dropline 1"
Overlay chart droplines	"Dropline 2"
Main chart hi-lo lines	"Hiloline 1"
Overlay chart hi-lo lines	"Hiloline 2"
Data associated with point x in series n	"SnPx"
Text attached to point x of series n	"Text SnPx"
Series title text of series n of an area chart	"Text Sn"

SELECT.END(*direction#*)

Changes the active cell.

Moves the active cell to the edge of the next block, in the direction specified by *direction#*:

Direction#	Direction
1	Left (same as Ctrl-Left arrow)
2	Right (same as Ctrl-Right arrow)
3	Up (same as Ctrl-Up arrow)
4	Down (same as Ctrl-Down arrow)

SELECT.LAST.CELL( )

Selects the cell at the end of a document.

Selects the cell at the intersection of the last row and last column in your document that contains a formula, value, format, or is referred to in a formula.

SHOW.ACTIVE.CELL( )

Displays the active cell.

Works the same as pressing Ctrl-Backspace; scrolls the active window so the active cell becomes visible.

SHOW.CLIPBOARD( )

Displays the Clipboard.

Works the same as choosing the Run command on the Control menu, and selecting Clipboard. Included for compatibility with macros written with *Microsoft Excel* for the Apple Macintosh.

STYLE(*bold,italic*)

STYLE?(*bold,italic*)

Changes font.

If *bold* is TRUE, *Excel* finds an available bold font and changes the font of the current selection to the bold font. If *italic* is TRUE, it changes the font of the current selection to an available italic font. If no appropriate font is available, *Excel* uses the most similar font available.

This function is included for compatibility with macros written with *Microsoft Excel* for the Apple Macintosh.

UNLOCKED.NEXT( )

Moves to the next unlocked cell.

UNLOCKED.PREV( )

Moves to the previous unlocked cell.

Work the same as pressing Tab or Shift-Tab to move the active cell to the next or previous unlocked cell in a protected worksheet.

VLINE(*numberrows*)

Vertically scrolls the active window by rows.

Scrolls the active window vertically the number of rows specified in *numberrows*. If *numberrows* is positive, *Excel* scrolls down; if *numberrows* is negative, *Excel* scrolls up.

VPAGE(*numberwindows*)

Vertically scrolls the active window one windowful at a time.

Scrolls the active window vertically the number of windows specified in *numberwindows*. If *numberwindows* is positive, *Excel* scrolls down. If *numberwindows* is negative, *Excel* scrolls up.

VSCROLL(*scroll,value*)

Vertically scrolls the document by percentage or by row number.

VSCROLL lets you scroll to the top or bottom of your window, or anywhere between. If *value* is TRUE, VSCROLL scrolls to the row represented by the number you specify as *scroll*. If *value* is FALSE or omitted, VSCROLL scrolls to the position represented by the fraction given in *scroll*. If *scroll* is 0, VSCROLL scrolls to the top row (row 1); if *scroll* is 1, it scrolls to the bottom of the window (row 16384).

To scroll to a specific row, either use the form VSCROLL(*rownumber*,TRUE) or VSCROLL(*rownumber*/16384).

Examples

Assuming you're starting from A1, the following uses of VSCROLL all scroll to row 4096, 25 percent of the way down the window:

HSCROLL(4096,TRUE)

HSCROLL(25%)

HSCROLL(.25,FALSE)

HSCROLL(4096/16384)

Customizing Functions

ADD.BAR( )

Adds a custom menu bar.

Creates an empty menu bar, and if successful, returns the bar ID number. If 15 menu bars (the maximum number of custom menu bars allowed) have already been defined, ADD.BAR returns the error message #VALUE!

ADD.BAR doesn't display the new bar. To see the bar, use the SHOW.BAR function.

ADD.COMMAND(*bar#*,*menuposition*,*menureference*)

Adds a custom command.

ADD.COMMAND( ) adds to the menu one or more custom commands described in the menu construction area *menureference*, at *menuposition* in the bar number indicated in the argument *bar#*. *Menureference* must be a reference to a macro sheet that describes the new command.

Menuposition can be the number of a menu or the text name of a menu. *Bar#* can be the number of one of the built-in menu bars or the ID number returned by the previously executed ADD.BAR function. The command position of the first command added is returned by the ADD.COMMAND.

Built-in menu bar numbers are:

Bar Number

1	Worksheet and macro menu, full menus
2	Chart menu, full menus
3	Nil menu (menu displayed when no documents are open)
4	Info window menu
5	Worksheet and macro menu, short menus
6	Chart menu, short menus

ADD.MENU(*bar#,menureference*)

Adds a custom menu.

Adds a menu described in the menu construction area *menureference* to the bar with the bar ID number *bar#*. *Menureference* must refer to a macro sheet that describes the new menu.

Bar# can be the number of one of the built-in menu bars or the ID number returned by the previously executed ADD.BAR function.

If ADD.MENU is successful, the menu is added immediately to the right of the existing menus on bar *bar#*, and ADD.MENU returns the position number of the new menu.

ALERT(*messagetext,type#*)

Displays a dialog box.

Use this function if you want to display a custom dialog box and have the user choose a button.

The dialog box contains the text you specify as *messagetext*, and the type of box depends on the number you specify as *type#*:

Type#	Use	Dialog Box
1	Telling the user to make a choice	Figure 4-2
2	Presenting information	Figure 4-3
3	Error message where no choice is available	Figure 4-4

Figure 4-2. Choice Dialog Box

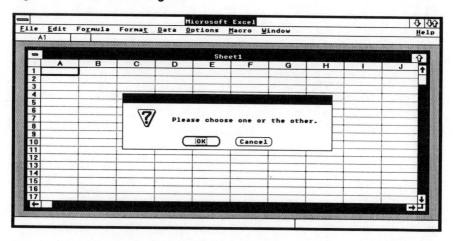

Figure 4-3. Information Dialog Box

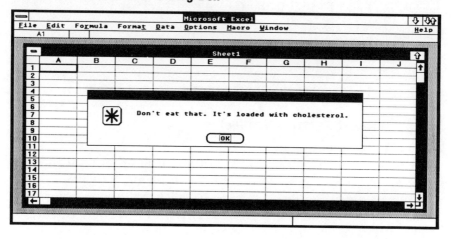

Figure 4-4. Error Dialog Box

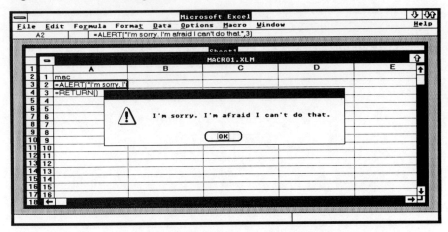

ALERT returns the logical value TRUE if the user chooses the OK bar, and FALSE if the Cancel bar is chosen.

Examples

=ALERT("I'm sorry, I'm afraid I can't do that.",3) (see Figure 4-4)

=ALERT("Data entered will affect other worksheets.",1)

APP.ACTIVATE (*titletext,waitvalue*)

Starts another application.

Use this function to activate another application with the title bar *titletext*. If *titletext* is omitted, the function activates *Excel*.

The argument *waitvalue* is used to tell *Excel* to wait before starting the application. If *waitvalue* is TRUE or is omitted, *Excel* flashes a message indicating it is waiting. If *waitvalue* is FALSE, *Excel* activates the application immediately.

BEEP(*number*)

Sounds a warning beep.

BEEP triggers production of an audible tone. Depending on your hardware, you may be able to use the argument number to specify different tones. The *number* argument may contain a value from 1 to 4, and is interpreted by your hardware as a beep tone. Some hardware (the IBM PC for instance) interprets all numbers used with BEEP as the same tone.

CALL(*calltext, argument1, . . .*)

Calls the *Microsoft Windows* library

CALL is recommended for use only by programmers expert in using the *Microsoft Windows* dynamic library. Incorrect use could cause damage to your system's operation.

CALL works with the macro function REGISTER, which sets up the parameters for CALL. In using REGISTER, you specify the name of the module and the procedure you want to use, as well as a text value describing the number and data types of arguments you want to give, and the data type of the return value. REGISTER returns the value of *calltext* to use with the CALL function.

CANCEL.KEY(*enable,macroreference*)

Alters the Esc key.

This function lets you temporarily disable the Esc key while a macro runs. If *enable* is FALSE or omitted, pressing Esc while a macro is running will not interrupt it. If *enable* is TRUE and *macroreference* is omitted, the Esc key is reactivated. If *enable* is TRUE and you specify *macroreference*, execution jumps to the specified macro location if you press Esc.

CANCEL.KEY only lasts for the duration of the currently running macro. Once the macro stops, the Esc key is reactivated.

CHECK.COMMAND(*bar#,menuposition,commandposition,check*)

Marks a command.

This function adds or removes a check mark beside the command designated. *Bar#* is either the number of one of the *Excel* built-in menu bars, or the number returned by the previously executed ADD.BAR function. *Menuposition* is either the number of the menu or the text form of the menu name. *Commandposition* is either the number of the command or the text form of the command title.

If *check* is TRUE, this function checks the command; if *check* is FALSE, it removes the check mark.

A checkmark does not affect the execution of the command. Its primary use is to indicate a command or option is in effect.

DELETE.BAR(*bar#*)

Deletes a custom menu bar.

Deletes the custom menu bar numbered *bar#*. *Bar#* must be the number returned by the previously ADD.BAR function, and may not be the currently displayed menu bar.

DELETE.COMMAND(*bar#,menuposition,commandposition*)

Deletes a command.

Deletes the command in the position specified. *Bar#* is either the number of one of the *Excel* built-in menu bars, or the number returned by the previously executed ADD.BAR function. *Menuposition* is either the number of the menu or the text form of the menu name. *Commandposition* is either the number of the command or the text form of the command title.

If the specified command does not exist, the function returns the error message #VALUE!

When a command is deleted, the number used for *commandposition* for all commands after that is decreased by 1.

DELETE.MENU(*bar#,menuposition*)

Deletes a menu.

Deletes the menu at *menuposition* in the bar identified by *bar#*. *Menuposition* is either the number of the menu or the text form of the menu name. *Bar#* is either the number of one of the *Excel* built-in menu bars, or the number returned by the previously executed ADD.BAR function.

If the menu specified by *menuposition* doesn't exist, the function returns the error message #VALUE!

When a menu has been deleted, the number used for *menuposition* for all menus to the right of that menu is decreased by 1.

DIALOG.BOX(*dialogreference*)

Displays a custom dialog box.

Displays the dialog box described in the construction area described in *dialogreference*, which may be on a macro sheet or a worksheet. The area pointed to by *dialogreference* must be seven columns wide and at least two rows high.

If the OK bar in the dialog box is chosen, the function enters values in the fields as specified in the *dialogreference* area, and returns the item number of the button pressed. Items are numbered sequentially, starting with the item in the second row in *dialogreference*. If the Cancel button in the dialog box is chosen, the function returns FALSE.

If *dialogreference* is invalid, the function returns the error message #VALUE!, and when the macro is run, displays a message indicating the cell in which the error was found.

DISABLE.INPUT(*logicalvalue*)

Stops all input to *Excel*.

If *logicalvalue* is TRUE, the function blocks all input from the keyboard and mouse, except input to displayed dialog boxes. If *logicalvalue* is FALSE, input is reenabled.

ECHO(*logicalvalue*)

Toggles screen update on and off.

If *logicalvalue* is TRUE or omitted, the function turns on screen updating while a macro is running. If *logicalvalue* is FALSE, screen updating is turned off. Screen updating resumes automatically when a macro ends.

ECHO is particularly useful when running a large command macro, since turning off screen updating lets the macro run faster.

ENABLE.COMMAND(*bar#*, *menuposition*, *commandposition*, *enable*)

Toggles the graying of a custom command.

Enables or disables the command identified by the arguments. *Bar#* is either the number of one of the *Excel* built-in menu bars, or the number returned by the previously executed ADD.BAR function. *Menuposition* is either the number of the menu or the text form of the menu name. *Commandposition* is either the number of the command to be checked or the text form of the command title. If *commandposition* is 0, the entire menu is enabled or disabled.

If *enable* is TRUE, the function enables the command. If *enable* is FALSE, the command is disabled. Disabled commands appear *grayed*, and cannot be executed.

If the specified command is one of *Excel's* built-in commands, or does not exist, the function returns the error message #VALUE!

ERROR(*enable,macroreference*)

Specifies an action to take if an error occurs while a macro is running.

If *enable* is FALSE, all error checking is disabled. When error checking of a macro has been disabled and an error is encountered, *Excel* ignores it and continues.

If *enable* is TRUE, and *macroreference* is omitted, normal error checking occurs. This means a dialog box appears when an error is encountered, permitting you to halt execution, single-step through the macro, or continue normal running. If *enable* is TRUE and *macroreference* specifies the reference of a macro, that macro will be run when an error is encountered.

Warning: Both ERROR(TRUE,*macroreference*) and ER-ROR(FALSE) result in no warning messages at all. ER-ROR(FALSE) also supresses the warning messages normally displayed if you attempt to close an unsaved document.

EXEC(*programtext,window#*)

Starts another application.

Starts the program named in the argument *programtext* as a separate program running under *Microsoft Windows* version 2.0. *Programtext* uses the same form of arguments as the File Run command in the Windows MS-DOS Executive.

Window# specifies how the window holding the program should appear:

Window	Type
1	Normal window
2	Minimized window
3	Maximized window

If omitted, *window#* is assumed to be 2.

If the EXEC function is successful, it returns the task ID number of the program started. The task ID number identifies the program running under *Microsoft Windows* version 2.0 or higher. If the function is unsuccessful, it returns the error message #VALUE!

EXECUTE(*channel#,executetext*)

Carries out a command in another application.

The EXECUTE function executes whatever commands are described in *executetext* in the application that's connected through *channel#*. The channel so designated must already have been opened by the INITIATE macro function.

This function works only if you're running *Microsoft Windows* version 2.0 or higher.

EXECUTE returns the following error messages if unsuccessful:

Message	Meaning
#VALUE!	*Channel#* isn't a valid channel number.
#N/A!	The application is doing something else.
#DIV/0!	The application doesn't respond, so you've pressed Esc to cancel the command.
#REF!	The application refuses the EXECUTE request.

FCLOSE(*file#*)

Closes a text file.

Closes the file that's been opened with FOPEN. *File#* is the number of the file, and has been returned when FOPEN is completed successfully.

FOPEN(*filetext,access#*)

Opens a text file.

FOPEN opens the file named *filetext,* and returns a file number. The argument *access#* specifies the type of access to allow to the file:

Access#	Type of Access
1	Read/write access
2	Read-only access
3	Create new file, with read/write access

If the file doesn't exist and *access#* is 3, FOPEN creates a new file. If it doesn't exist and *access#* is 1 or 2, or if FOPEN can't open the file, FOPEN returns the error message #N/A!

FPOS(*file#*,*position#*)

Returns position in a text file.

Once a file has been opened with FOPEN and *file#* returned, the FPOS function looks in the file so identified and positions the file (for further activity, such as reading or writing) at *position#* within the file. (The first byte of the file is considered position 1.)

FREAD(*file#*,*#characters*)

Reads characters from a text file.

Reads *#characters* from the file file#, where *file#* is the number returned when FOPEN was used to open the file.

If FREAD is successful, it returns the text read. If *file#* isn't a valid file number, it returns the error message #VALUE! If FREAD can't read the document, or if it reaches the end of the file, it returns the error message #N/A!

FREADLN(*file#*)

Reads a line from a text file.

FREADLN starts at the current file position (see FPOS) in the file identified by *file#* and reads until it encounters an End of Line character or equivalent. The file must have been opened with FOPEN, and file# is the number returned by that function.

FSIZE(*file#*)

Returns the size of a text file.

Returns the number of characters in the file identified by *file#*, which is the number returned by the function FOPEN.

If *file#* is not a valid file number, FSIZE returns the error message #VALUE!

FWRITE(*file#*,*text*)

Writes characters to a text file.

FWRITE writes the characters in text to the file identified by *file#*, starting at the current position (see FPOS). The file must have been opened by FOPEN, which returns *file#*.

If *file#* is not a valid file number, FWRITE returns the error message #VALUE! If it can't write to the file, it returns the error message #N/A!

FWRITELN(*file#*, *text*)

Writes line to a text file.

FWRITELN writes the characters specified in text to the file identified by *file#*, starting at the current position in that file (see FPOS). The characters written are followed by a carriage return and a line feed. The file must have been opened by FOPEN, which returns *file#*. If *file#* is not a valid file number, FWRITELN returns the error message #VALUE! If it can't write to the file, it returns the error message #N/A!

HELP(*helptext*)

Displays a customized Help topic.

When used as a macro function, HELP displays the Help topic specified as *helptext*, where *helptext* is a reference to a topic in a custom help file in the form *filename!topic#*. If you omit *helptext*, HELP displays the normal *Excel* Help index.

INITIATE(*applicationtext*, *topictext*)

Opens a channel to another application.

INITIATE opens a DDE channel to another application, but it doesn't start the application. *Applicationtext* is the DDE name of the application you want. *Topictext* describes what you want to access, which can be a filename, or whatever is appropriate for the application.

If INITIATE is successful, it returns the number of the open channel, and all subsequent DDE macro functions will use this number when specifying a channel.

When an application is running, it will have a task number; if more than one instance of the application is running, this task number is necessary to identify which instance you want. If you don't specify a task number and more than one instance is running, INITIATE displays a dialog box, allowing you to identify the instance you want.

INPUT(*prompt*, *type*, *title*, *default*, *xposition*, *yposition*)

Displays a dialog box.

INPUT displays a dialog box and returns the information in the dialog box. *Prompt* and *type* are required arguments, and are text. *Title*, *default*, *xposition*, and *yposition* are optional; *title* is text and the other three arguments must be numbers.

INPUT is one way you can design a custom dialog box, and is particularly useful for prompting the user to enter data.

An INPUT dialog box can be seen in Figure 4-5.

Figure 4-5. INPUT Dialog Box

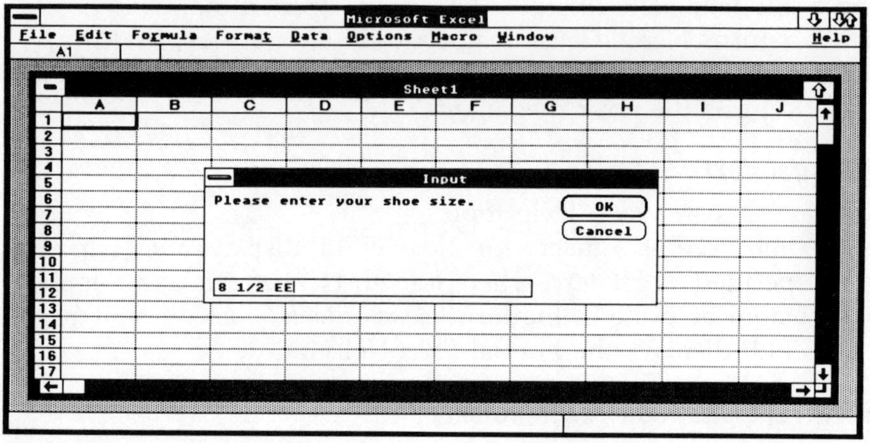

If you omit *title*, *Excel* assumes the title is *Input*. If you omit *xposition* or *yposition*, *Excel* assumes they are 0 and centers the dialog box.

The argument type refers to the data type that's expected to be entered:

Number	Data type
0	Formula
1	Number
2	Text
4	Logical
8	Reference
16	Error
64	Array

Excel allows you to indicate a combination of types by summing the numeric values. For instance, if you want the input box to accept numbers, text, or logical values, but not cell references, set type = 7.

When you set type = 8, INPUT returns the absolute cell reference. When you set type = 0, INPUT returns the formula as text, with any references set in R1C1 style.

136

If the information entered by the user isn't the correct type, *Excel* tries to translate it to the correct type. If it can't, it displays an error message.

MESSAGE(*logical, text*)

Displays a message in status bar.

Toggles the display or removal of a message (*text*) in the status bar. Any message displayed with MESSAGE stays in the status bar until removed by another MESSAGE.

If *logical* is TRUE, *Excel* displays text in the status bar. If *text* is the empty text value (" "), any message currently displayed in the status bar is removed. If *logical* is FALSE, any message in the status bar is removed and the status bar is re-enabled to handle normal command help messages.

ON.DATA(*documenttext, macrotext*)

Runs a macro when data is sent to *Excel* by another application.

ON.DATA lets you automatically update a document whenever it receives new data. *Macrotext* is the name of the macro started when new data is sent by another application to the document specified by *documenttext. Macrotext* must be a text form of R1C1-style reference.

If the incoming data causes recalculation, *Excel* first recalculates, then starts the specified macro.

ON.DATA stays in effect until it's turned off or until you exit *Excel*. If you close the macro sheet containing *macrotext*, an error message is generated when data is sent to the document named in *documenttext*. To turn off ON.DATA, omit the *macrotext* argument.

ON.KEY(*keytext, macrotext*)

Runs a macro when a particular key is pressed.

ON.KEY lets you set up an autokey initiation of your macro. When you press the key specified in *keytext*, the macro specified in *macrotext* is run.

The key specified in *keytext* must be in a form *Excel* can understand. The Appendix on pages 373–375 of the *Microsoft Excel Functions and Macros* manual explains how to specify keys.

Macrotext must be a text form of R1C1-style reference. If *macrotext* is empty text (" "), nothing happens when the key is pressed. If *macrotext* is omitted, *keytext* reverts to its normal meaning.

ON.KEY remains in effect until you turn it off or you quit *Excel*.

ON.TIME(*time, macrotext, tolerance, insertvalue*)

Runs a macro at a certain time.

ON.TIME lets you set up your worksheet so a macro is run at a specific time. It uses the time portion of the serial number, which is automatically updated to current date and time when you turn on your machine.

Macrotext is the R1C1-style reference to the macro that is to be run. If *insertvalue* is TRUE or is omitted, the macro will be run at the time specified. If *insertvalue* is FALSE, any prior requests to execute the specified macro at the specified time are ignored.

The *time* argument can be a number less than one; if so, *Excel* will assume the macro is to be run every day at the time specified. If the specified time occurs and the macro specified is not in memory, the function is ignored. If two identical ON.TIME statements are present, the first is executed, and the second is ignored and returns the error message #N/A!

The *tolerance* parameter is used to allow *Excel* to leave one of the modes where this function can be executed, then return and still run the function. If the specified time occurs and *Excel* is not in READY, COPY, CUT, or FIND mode, *Excel* waits for the length of time specified by *tolerance* (a date/time serial number). If *Excel* doesn't return to one of these modes within the length of time specified, the request is canceled.

ON.WINDOW(*windowtext, macrotext*)

Runs a macro when a window is changed.

ON.WINDOW starts the macro specified in *macrotext* whenever the window specified in *windowtext* is activated. Both arguments must be enclosed in double quotes.

If *windowtext* is omitted, *Excel* starts the macro specified whenever any window is activated, except for those windows named in other ON.WINDOW functions.

POKE(*channel#,itemtext,datareference*)

Sends data to another application.

POKE lets you send data from *Excel* to another application while both *Excel* and the other application are running.

POKE uses the channel number returned by the INITIATE function. *Itemtext* is the specification within the other application where the data is to go, and *datareference* is the reference to the cell or cell range where the *Excel* data is to be found.

If POKE is not successful because the channel number was not valid, it returns the error message #VALUE! If POKE is refused, it returns the error message #REF! If the application you're trying to send data to does not respond and you press the Esc key to cancel the request, POKE returns the error message #DIV/0!

REGISTER(*moduletext,proceduretext,argumenttext*)

Accesses *Microsoft Windows* library.

This is a very powerful function that returns a text value to be used by the CALL function, which in turn can then be used to access the *Microsoft Windows* dynamic library. Basically a system-level command, it must be used with considerable care, or it could cause system operation errors.

The argument *moduletext* contains the name of the *Microsoft Windows* dynamic library that contains the procedure you want. *Proceduretext* is the text form of the procedure name you want. *Argumenttext* is a character string with argument codes concatenated with return type codes.

REGISTER is a complex function, requiring system-level understanding of the *Microsoft Windows* dynamic library.

RENAME.COMMAND(*bar#,menuposition,commandposition,nametext*)

Renames command.

Assigns the name specified in *nametext* to a command at a specified position on a specified menu. *Menuposition* can either be the number of a menu or its name as text. *Commandposition* can either be the number of the command being renamed or its title as text. If *commandposition* is 0, the menu is renamed.

Bar# is either the number of the built-in menu bars or the number returned by the previously executed ADD.BAR function.

If the command specified doesn't exist, the function returns the error message #VALUE!.

REQUEST(*channel#*, *itemtext*)

Returns data from another application.

REQUEST gets the data specified by *itemtext* from the application connected via *channel#*. *Channel#* is the number of a channel that's already been opened by INITIATE. REQUEST returns data as an array.

If the channel number specified is not valid, REQUEST returns the error message #VALUE! If the request is refused, it returns the error message #REF! If the application is busy, the function returns the error value #N/A! If the application doesn't respond and you press the Esc key to cancel the function, it returns the error message #DIV/0!

SEND.KEYS(*keytext*, *waitvalue*)

Sends a key sequence to an application.

SEND.KEYS lets you send a keystroke sequence to another application, just as if you had pressed the keys in that application. The keys should be in the form described in the Appendix (pages 373–375) of the *Excel Functions and Macros* reference manual.

If *waitvalue* is TRUE, *Excel* waits for the keys to be processed before returning control to the calling macro. If *waitvalue* is FALSE or omitted, the macro continues without waiting for the other application to process the keys.

SET.NAME(*nametext*, *value*)

Defines a name as a certain value.

SET.NAME is the same as equating a named variable with a constant, a logical value, or a reference. If the argument called *value* is omitted, the name *nametext* is deleted.

If you use SET.NAME to define *nametext* as a reference, it will be the text version of that reference, not the value. If you want the value of that reference, use the DEREF function.

SET.VALUE(*reference*, *values*)

Enters values in a cell.

SET.VALUE changes the value of the cell or cells specified in reference to the values specified in the argument *values*. If a cell already contains a formula, it's ignored.

The cells referred to by *reference* must be cells on the current macro sheet. If *reference* is a range, *values* should be an array of numbers of an equivalent size. If there is a mismatch, *Excel* expands the array to fit the range.

SHOW.BAR(*bar#*)

Displays a menu bar.

SHOW.BAR displays the menu bar specified by *bar#*, where *bar#* can be either one of the built-in menu bars, or the number returned by the previously executed ADD.BAR. If *bar#* is omitted, *Excel* displays a standard bar, depending on which window is active:

Active Window	Standard bar
Worksheet or macro sheet (full menus)	1
Chart (full menus)	2
No active window	3
Info window	4
Worksheet or macro sheet (short menus)	5
Chart (short menus)	6

STEP( )

Single-steps through a macro.

STEP starts single-step processing of a macro, displaying a dialog box for each macro instruction, and letting you choose whether to execute the next instruction, halt the macro, or continue normal processing of the instructions. Single-stepping is particularly useful when debugging a macro.

You can also single-step through a macro by pressing the Esc key while the macro is running.

TERMINATE(*channel#*)

Closes a channel to another application.

TERMINATE is the opposite of INITIATE, and closes the channel specified by *channel#*. If TERMINATE is not successful, it returns the error message !VALUE!

WAIT(*serialnumber*)

Stops a macro from running.

WAIT suspends execution of a macro for the amount of time specified in *serialnumber*. *Serialnumber* is the serial number value of the specified date and time.

Control Functions

ARGUMENT(*nametext,datatype#,reference*)

Describes arguments to a macro.

The ARGUMENT function lets you use named values as arguments in macro functions. These named values will be used wherever the name is referenced in a function macro.

Nametext is the name you want to assign to the argument. It may also be the name of the cells containing the argument, if you're using reference. *Datatype#* is a code number specifying the type of entry. (See the INPUT function explanation for *datatype#* values.) The *reference* argument tells *Excel* where you want it to store the value that will be passed to the macro.

BREAK( )

Gets out of a FOR-NEXT or WHILE-NEXT loop.

When BREAK is encountered, processing of a FOR-NEXT or WHILE-NEXT loop stops, and macro execution returns to the statement following the NEXT statement at the end of the current loop.

FOR(*counter,start#,end#,increment*)

Starts a FOR-NEXT loop.

A loop in a macro allows you to perform some set of actions a finite number of times. A loop means a set of instructions is repeated, usually with one or more changes to some counter or other variable, until some specified condition occurs.

Looping is a bit like doing situps as part of an exercise program: You repeat the situp exercise each time until you've completed a certain number, and then you can stop and go on to something else.

A FOR statement begins the loop; a NEXT statement marks the end of the loop and the point at which control either returns to the beginning of the loop (if the end-condition hasn't been met) or proceeds with statements that follow the loop.

Loop processing starts at the begin-point and goes to the statement immediately preceding the NEXT statement. When the end-condition has been met, processing is allowed to get past the NEXT statement.

Arguments that accompany a FOR-NEXT loop:

Counter is the name of the variable that counts the number of times the loop has been performed; when its value exceeds that of *end#*, control passes outside of the loop.

Start# is an optional argument. It's assumed to be 1 unless otherwise specified. *Start#* is the value to which *counter* is set when the loop begins.

End# is the value against which counter is compared after each iteration of the loop. Until the value in *counter* is greater than *end#*, looping continues.

Increment is the value by which *counter* is incremented on each pass through the loop.

GOTO(*reference*)

Jumps to another cell.

The GOTO function works the same as pressing F5: It tells *Excel* to jump to the upper left cell specified in the argument named reference and continue processing there.

Reference must be a cell or cell range on an open macro sheet, though it doesn't have to be the same macro sheet as the one on which the GOTO statement occurs.

HALT( )

Stops one or more macros from running.

HALT stops all macro action. It's particularly useful for stopping processing when an error occurs. When you use HALT, you should combine it with some function that produces a message, so the user knows why everything has stopped.

NEXT( )

Ends a FOR-NEXT or WHILE-NEXT loop.

NEXT is the last statement in a loop. It marks the point at which control either returns to loop processing, or continues on to other instructions, depending on the current state of the counter. (See FOR and WHILE.)

RESTART(*level#*)

Removes return addresses from the stack.

When you jump from the middle of one macro to the beginning of another, *Excel* stores the address of the last instruction in the macro you left as the return address. If you then jump from the second macro to a third, it keeps track of that return address as well. That list of return adresses is known as a *stack*.

When you want to return to the calling macro, *Excel* consults this stack. A level 1 return means control returns to the macro that directly called the macro you're in. If, however, you want to return to some other macro that was in the chain of nested calls, you need to specify a different level.

You may, however, wish to remove some return addresses from that stack. RESTART lets you do that by level number, where level 1 is the most recent call, level 2 is the call or set of calls before that, and so on. If the *level#* argument is omitted, *Excel* removes all return addresses from the stack. Thus, when a RETURN function is encountered, the macro will stop running instead of returning control to the macro that called it.

RESULT(*type#*)

Specifies the data type of a function macro's return value.

RESULT is usually used at the beginning of a macro to specify what kind of return value is expected. The kind of return value is specified by a code number (shown below).

Type#	Data Type
1	Number
2	Text
4	Logical
8	Reference
16	Error
64	Array

Type# can be a sum of the codes, indicating that a combination of types is allowable. For instance, if *type#* = 7 (the default), the return value may be a number, text, or a logical value.

RETURN(*value*)

Returns control to whatever started the macro.

RETURN is normally the last instruction in a function or command macro It tells *Excel* that control is to return to whatever called the macro. This may be the user (using the Macro Run command or a shortcut key), a formula, or another macro.

Use of the *value* argument depends on whether the macro is a command macro or a function macro. In a command macro run by the user, don't specify value. In a function macro, *value* specifies the return value associated with this macro.

WHILE(*testvalue*)

Starts a WHILE-NEXT loop.

WHILE begins a loop of instructions that ends with a NEXT statement. WHILE continues to loop until *testvalue* is FALSE, unlike a FOR-NEXT loop, where the exit from the loop is determined by a counter.

If *testvalue* is FALSE the first time, execution skips to the matching NEXT instruction and proceeds with the instruction after it. Thus, if the value is FALSE, the WHILE-NEXT loop won't execute.

Value-Returning Functions

ABSREF(*referencetext,reference*)

Returns the absolute reference of a cell.

ABSREF lets you determine the reference of one cell by describing its position relative to another cell. *Referencetext* must be in R1C1-style, a relative reference, and in text form: "R[− 2]C[− 2]". If *reference* is a cell range, *referencetext* is assumed to be relative to the upper left corner of *reference*.

Examples

ABSREF("R[− 2]C[− 2]",D5) = B3

ABSREF("R[− 1]C[− 1]",D10:E150 = C9

ACTIVE.CELL( )

Returns the reference of the active cell.

ACTIVE.CELL returns the reference of the active cell as an external reference. ACTIVE.CELL is particularly useful when you're working with linked worksheets and need to communicate the value or position of the active cell to an external file.

Normally the value returned by ACTIVE.CELL will be the value contained in the active cell, since that's how it's usually translated. If you want the reference instead, use REFTEXT to convert the active cell reference to text, which can then be stored or manipulated.

CALLER( )
Returns the reference of the cell that started the function macro.

Unlike RETURN, CALLER returns the reference of the cell that contained the function that called the currently running macro. If the function was part of an array formula, CALLER returns the range reference. If the currently running macro is a command macro started by the user, CALLER returns the error message #REF!

DEREF(*reference*)
Returns the value of a cell in a reference.

In most cases, a reference to a cell returns the value of that cell. If, however, you've used a function such as SET.NAME, references are not always converted to values. In those cases, the DEREF function returns a value. If the argument *reference* is a reference to a single cell, DEREF returns the value of that cell. If *reference* is a range of cells, DEREF returns the array of values in those cells.

DOCUMENTS( )
Returns the names of open documents.

DOCUMENT returns the names of all open files in alphabetical order as an array of text values. It's frequently used with INDEX to select individual filenames for other uses.

FILES(*directoryname*)
Returns the names of files in a specific directory.

FILES gives you a horizontal text array of the filenames in the directory you specify. You can use the wildcard characters * and ? in the FILES argument. Up to 256 filenames can be returned. If *directoryname* is not specified, it's assumed to be *.*.

GET.BAR( )

Returns the number of the active menu bar.

Built-in menu bar numbers are:

Number	Built-in Menu Bar
1	Worksheet and macro menu, full menus
2	Chart menu, full menus
3	Nil menu (menu displayed when no documents are open)
4	Info window menu
5	Worksheet and macro menu, short menus
6	Chart menu, short menus

GET.CELL(*infocode,reference*)

Returns information about a cell.

GET.CELL tells you about the location, contents, or formatting of the upper-left cell in *reference*. If the argument called reference is omitted, it's assumed to be the current selection.

The argument *infocode* specifies what kind of information you want:

Infocode	Result
1	Reference of upper-left cell in area specified, as text
2	Row number of the top cell in reference
3	Column number of the leftmost cell in reference
4	The same as TYPE(reference)
5	Contents of reference
6	The formula in reference, as text
7	Format of cell, as text
8	Cell's alignment:
	1 = General
	2 = Left
	3 = Center
	4 = Right
	5 = Fill
9	If cell has left border, returns TRUE; otherwise FALSE
10	If cell has right border, returns TRUE; otherwise FALSE
11	If cell has top border, returns TRUE; otherwise FALSE

147

Infocode	Result
12	If cell has bottom border, returns TRUE; otherwise FALSE
13	If cell is shaded, returns TRUE; otherwise FALSE
14	If cell is locked, returns TRUE; otherwise FALSE
15	If cell is hidden, returns TRUE; otherwise FALSE
16	Column width of the cell, measured in characters of Font 1
17	Row height of cell, in points
18	Name of font, as text
19	Size of font, in points
20	If cell is bold, returns TRUE; otherwise FALSE
21	If cell is italic, returns TRUE; otherwise FALSE
22	If cell is underlined, returns TRUE; otherwise FALSE
23	If cell is overstruck, returns TRUE; otherwise FALSE

GET.CHART.ITEM(*xyindex,pointindex,code*)

Returns the location of a chart element in a chart window.

This function returns the vertical or horizontal position of a point on a chart element. The argument *xyindex* is a code number: 1 for horizontal coordinate of the position, or 2 for the vertical coordinate.

Pointindex specifies the point on the chart object, as shown below. If the selected object is a point, *pointindex* must be 1. If *pointindex* is omitted, it's assumed to be 1.

The value given for *code* is in text form, and is the same as shown under SELECT, discussed earlier.

If the selected object is any line other than a data line, these values are used for pointindex:

Pointindex	Chart Object Position
1	Lower left
2	Upper right

If the selected object is a rectangle or an area in an area chart, these values are used for pointindex:

Pointindex	Chart Object Position
1	Upper left
2	Upper middle
3	Upper right
4	Right middle
5	Lower right
6	Lower middle
7	Lower left
8	Left middle

If the selected object is an arrow, these values are used for *pointindex:*

Pointindex	Chart Object Position
1	Base
2	Head

If the selected object is a pie slice, these values are used for *pointindex:*

Pointindex	Chart Object Position
1	Outermost counterclockwise point
2	Outer center point
3	Outermost clockwise point
4	Midpoint of the most clockwise radius
5	Center point
6	Midpoint of the most counterclockwise radius

GET.DEF(*definition, document*)

Returns a name matching a definition.

Returns the text version of the name that matches whatever is in definition, which may be a part of document. *Definition* may be a reference, but if so must be in R1C1 style.

GET.DOCUMENT(*infotype, nametext*)

Returns information about a document.

Depending on the code you specify in infotype, GET.DOCUMENT returns information about the document you identify in *nametext*. If *nametext* is omitted, it's assumed to be the active document.

Infotype	Result
1	Name of the document as text; doesn't include drive, directory, or window number.

149

Infotype	Result
2	Path name of directory containing *nametext*. If *nametext* has not yet been saved, returns the error message #N/A!
3	Returns: 1 If the document is a worksheet 2 If the document is a chart 3 If the document is a macro sheet 4 If the active window is the Info window
4	TRUE if changes have been made to the document since it was last saved; FALSE if no changes have been made.
5	TRUE if access is read-only; FALSE otherwise.
6	TRUE if file protected; FALSE otherwise.
7	TRUE of contents are protected; FALSE otherwise.
8	TRUE if document windows are protected; FALSE otherwise.

The four infotypes shown below apply only to charts:

9	Code number indicating type of chart: 1 Area 2 Bar 3 Column 4 Line 5 Pie 6 Scatter
10	Code number (same as with infotype 9) indicating type of overlay chart. If there is no overlay chart, returns #N/A!
11	Number of series in main chart.
12	Number of series in overlay chart.

The remaining infotype values apply only to worksheets and macro sheets:

9	Row number of first row used. If document is empty, returns 0.
10	Row number of last row used. If document is empty, returns 0.

150

Infotype	Result
11	Column number of first column used. If document is empty, returns 0.
12	Column number of last column used. If document is empty, returns 0.
13	Number of windows.
14	Code number indicating calculation mode: 1 Automatic 2 Automatic except tables 3 Manual
15	TRUE if iteration is enabled; otherwise FALSE.
16	Maximum number of iterations.
17	Maximum change between iterations.
18	TRUE if updating remote reference is enabled; FALSE otherwise.
19	TRUE if set to Precision as Displayed; FALSE otherwise.
20	TRUE is document is using 1904 date system; FALSE otherwise.
21	Four-item horizontal text array of the names of the four fonts.
22	Four-item horizontal number array of the sizes of the four fonts

GET.FORMULA(*reference*)

Returns the contents of a cell.

GET.FORMULA returns the contents of *reference* as it would appear in the formula bar. The contents are returned as text. If the formula contains references, they are returned in R1C1-style.

GET.NAME(*nametext*)

Returns the definition of a name.

GET.NAME returns a name's definition as it would appear in the Refers to text box Formula Define Name command. *Nametext* can be a name on a macro sheet, or an external reference to a name defined on a document.

If the definition of nametext contains references, they are returned in R1C1-style.

GET.NOTE(*cellreference,start,count*)

Returns characters from a note.

GET.NOTE returns count number of characters from the cell identified by *cellreference*, beginning at the character numbered *start*. If *start* is omitted, it's assumed to be 1. If *count* is omitted, it's assumed to be the length of the note attached to *cellreference*.

GET.WINDOW(*infotype,nametext*)

Returns information about a window.

Depending on the code you specify in *infotype*, GET.WINDOW returns information about the window you identify in *nametext*. If *nametext* is omitted, it's assumed to be the active window.

Use *infotype* to specify what kind of information you want. *Infotypes* 1 through 7 apply to all windows, and 8 through 17 apply to worksheets and macro sheets. *Infotypes* 13 through 17 return numeric arrays that specify what rows or columns are at the edges of the panes in the specified window.

Infotype	Results
1	Name of document in the window specified in *nametext*, as text.
2	Number of window specified.
3	Number of points from the left edge of your screen to the left edge of the window (*x* position).
4	Number of points from the top edge of your screen to the top edge of the window (*y* position).
5	Width, measured in points.
6	Height, measured in points.
7	TRUE if window is hidden; otherwise FALSE.
8	TRUE if formulas are displayed; otherwise FALSE.
9	TRUE if gridlines are displayed; otherwise FALSE.
10	TRUE if row and column headings are displayed; otherwise FALSE.
11	TRUE if zeros are displayed; otherwise FALSE.
12	Code number 0–8 giving the color of gridlines and headlines, corresponding to colors shown in

Infotype	Results
	the Options Display dialog box. (Zero is equivalent to the Automatic Display option.)
13	The leftmost column of each pane, as an array.
14	The top row of each pane, as an array.
15	The rightmost column of each pane, as an array.
16	The bottom row of each pane, as an array.
17	Returns the active pane number.

GET.WORKSPACE(*infotype*)

Returns information about the workspace.

Depending on the code you specify in *infotype*, GET.WORKSPACE returns information about your workspace.

Use *infotype* to specify what kind of information you want.

Infotype	Result
1	Name and version number of the environment in which *Excel* is running, as text.
2	Version number of *Excel*, as text.
3	If auto-decimal is set, returns the number of decimals; otherwise 0.
4	TRUE if in R1C1 mode; FALSE if in A1 mode.
5	TRUE if scroll bars are displayed; otherwise FALSE.
6	TRUE if status bar is displayed; otherwise FALSE.
7	TRUE if formula bar is displayed; otherwise FALSE.
8	TRUE if remote requests are enabled; otherwise FALSE.
9	Returns alternate menu key as text; returns #N/A! if no alternate menu key is set.
10	Special mode code number: 1 Data Find 2 Copy 3 Cut 0 No special mode
11	Number of points from the left edge of the screen to the left edge of the *Excel* window (*x* position).

Infotype	Result
12	Number of points from the top edge of the screen to the top edge of the *Excel* window (*y* position).
13	Usable workspace width, in points.
14	Usable workspace height, in points.
15	Maximize/minimize code number:

     1 *Excel* is neither maximized nor minimized
     2 Minimized
     3 Maximized

16	Number of kilobytes of memory free.
17	Total number of kilobytes of memory available to *Excel*.
18	TRUE if math coprocessor is present; otherwise FALSE.
19	TRUE if mouse is present; otherwise FALSE.

LINKS(*docname*)

Returns the names of all linked documents.

LINKS returns a horizontal array of the names of all documents referred to by external references in the document specified by *docname*. If *docname* is omitted, it's assumed to be the active document. If the document identified by *docname* contains no external references, LINKS returns the error message #N/A!

NAMES(*docname*)

Returns an array of defined names on a document.

NAMES returns a horizontal text array of all names defined on *docname*. If *docname* is omitted, it's assumed to be the active document.

OFFSET(*reference,rows,columns,height,width*)

Returns a reference offset from a given reference.

OFFSET returns an array whose dimensions are indicated by the values in *height* and *width* at an offset from the cell or array indicated in *reference*. This offset is indicated in the arguments *rows* and *columns*. If *height* or *width* are omitted, they are assumed to be the same dimensions as *reference*.

If the offset parameters go over the edge of the worksheet, OFFSET returns the #REF! error message. If *reference* is a multiple value, the function returns the error message #VALUE!

REFTEXT(*reference,a1*)

Converts a reference into text.

Converts reference to an absolute reference, as text. If *a1* is TRUE, REFTEXT returns it in A1-style; if FALSE or omitted, REFTEXT returns it in R1C1-style.

RELREF(*reference,comparison*)

Returns a relative reference.

RELREF compares the value in the argument called *comparison* to the argument called *reference* and returns a relative reference, in R1C1-style, as text.

Example

RELREF(B3,C4) = "R[− 1]C[− 1]"

SELECTION( )

Returns the reference of a selection.

SELECTION returns the reference of a selection as an external reference.

Normally the value returned by SELECTION is converted to a value rather than stored as a reference. If you want the reference rather than the value, use REFTEXT to convert the reference to text, which can then be further manipulated.

TEXTREF(*text,a1*)

Converts text to a reference.

Converts the text specified to a cell reference. If *a1* is TRUE, *text* is assumed to be in A1-style; if *a1* is FALSE or omitted, *text* is assumed to be in R1C1-style.

WINDOWS( )

Returns the names of open windows.

WINDOWS returns a horizontal text array of all windows on your screen, in order by level. The active window is the first named; the window directly under that is the second, and so forth.

Part 3
The Models

Chapters 5 through 10 contain sample models that can be used in business situations. Chapter 5 shows you some basic financial statements: the income statement, the balance sheet, and the cash flow statement.

Chapter 6 presents four accounting models; Chapter 7 shows three models in the area of finance; and Chapter 8 offers some manufacturing models. Chapter 9 shows some models that can be used with investments; and Chapter 10 gives some ideas about using models in statistical analysis.

In each chapter you'll be led step by step through the construction of a worksheet. Each worksheet model is shown both in completed form and as a cell-by-cell listing of contents. There are also some comments about things you can do to alter the model so it fits your needs.

You'll also see how to construct one or more of the models in each chapter as a macro, and illustrate some of the ways you can use macros to make your work more efficient. Macro techniques such as automatic calling, prompting for input, looping, and other facilities are illustrated.

Chapter 5

The Basic Financial Statements

The income statement, the balance sheet, and the cash flow statement are three of the most basic financial statements. They are different pictures of a business entity's financial health. They can be used with large and small businesses, and with some minor modifications even with personal data.

The income statement looks solely at income and expenses—where the money came from, and where it went. Its concern is the basic formula:

Income − Expenses = Profit

As such, it isn't concerned with a breakdown of income into accounts receivable, cash, or other forms of income. It may be divided into categories, such as sales from Product A, Product B, and Product C, and income from services or income from interest, or even income from sale of assets. However, it considers all income as Income. Likewise, the expense part of the income statement considers all expenses to be money spent, whether it's been allocated to an accrual account, such as for payroll or other taxes, or directly spent on such things as wages, rent, or supplies. You get profit (or net income) when you subtract all expenses from all income.

Within an income statement, some income and expense items are grouped into other categories. For instance, when you subtract the cost of commissions from total sales, you have a figure some people call Net Sales. When you subtract the cost of goods sold from the revenue derived from selling those products, you have an interim profit called Gross Profit or Gross Margin. When you subtract operating expenses and depreciation expenses from the Gross Profit, you have an Operating Profit. When you subtract any interest expense from the Operating Profit, you have Net Income Before Taxes, or Profit Before Income Taxes. When you subtract income taxes from that, you have Net Income, commonly called the "bottom line."

A balance sheet looks at assets and liabilities, and regards net income for the period only as one of the assets. It reports the financial condition for the entity as of the last day of the period for which the income statement was done.

A balance sheet is concerned with the basic formula

Assets = Liabilities + Equity

It isn't concerned with how income or expenses flowed into or out of any of the categories mentioned. The only thing that counts in a balance sheet is the amount in that category at the time and date (usually midnight the last day of the reporting period) the amounts in the balance sheet were reported.

There are some fairly standard categories for a balance sheet:

• Assets are composed of current assets, fixed assets, and other assets. Current assets are cash and other assets that could be converted into cash in a short period of time, usually 60 days. Fixed assets are longer-term assets, such as buildings, land, and equipment. Other assets are things that could generate money if necessary, but can't be clearly categorized as either current or fixed assets.
• Liabilities list current liabilities and long-term liabilities. Current liabilities are amounts that will have to be paid within one year of the date of the balance sheet. Long-term liabilities are amounts that are to be paid more than one year after the balance sheet date.
• Equity shows two kinds of owner's equity: paid-in capital, and retained earnings. Paid-in capital comes when stockholders buy stock in the company, thereby investing capital in the company. When the Net Income earned by the business is distributed to the owners, this is called dividends, and any of this money left after distribution of dividends is called Retained Earnings.

A cash flow statement shows sources of cash and where it went, along with an ending balance, taken at midnight the last day of the reporting period. However, cash flow does not take into account receivables, nor such assets as inventory or equipment that could be used to create more sales. As such, net cash received during the reporting period is usually not the same as sales or revenue, and cash disbursements for the same period don't necessarily reflect a company's relative financial health.

Further, a cash flow statement must make a distinction between cash received as a result of sales and spent in order to create goods or services, and cash received as a result of loans or capital investment in the company. The latter is frequently spent on long-term assets such as equipment or Research and Development projects.

The Income Statement

In this section, we'll construct a basic income statement for a company that sells scuba, snorkeling, and surfing equipment, and makes a few of the items it sells. Its income comes partly from the sales of products and partly from the lessons it gives. You'll see several interim profits, until at the bottom we calculate the final Net Income.

With a blank worksheet on your screen, type the title information in column A, as shown. (Don't worry about centering. We'll move these lines later, if necessary.) In rows 1, 2, and 3, type these lines:

Bayside Water Sports, Inc.

Income Statement

October 1, 1987 – September 30, 1988

A title is important on a financial statement because it identifies the business entity (in this case, Bayside Water Sports, Inc.), the type of financial statement (Income Statement), and the period being reported.

Skip the next line, and in row 5, type the word INCOME. The next section will detail where the income comes from, and will include deductions for the commissions you pay to the teachers who sell your equipment, and for the cost of materials and supplies bought to produce the equipment sold.

Notice that some items are spelled out in column A, and others are in column B. There are several schools of thought about showing income and expenses this way. We've chosen this one because it's simple. Major items of an income statement are in column A, and supporting details are in column B. You may also wish to rearrange the figures in a similar manner: Major items could be in column E and supporting details in column D.

Move to row 7 and from there, type the row headings as shown below:

Figure 5-1. Row Headings, Income Statement

	A	B	C	D
1	Bayside Water Sports, Inc.			
2	Income Statement			
3	October 1, 1987 - September 30, 1988			
4				
5	INCOME			
6				
7	Sales			
8		Scuba/snorkel equip.		
9		Surfboards		
10		Windsurfers		
11		Lessons		
12		Less commissions		
13				
14		Net Sales Revenue		
15	Cost of Goods			
16				
17	Gross Margin			
18				
19	EXPENSES			
20				
21	Operating Expenses			
22		Rent		
23		Utilities		
24		Phone		
25		Wages		
26		Payroll taxes		
27		Advertising		
28		Supplies		
29		Equipment		
30		Transportation		
31				
32				
33		Depreciation		
34				
35		Total Operating Exp.		
36				
37	NET OPERATING INCOME			
38		Interest Expense		
39				
40	NET INCOME BEFORE TAXES			
41		Income Taxes		
42				
43	NET INCOME			

Your next task is to enter the figures for each of the rows. The first time you construct this worksheet, use the figures shown. Thereafter you can substitute any data you like. Enter data as follows:

Scuba/snorkel equip.	255375
Surfboards	138152
Windsurfers	215339
Lessons	72400
Less commissions	4200
Cost of Goods	114278

162

Leave the space for Net Sales Revenue blank for now.

You'll be adding the first four lines, and subtracting the commission figure in order to determine Net Sales Revenue. In D14 type the formula

= SUM(D8:D11) − D12

and press the Enter key. *Excel* computes the total, which appears in D14.

To make it obvious you're adding up a column of figures, type a summary line in D13. To make sure *Excel* doesn't think it's a mistyped formula, type nine hyphens:

- - - - - - - - -

You'll use this line again, in several other places. Once typed, all you have to do is copy it where you want it to go. For instance, with the active cell in D13, choose the Edit Copy command. (*Excel* assumes the active cell contains the material you want copied.) You'll need another summary line in D16, so move the active cell there, and press the Enter key. Note that *Excel* has now copied the summary line to the new location.

To determine the figure for Gross Margin, move the active cell to D17 and type the formula:

= D14 − D15

This completes the income section of the Income Statement.

The next section, starting on row 19, details how the income was spent. In D22 through D30 type the figures shown below:

Rent	56000
Utilities	14376
Phone	12843
Wages	112540
Payroll taxes	39564
Advertising	48450
Supplies	14588
Equipment	39845
Transportation	23675

While you're entering data, also enter the following:

in D33	**45000**
in D38	**75000**
in D41	**68363**

Next, copy the summary lines where they'll be needed. Move the active cell to one of the two current locations of the summary line (either D13 or D16), and choose the Edit Copy command. Now move the active cell to D31 and press the Enter key.

Since the summary line is now in D31, this cell can be used as the source for the next copy operation. Again, choose the Edit Copy command, move the active cell to D34, and press the Enter key. Repeat this action so summary lines are placed in D36, D39, and D42.

The next series of steps involves calculating the interim totals and the final Net Income. All involve formulas, since the data has already been entered. You can either type the cell locations involved in these formulas, or use Point mode to select and place their reference in the formula. We'll use Point mode in this exercise.

With the active cell in:

D32   Type an equals sign, then SUM, then a left parenthesis. Use the up-arrow key or your mouse to make D22 the active cell, type a colon (:), make D30 the active cell, type a right parenthesis, and press the Enter key. The formula =SUM(D22:D30) appears in the formula bar, and the results appear in D32.

D35   Type an equals sign, point to D32, type a minus sign, point to D33, and press the Enter key. The formula =D32−D33 appears in the formula bar.

D37   Type an equals sign, point to D17 (the figure for Gross Margin), type a minus sign, point to D35, and press the Enter key. The formula =D17−D35 appears in the formula bar.

D40   Type an equals sign, point to D37, type a minus sign, point to D38, and press the Enter key. The formula =D37−D38 appears in the formula bar.

D43   Type an equals sign, point to D40, type a minus sign, point to D41, and press the Enter key. The formula =D40−D41 appears in the formula bar.

The only thing left is to format the numbers so they're more readable. In this example, we chose #,##0 format (no decimals). You might wish to use $#,##0 or $#,##0.00 format. To format the numbers, press F8 and highlight everything from D8 to D43; then choose the Format Number command and choose the format you want.

The finished income statement worksheet looks like Figure 5-2.

Figure 5-2. Completed Income Statement

	A	B	C	D
1	Bayside Water Sports, Inc.			
2	Income Statement			
3	October 1, 1987 - September 30, 1988			
4				
5	INCOME			
6				
7	Sales			
8		Scuba/snorkel equip.		255,375
9		Surfboards		138,152
10		Windsurfers		215,339
11		Lessons		72,400
12		less commissions		4,200
13				----------
14		Net Sales Revenue		677,066
15	Cost of Goods			114,278
16				----------
17	Gross Margin			562,788
18				
19	EXPENSES			
20				
21	Operating Expenses			
22		Rent		56,000
23		Utilities		14,376
24		Phone		12,843
25		Wages		112,540
26		Payroll taxes		39,564
27		Advertising		48,450
28		Supplies		14,588
29		Equipment		39,845
30		Transportation		23,675
31				----------
32				361,881
33		Depreciation		45,000
34				----------
35		Total Operating Exp.		316,881
36				----------
37	NET OPERATING INCOME			245,907
38		Interest Expense		75,000
39				----------
40	NET INCOME BEFORE TAXES			170,907
41		Income Taxes		68,363
42				----------
43	NET INCOME			102,544

Now that you have a template for an income statement, you can save the original version and then make as many modifications as you want and save them as different versions. If you insert or delete rows, the formulas will be adjusted automatically. New rows can indicate income or expenses in more detail.

If all your figures are kept in one column, you may wish to expand the worksheet to the right, and make the Income Statement a monthly worksheet, showing each month's figures. The same formulas apply. If you copy the formulas and summary lines to the right, you'll find the formulas adjust to reflect their new locations.

You may also wish to reduce the column width of Column A, so the data in column B doesn't appear indented as far.

Figure 5-3 is an example of the same worksheet, showing three months' activity, with Column A adjusted to five characters wide.

Figure 5-3. Three Month Income Statement

	A	B	C	D	E	F
1			Bayside Water Sports, Inc.			
2			Income Statement			
3						
4				Jul-88	Aug-88	Sep-88
5	INCOME					
6						
7	Sales					
8		Scuba/snorkel equip.		65,223	68,232	51,220
9		Surfboards		14,255	15,243	8,453
10		Windsurfers		17,846	14,236	10,335
11		Lessons		8,460	8,715	2,850
12		less commissions		605	645	225
13				----------	----------	----------
14		Net Sales Revenue		105,179	105,781	72,633
15	Cost of Goods			22,535	20,355	16,545
16				----------	----------	----------
17	Gross Margin			82,644	85,426	56,088
18						
19	EXPENSES					
20						
21	Operating Expenses					
22		Rent		4,665	4,665	4,665
23		Utilities		1,050	1,164	987
24		Phone		1,185	1,195	1,052
25		Wages		9,574	9,514	9,418
26		Payroll taxes		2,872	2,854	2,825
27		Advertising		5,265	5,175	4,936
28		Supplies		1,401	1,378	1,184
29		Equipment		5,322	4,922	1,618
30		Transportation		3,589	3,275	2,674
31				----------	----------	----------
32				34,923	34,142	29,359
33		Depreciation		3,750	3,750	3,750
34				----------	----------	----------
35		Total Operating Exp.		31,173	30,392	25,609
36				----------	----------	----------
37	NET OPERATING INCOME			51,471	55,034	30,479
38		Interest Expense		6,500	6,150	6,050
39				----------	----------	----------
40	NET INCOME BEFORE TAXES			44,971	48,884	24,429
41		Income Taxes		17,988	19,554	9,772
42				----------	----------	----------
43	NET INCOME			26,983	29,330	14,657

Balance Sheet

As mentioned with the Income Statement, the data for our hypo-thetical company shows relative financial health. An income statement shows profit/loss, but a balance sheet offers a more complete picture that takes assets, accruals, and other factors into consideration.

This section will show you how to construct a balance sheet on a worksheet, and then will give you a macro that automates part of that procedure.

This balance sheet uses data that differs from that used for the income statement, although it comes from the same set of books. For instance, the income figures used to compute the Net Sales Revenue don't show how much is cash and how much is accounts receivable; it's shown there as all income. The balance sheet breaks that down into cash and receivables. The supplies and equipment expenses on the income statement only show that these categories of things were bought; it doesn't show that they went into inventory, plant and equipment, or were used during the month in the process of producing items that were then sold.

This balance sheet also reflects other financial data that don't appear on an income statement: the amount of long-term debt, or the amount stockholders paid in as capital to start the com-pany. The plant and equipment figure takes into account the de-preciation shown as an expense on the income statement, plus the value of any equipment added during the month.

The balance sheet also reflects some changes in column width: Column A is 30 characters wide, and the rest of the col-umns are 12 characters wide. Change the default column widths with the Format Column Width command.

Enter the row and column labels as shown in Figure 5-4.

Figure 5-4. Balance Sheet Labels

	A	B	C	D
1	Balance Sheet for Year 87-88			
2				
3		1-Jul-88	1-Aug-88	1-Sep-88
4				
5	Assets			
6				
7	Cash			
8	Accounts Receivable: Trade			
9	Accounts Receivable: Other			
10	Inventory			
11	Other Current Assets			
12		---------	---------	---------
13	Total Current Assets			
14				
15	Plant and Equipment			
16		---------	---------	---------
17	Total Assets			
18				
19	Liabilities and Equity			
20				
21	Accounts Payable			
22				
23	Accrued Liabilities			
24	Income Tax			
25	Commissions			
26	Other Accruals			
27				
28	Loans/Other Liabilities			
29				
30	Long Term Debt			
31		---------	---------	---------
32	Total Liabilities			
33				
34				
35	Stockholder Equity			
36	Net Income Year-to-Date			
37		---------	---------	---------
38	Total Equity			
39		---------	---------	---------
40	Total Liabilities and Equity			
41				
42	'==============================	==========	==========	==========
43	Ratios			
44				
45	Current Ratio			
46	Acid Test Ratio			
47	Return on Total Assets			

Notice that the figure on line 36, Net Income Year-to-Date, is a cumulative figure. It uses the Net Income figure on line 43 of the Income Statement, and adds each month's figure to the total for the year. If you use the Income Statement template to create a worksheet each month, you can use an external reference in the formula in this worksheet to pick up the figure on the Income Statement file. (External references are discussed in detail in a companion book, *Using PCExcel*, and in the guide that comes as part of the *Excel* package.)

The ratios at the bottom are commonly used percentages, often preferred by banks and analysts to determine a company's financial health. Current Ratio is the ratio of current assets to current liabilities. Acid Test Ratio, or quick ratio, is the result of current assets minus inventory, divided by current liabilities. Return on Total Assets is net income divided by total assets.

Once the labels have been entered, there are only five formulas to enter, plus the three for the ratios. The formulas, like the summary lines, can be copied from one cell to the other cells where they'll be used. The formulas are entered in the rows shown below, in column B. Once entered, you should copy them to columns to the right for as many months as you wish the balance sheet to contain.

Row	Formula to Enter
Row 13	=SUM(B7:B11)
Row 17	=B13+B15
Row 32	=SUM(B21:B30)
Row 38	=B35+B36
Row 40	=B32+B38
Row 45	=B13/SUM(B21:B26)
Row 46	=(B13−B10)/SUM(B21:B26)
Row 47	=B36/B17

Once the formulas have been entered, you can enter the data. You can ignore the error messages; they'll disappear once there's data to work with. You may wish to use the figures shown in Figure 5-5, or enter your own.

Figure 5-5. Completed Balance Statement

	A	B	C	D
1	Balance Sheet for Year 87-88			
2				
3		1-Jul-88	1-Aug-88	1-Sep-88
4				
5	Assets			
6				
7	Cash	42,355	37,113	36,144
8	Accounts Receivable: Trade	74,322	79,340	87,334
9	Accounts Receivable: Other	1,215	1,665	10,224
10	Inventory	167,533	152,239	143,122
11	Other Current Assets	14,223	12,133	10,125
12		---------	---------	---------
13	Total Current Assets	299,648	282,490	286,949
14				
15	Plant and Equipment	51,233	51,074	50,224
16		---------	---------	---------
17	Total Assets	350,881	333,564	337,173
18				
19	Liabilities and Equity			
20				
21	Accounts Payable	17,233	19,334	20,345
22				
23	Accrued Liabilities			
24	Income Tax	18,788	7,511	8,326
25	Commissions	63,499	26,195	13,413
26	Other Accruals	4,378	4,211	4,119
27				
28	Loans/Other Liabilities			
29				
30	Long Term Debt	50,000	50,000	50,000
31		---------	---------	---------
32	Total Liabilities	153,898	107,251	96,203
33				
34				
35	Stockholder Equity	35,000	35,000	35,000
36	Net Income Year-to-Date	161,983	191,313	205,970
37		---------	---------	---------
38	Total Equity	196,983	226,313	240,970
39		---------	---------	---------
40	Total Liabilities and Equity	350,881	333,564	337,173
41				
42	'=============================	==========	==========	==========
43	Ratios			
44				
45	Current Ratio	2.88	4.93	6.21
46	Acid Test Ratio	1.27	2.28	3.11
47	Return on Total Assets	0.46	0.57	0.61

Using a Macro to Create a Balance Sheet Template

Once you've created a worksheet template with *Excel,* you can use it over and over again, substituting new figures after clearing the old ones. (Don't use the Edit Delete command, or you'll erase the formulas as well.)

Another solution, one that actually works more quickly, is to use a macro program to construct the labels and formulas part of the worksheet, leaving it ready for you to enter data. We've created one such macro program, shown in Figure 5-6.

Figure 5-6. BALSHT.XLM Macro

	A
1	BalanceSheet
2	=COLUMN.WIDTH(35)
3	=SELECT("R2C2")
4	=COLUMN.WIDTH(12)
5	=SELECT("R2C3")
6	=COLUMN.WIDTH(12)
7	=SELECT("R2C4")
8	=COLUMN.WIDTH(12)
9	=SELECT("R2C5")
10	=COLUMN.WIDTH(12)
11	=SELECT("R2C6")
12	=COLUMN.WIDTH(12)
13	=SELECT("R2C7")
14	=COLUMN.WIDTH(12)
15	=SELECT("R2C8")
16	=COLUMN.WIDTH(12)
17	=SELECT("R2C9")
18	=COLUMN.WIDTH(12)
19	=SELECT("R2C10")
20	=FORMULA("")
21	=SELECT("R2C10")
22	=COLUMN.WIDTH(12)
23	=SELECT("R2C11")
24	=COLUMN.WIDTH(12)
25	=SELECT("R2C12")
26	=COLUMN.WIDTH(12)
27	=SELECT("R2C13")
28	=COLUMN.WIDTH(12)
29	=SELECT("R1C1")
30	=FORMULA("Balance Sheet for Year 87-88")
31	=SELECT("R2C1")
32	=COLUMN.WIDTH(25)
33	=FORMAT.FONT("Helv",10,TRUE,FALSE,FALSE,FALSE)

	A
34	=SELECT("R1C1")
35	=FORMAT.FONT("Helv",10,TRUE,FALSE,FALSE,FALSE)
36	=SELECT("R1C1")
37	=COLUMN.WIDTH(30)
38	=DISPLAY(FALSE,FALSE,TRUE,TRUE,0)
39	=SELECT("R2C1")
40	=BORDER(FALSE,FALSE,FALSE,FALSE,FALSE,FALSE)
41	=SELECT("R2C1")
42	=BORDER(FALSE,FALSE,FALSE,FALSE,FALSE,FALSE)
43	=SELECT("R2C1")
44	=FORMULA(" ")
45	=SELECT("R2C1:R2C13")
46	=BORDER(FALSE,FALSE,FALSE,FALSE,FALSE,FALSE)
47	=SELECT("R2C1:R2C13")
48	=BORDER(FALSE,FALSE,FALSE,FALSE,FALSE,TRUE)
49	=SELECT("R3C2")
50	=FORMULA("October")
51	=SELECT("R3C3")
52	=FORMULA("November")
53	=SELECT("R3C4")
54	=FORMULA("December")
55	=SELECT("R3C5")
56	=FORMULA("January")
57	=SELECT("R3C6")
58	=FORMULA("February")
59	=SELECT("R3C7")
60	=FORMULA("March")
61	=SELECT("R3C8")
62	=FORMULA("April")
63	=SELECT("R3C9")
64	=FORMULA("May")
65	=SELECT("R3C10")
66	=FORMULA("June")
67	=SELECT("R3C11")
68	=FORMULA("July")
69	=SELECT("R3C12")
70	=FORMULA("August")
71	=SELECT("R3C13")
72	=FORMULA("September")
73	=SELECT("R3C1:R3C13","R3C13")
74	=BORDER(FALSE,FALSE,FALSE,FALSE,FALSE,FALSE)
75	=SELECT("R4C1:R4C13","R4C13")
76	=BORDER(FALSE,FALSE,FALSE,FALSE,FALSE,TRUE)
77	=SELECT("R5C1")
78	=FORMULA("Assets")
79	=SELECT("R5C1")
80	=FORMAT.FONT("Helv",10,TRUE,FALSE,FALSE,FALSE)
81	=SELECT("R7C1")
82	=FORMULA(" Cash")
83	=SELECT("R8C1")
84	=FORMULA(" Accounts Receiveable: Trade")
85	=SELECT("R9C1")
86	=FORMULA(" Accounts Receiveable: Other")
87	=SELECT("R10C1")
88	=FORMULA(" Inventory")
89	=SELECT("R11C1")
90	=FORMULA(" Other Current Assets")
91	=SELECT("R13C1")
92	=FORMULA(" Total Current Assets")
93	=SELECT("R15C1")
94	=FORMULA("Plant and Equipment")
95	=SELECT("R17C1")
96	=FORMULA(" Total Assets")
97	=SELECT("R19C1")
98	=FORMULA("Liabilities and Equity")
99	=SELECT("R19C1")

	A
100	=FORMAT.FONT("Helv",10,TRUE,FALSE,FALSE,FALSE)
101	=SELECT("R21C1")
102	=FORMULA(" Accounts Payable")
103	=SELECT("R23C1")
104	=FORMULA(" Accrued Liabilities")
105	=SELECT("R24C1")
106	=FORMULA(" Income Tax")
107	=SELECT("R25C1")
108	=FORMULA(" Commissions")
109	=SELECT("R26C1")
110	=FORMULA(" Other Accruals")
111	=SELECT("R28C1")
112	=FORMULA(" Loans/Other Liabilities")
113	=SELECT("R30C1")
114	=FORMULA(" Long Term Debt")
115	=SELECT("R32C1")
116	=FORMULA(" Total Liabilities")
117	=SELECT("R35C1")
118	=FORMULA(" Stockholder Equity")
119	=SELECT("R36C1")
120	=FORMULA("Net Income Year-to-Date")
121	=SELECT("R36C1")
122	=FORMULA(" Net Income Year-to Date")
123	=SELECT("R38C1")
124	=FORMULA(" Total Equity")
125	=SELECT("R40C1")
126	=FORMULA("Total Liabilities and Equity")
127	=SELECT("R39C1:R39C13")
128	=BORDER(FALSE,FALSE,FALSE,FALSE,FALSE,TRUE)
129	=SELECT("R37C1:R37C13")
130	=BORDER(FALSE,FALSE,FALSE,FALSE,FALSE,TRUE)
131	=SELECT("R31C1:R31C13")
132	=BORDER(FALSE,FALSE,FALSE,FALSE,FALSE,TRUE)
133	=SELECT("R16C1")
134	=SELECT.END(2)
135	=SELECT.END(2)
136	=SELECT("R16C255")
137	=SELECT.END(1)
138	=SELECT("R16C1:R16C13")
139	=BORDER(FALSE,FALSE,FALSE,FALSE,FALSE,TRUE)
140	=SELECT("R12C1:R12C13")
141	=BORDER(FALSE,FALSE,FALSE,FALSE,FALSE,TRUE)
142	=SELECT("R42C1:R42C13")
143	=BORDER(FALSE,FALSE,FALSE,FALSE,FALSE,TRUE)
144	=SELECT("R43C1")
145	=FORMULA("Ratios")
146	=FORMAT.FONT("Helv",10,TRUE,FALSE,FALSE,FALSE)
147	=SELECT("R45C1")
148	=FORMULA("Current Ratios")
149	=SELECT("R46C1")
150	=FORMULA("Acid Test Ratio")
151	=SELECT("R47C1")
152	=FORMULA("Return on Total Assets")
153	=SELECT("R13C2")
154	=FORMULA("=SUM(R[-6]C:R[-2]C)")
155	=COPY()
156	=SELECT("R13C3:R13C13")
157	=PASTE()
158	=CANCEL.COPY()
159	=SELECT("R17C2")
160	=FORMULA("=R[-4]C[-1]+R[-2]C[-1]")
161	=SELECT("R15C2")
162	=FORMULA("#VALUE!")
163	=SELECT("R17C2")
164	=FORMULA("=R[-4]C+R[-2]C")
165	=COPY()

	A
166	=SELECT("R17C3")
167	=SELECT.END(2)
168	=SELECT.END(2)
169	=SELECT("R17C255")
170	=SELECT.END(1)
171	=SELECT("R17C3:R17C13")
172	=PASTE()
173	=CANCEL.COPY()
174	=SELECT("R15C2")
175	=FORMULA("")
176	=SELECT("R32C2")
177	=FORMULA("=R[-11]C+(SUM(R[-8]C:R[-6]C))+R[-4]C+R[-2]C")
178	=COPY()
179	=SELECT("R32C3:R32C13")
180	=PASTE()
181	=CANCEL.COPY()
182	=SELECT("R38C2")
183	=FORMULA("=R[-3]C+R[-2]C")
184	=SELECT("R40C2")
185	=FORMULA("=R[-8]C+R[-2]C")
186	=SELECT("R38C2")
187	=COPY()
188	=SELECT("R38C3:R38C13")
189	=PASTE()
190	=CANCEL.COPY()
191	=SELECT("R40C2")
192	=COPY()
193	=SELECT("R40C3:R40C13")
194	=PASTE()
195	=CANCEL.COPY()
196	=SELECT("R45C2")
197	=FORMULA("=R[-32]C")
198	=FORMULA("=R[-32]C/(R[-22]C+SUM(R[-19]C:R[-17]C))")
199	=COPY()
200	=SELECT("R45C3:R45C13")
201	=PASTE()
202	=CANCEL.COPY()
203	=SELECT("R46C2")
204	=FORMULA("(B13-B10)/(B23+SUM(B26:B28)+B30)")
205	=FORMULA("=(R[-33]C-R[-36]C)/(R[-23]C+SUM(R[-20]C:R[-18]C)+R[-16]C)")
206	=COPY()
207	=SELECT("R46C3:R46C13")
208	=PASTE()
209	=CANCEL.COPY()
210	=SELECT("R47C2")
211	=FORMULA("=R[-9]C/R[-30]C")
212	=COPY()
213	=SELECT("R47C3:R47C13")
214	=PASTE()
215	=CANCEL.COPY()
216	=SELECT("R7C2")
217	=BORDER(TRUE,FALSE,FALSE,FALSE,FALSE,FALSE)
218	=COPY()
219	=SELECT("R7C2:R11C13")
220	=PASTE()
221	=SELECT("R15C2:R15C13")
222	=PASTE()
223	=SELECT("R21C2:R21C13")
224	=PASTE()
225	=SELECT("R24C2:R26C13")
226	=PASTE()
227	=SELECT("R28C2:R28C13")
228	=PASTE()
229	=SELECT("R30C2:R30C13")
230	=PASTE()
231	=SELECT("R35C2:R36C13")

	A
232	=PASTE()
233	=SELECT("R37C1")
234	=SELECT("R1C1")
235	=SELECT("R7C2")
236	=SELECT("r1c1")
237	=SELECT("R7C2")
238	=RETURN()

This macro program was initially created with the Macro Record command while the Balance Sheet worksheet was being created, then cleaned up and modified somewhat with some formatting. When it's run, for instance, it will remove the grid lines in many instances (grid lines were restored for this book to improve clarity) and several shaded bars are used to separate categories of information.

The macro needs to be stored as a macro file before it can be used. Open a new macro file, type the macro instructions as shown, and save it with a filename. (*Excel* adds the extension .XLM to identify it as a macro program.)

To run the macro, open the macro file; then open a blank worksheet so the worksheet is the active window. (If you try to run the macro program while the macro is the active window, it will overwrite its own commands and the data will be useless.)

Choose the Macro Run command, and in the dialog box, choose the filename you've given this macro. Once you choose the OK bar, the macro program goes about creating the template shown in Figure 5-7.

Don't be surprised if the process takes a minute or two; there are over 230 steps in the macro. When the program ends, the active cell will be B7—the first cell where you will want to enter numbers. As you enter numbers in the column, the formulas will calculate interim results, some showing misinformation until you finish entering your data.

The macro program does not check that the figure for Total Assets in row 17 equals the figure shown for Total Liabilities and Equity in row 40. That's because this particular macro was constructed only to display the template, not to check the figures.

Figure 5-7. Balance Sheet Template Created with a Macro

	A	B	C	D	E	F
1	Balance Sheet for Year 87-88					
2						
3		October	November	December	January	February
4						
5	Assets					
6						
7	Cash					
8	Accounts Receiveable: Trade					
9	Accounts Receiveable: Other					
10	Inventory					
11	Other Current Assets					
12						
13	Total Current Assets	0	0	0	0	0
14						
15	Plant and Equipment					
16						
17	Total Assets	0	0	0	0	0
18						
19	Liabilities and Equity					
20						
21	Accounts Payable					
22						
23	Accrued Liabilities					
24	Income Tax					
25	Commissions					
26	Other Accruals					
27						
28	Loans/Other Liabilities					
29						
30	Long Term Debt					
31						
32	Total Liabilities	0	0	0	0	0
33						
34						
35	Stockholder Equity					
36	Net Income Year-to Date					
37						
38	Total Equity	0	0	0	0	0
39						
40	Total Liabilities and Equity	0	0	0	0	0
41						
42						
43	Ratios					
44						
45	Current Ratios	#DIV/0!	#DIV/0!	#DIV/0!	#DIV/0!	#DIV/0!
46	Acid Test Ratio	#DIV/0!	#DIV/0!	#DIV/0!	#DIV/0!	#DIV/0!
47	Return on Total Assets	#DIV/0!	#DIV/0!	#DIV/0!	#DIV/0!	#DIV/0!

Cash Flow Statement

A cash flow statement, the third of the basic financial statements, concentrates specifically in the in- and outflows of cash. It breaks sales down into cash and receivables, and shows when payment of bills will reduce the amount of available cash. It specifically warns if cash is likely to get too low to meet monthly commitments, like wages, payroll taxes, and interest on loans.

In the cash flow model shown here, you predict the percentage of sales that are cash and receivables. You also indicate what percentage of the month's bills are payable immediately, or can be put on 30, 60, or 90 day payment schedules. You also specify the minimum cash balance you want on hand, and the maximum

	G	H	I	J	K	L	M
1							
2							
3	March	April	May	June	July	August	September
4							
5							
6							
7							
8							
9							
10							
11							
12							
13	0	0	0	0	0	0	0
14							
15							
16							
17	0	0	0	0	0	0	0
18							
19							
20							
21							
22							
23							
24							
25							
26							
27							
28							
29							
30							
31							
32	0	0	0	0	0	0	0
33							
34							
35							
36							
37							
38	0	0	0	0	0	0	0
39							
40	0	0	0	0	0	0	0
41							
42							
43							
44							
45	#DIV/0!	#DIV/0!	#DIV/0!	#DIV/0!	#DIV/0!	#DIV/0!	#DIV/0!
46	#DIV/0!	#DIV/0!	#DIV/0!	#DIV/0!	#DIV/0!	#DIV/0!	#DIV/0!
47	#DIV/0!	#DIV/0!	#DIV/0!	#DIV/0!	#DIV/0!	#DIV/0!	#DIV/0!

limit to your revolving line of credit. For each month, you also enter the current short-term interest rate.

If you use this form as a cash flow projection, you can also specify the percent by which sales will increase each month, the percentage of sales that is to be allocated for the cost of goods, and the percentage for operating expenses. All percentages should be entered in xx.x format (for example, 17.2), not as decimal fractions.

The model calculates the total cash receipts and disbursements for the period, indicates whether you need to borrow against your credit limit, how much has been borrowed to date, and reports an ending cash balance. It also gives the total amounts of accounts receivable and payable, the remaining credit

177

available, and the total working capital available. Each month's ending totals are used in the next month's starting figures, and any cash over the minimum cash balance is assumed to have been used to pay any short-term borrowing.

When you initially use the model, you'll need to indicate the amounts of sales that were allocated in the prior month to cash, and 30-day, 60-day, and 90-day receivables. You'll also need to enter the same breakdown of accounts payable, as well as data for payment on long term debt, the short term interest rate (as a percentage), income taxes, and "other."

The model is initially set up to be used as a cash flow projection, with some of the amounts determined by formulas. If you want to use this as a cash flow analysis of actual amounts spent, enter actual data where known; the data will override the projected amounts, and be used in the calculations near the bottom.

Enter the row and column labels as shown in Figure 5-8.

Format the cell ranges D17:O29 and D31:O56 as 0 (no decimals).

The top part of the worksheet holds the assumptions. When this worksheet is used to project cash flows forward, the figures entered here play an important role in producing bottom-line figures. To produce the results shown in Figure 5-8, enter the data below. Note that some of the formulas have absolute cell references (such as $H$6 or $C$7) and some have relative references (D17 or E8). When a cell reference is shown as relative, it may be adjusted when you copy the formula it's in. When a cell reference is shown as absolute, no adjustment will be made.

C6	25
E6	26280
H6	2
C7	40
E7	39320
J7	41.8
C8	30
E8	30840
C9	5
E9	3560

H10	**20000**
C11	**50**
E11	**25000**
C12	**30**
E12	**15000**
J12	**44.6**
C13	**15**
E13	**7500**
C14	**5**
E14	**2500**
H14	**250000**

In the body of the worksheet, enter other data or formulas as follows:

D17	100000 (or whatever the initial sales amount is)
E17	= D17 + (D17*$H$6/100) (copy this formula into F17 through O17)
D19	= D17*$C$6/100 (copy this formula into E19 through O19)
D20	= E7 + E8 + E9
E20	= (D17*$C$7/100) + E8 + E9
F20	= (E17*$C$7/100) + (D17*$C$8/100) + E9
G20	= (F17*$C$7/100) + (E17*$C$8/100) + (D17*$C$9/100) (copy this formula into H20 through O20)
D22	= D19 + D20 (copy this formula into E22 through O22)
D27	= J7* (E11 + E12 + E13 + E14)/100
E27	= $C$11/100*($J$7/100*E17) + $C$12/100*($J$7/100*D17) + $C$13/100*($J$7/100*D17) + $C$14 /100*($J$7/100*D17)
F27	= $C$11/100*($J$7/100*F17) + $C$12/100*($J$7/100*E17) + $C$13/100*($J$7/100*D17) + $C$14 /100*($J$7/100*D17)
G27	= $C$11/100*($J$7/100*G17) + $C$12/100*($J$7/100*F + 17) + $C$13/100*($J$7/100*E17) + $C$1 4/100*($J$7/100*D17) (copy this formula into H27 through O27)
D28	= D17*($J$12/100) (copy this formula into E28 through O28)
D29	2500 (substitute whatever figure you want to use for payments on long term debt; copy this figure into E29 through O29)
D30	14 (substitute whatever figure is the going rate for short-term loans; use the same figure or revise it as appropriate for cells E30 through O30; also format D30:O30 as 0.00)

Figure 5-8. Cash Flow with Labels

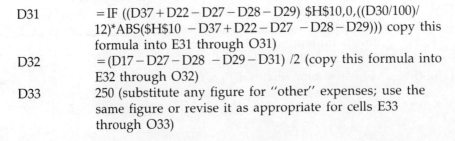

	A	B	C	D	E	F	G	H	I
1	Cash Flow Analysis								
2									
3	Assumptions:								
4					For		Sales		
5	For any month:		% of Sales		Prior Month		Increase		Cost of
6	Cash Sales						Per Month		Goods (%
7	30-day Collect						(%)		of Sales)
8	60-day Collect								
9	90-day Collect						Minimum		
10							Cash Bal.		Operating
11	Payable Immed.								Expenses
12	30-day Payable						Maximum		(% Sales)
13	60-day Payable						Credit		
14	90-day Payable						Limit:		
15									
16				1-Jan-80	1-Feb-80	1-Mar-80	1-Apr-80	1-May-80	1-Jun-80
17	Sales								
18	==========	==========	==========	==========	==========	==========	==========	==========	==========
19	Cash								
20	Receivables								
21				----------	----------	----------	----------	----------	----------
22	Total Cash Receipts								
23									
24									
25	Cash Disbursements								
26	==========	==========							
27	Cost of Goods								
28	Operating Expenses								
29	Payment on Long Term Debt								
30	Shot Term Int. Rate (%)								
31	Interest on Credit Line								
32	Income Taxes								
33	Other								
34									
35	Total Cash Disbursements								
36	==========	==========	==========	==========	==========	==========	==========	==========	==========
37	Beginning Cash Balance								
38	Net Cash this Period								
39									
40	Balance before Loan								
41	Amt. under Min. Balance								
42									
43	Borrowing This Month								
44	Current Credit Line Used								
45									
46	Ending Cash Balance								
47	==========	==========	==========	==========	==========	==========	==========	==========	==========
48	Net Balances								
49									
50	Cash								
51	Accounts Receivable								
52									
53	Accounts Payable								
54	Credit Line Available								
55									
56	Working Capital Available								

D31   = IF ((D37 + D22 − D27 − D28 − D29) $H$10,0,((D30/100)/ 12)*ABS($H$10 − D37 + D22 − D27 − D28 − D29))) copy this formula into E31 through O31)

D32   = (D17 − D27 − D28 − D29 − D31) /2 (copy this formula into E32 through O32)

D33   250 (substitute any figure for "other" expenses; use the same figure or revise it as appropriate for cells E33 through O33)

	J	K	L	M	N	O
1						
2						
3						
4						
5						
6						
7						
8						
9						
10						
11						
12						
13						
14						
15						
16	1-Jul-80	1-Aug-80	1-Sep-80	1-Oct-80	1-Nov-80	1-Dec-80
17						
18	==========	==========	==========	==========	==========	==========
19						
20						
21	----------	----------	----------	----------	----------	----------
22						
23						
24						
25						
26						
27						
28						
29						
30						
31						
32						
33						
34						
35						
36	==========	==========	==========	==========	==========	==========
37						
38						
39						
40						
41						
42						
43						
44						
45						
46						
47	==========	==========	==========	==========	==========	==========
48						
49						
50						
51						
52						
53						
54						
55						
56						

D35   = D27 + D28 + D29 + D31 + D32 + D33 (copy this formula into E35 through O35)

D37   20000 (substitute any figure for opening cash balance)

E37   = D46 (copy this into F37 through O37)

D38   = D22 − D35 (copy this formula into E38 through O38)

D40   = D37 + D38 (copy this formula into E40 through O40)

D41   = IF(D40$H$10,0,$H$10 − D40) (copy this formula into E41 through O41)

D43   = D41 (copy this into E43 through O43)

181

D44	= D43
E44	= D44 + E43 (copy this formula into F44 through O44)
D46	= D40 + D43 (copy this formula into E46 through O46)
D50	= D40 (copy this into E50 through O50)
D51	= D17 − ($C$6/100*D17) (copy this formula into E51 through O51)
D53	= E12 + E13 + E14
E53	= E27 − ($C$11/100*$J$7/100*$E$17) (copy this formula into F53 through O51)

Figure 5-9. Completed Cash Flow Statement

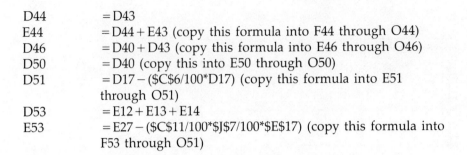

	A	B	C	D	E	F	G	H	I
1	Cash Flow Analysis								
2									
3	Assumptions:								
4					For		Sales		
5	For any month:		% of Sales		Prior Month		Increase		Cost of
6	Cash Sales		25		26280		Per Month	2	Goods (%
7	30-day Collect		40		39320		(%)		of Sales)
8	60-day Collect		30		30840				
9	90-day Collect		5		3560		Minimum		
10							Cash Bal.	20000	Operating
11	Payable Immed.		50		25000				Expenses
12	30-day Payable		30		15000		Maximum		(% Sales)
13	60-day Payable		15		7500		Credit		
14	90-day Payable		5		2500		Limit:	250000	
15									
16				1-Jan-80	1-Feb-80	1-Mar-80	1-Apr-80	1-May-80	1-Jun-80
17	Sales			100000	102000	104040	106121	108243	110408
18	==========	==========	==========	==========	==========	==========	==========	==========	==========
19	Cash			25000	25500	26010	26530	27061	27602
20	Receivables			73720	74400	74360	77216	78760	80336
21				----------	----------	----------	----------	----------	----------
22	Total Cash Receipts			98720	99900	100370	103746	105821	107938
23									
24									
25	Cash Disbursements								
26	==========	==========							
27	Cost of Goods			20900	42218	42895	43711	44585	45477
28	Operating Expenses			44600	45492	46402	47330	48276	49242
29	Payment on Long Term Debt			2500	2500	2500	2500	2500	2500
30	Shot Term Int. Rate (%)			14.00	14.00	14.25	14.25	14.50	14.75
31	Interest on Credit Line			0	0	0	0	0	0
32	Income Taxes			16000	5895	6121	6290	6441	6594
33	Other			250	250	250	250	250	250
34									
35	Total Cash Disbursements			84250	96355	98169	100081	102053	104064
36	==========	==========	==========	==========	==========	==========	==========	==========	==========
37	Beginning Cash Balance			20000	34470	38015	40217	43882	47650
38	Net Cash this Period			14470	3545	2202	3665	3769	3874
39									
40	Balance before Loan			34470	38015	40217	43882	47650	51524
41	Amt. under Min. Balance			0	0	0	0	0	0
42									
43	Borrowing This Month			0	0	0	0	0	0
44	Current Credit Line Used			0	0	0	0	0	0
45									
46	Ending Cash Balance			34470	38015	40217	43882	47650	51524
47	==========	==========	==========	==========	==========	==========	==========	==========	==========
48	Net Balances								
49									
50	Cash			34470	38015	40217	43882	47650	51524
51	Accounts Receivable			75000	76500	78030	79591	81182	82806
52									
53	Accounts Payable			25000	20900	21577	22393	23267	24159
54	Credit Line Available			250000	250000	250000	250000	250000	250000
55									
56	Working Capital Available			334470	343615	346669	351079	355565	360171

D54   = $H$14 − D43 (copy this formula into E54 through O54)
D56   = D50 + D51 − D53 + D54 (copy this formula into E56
                through O56)

If all the formulas and data have been entered as shown above, the completed 12-month cash flow projection is as shown in Figure 5-9.

	J	K	L	M	N	O
1						
2						
3						
4						
5						
6						
7	41.8					
8						
9						
10						
11						
12	44.6					
13						
14						
15						
16	1-Jul-80	1-Aug-80	1-Sep-80	1-Oct-80	1-Nov-80	1-Dec-80
17	112616	114869	117166	119509	121899	124337
18	==========	==========	==========	==========	==========	==========
19	28154	28717	29291	29877	30475	31084
20	81942	83581	85253	86958	88697	90471
21	----------	----------	----------	----------	----------	----------
22	110096	112298	114544	116835	119172	121555
23						
24						
25						
26						
27	46387	47314	48261	49226	50211	51215
28	50227	51231	52256	53301	54367	55454
29	2500	2500	2500	2500	2500	2500
30	15.00	15.25	15.25	15.00	15.00	14.75
31	0	0	0	0	0	0
32	6751	6911	7075	7241	7411	7584
33	250	250	250	250	250	250
34						
35	106115	108207	110341	112518	114739	117003
36	==========	==========	==========	==========	==========	==========
37	51524	55506	59597	63799	68116	72550
38	3981	4091	4203	4317	4433	4552
39						
40	55506	59597	63799	68116	72550	77101
41	0	0	0	0	0	0
42						
43	0	0	0	0	0	0
44	0	0	0	0	0	0
45						
46	55506	59597	63799	68116	72550	77101
47	==========	==========	==========	==========	==========	==========
48						
49						
50	55506	59597	63799	68116	72550	77101
51	84462	86151	87874	89632	91425	93253
52						
53	25069	25996	26943	27908	28893	29897
54	250000	250000	250000	250000	250000	250000
55						
56	364899	369752	374731	379840	385082	390458

This is a fairly big model, and its size alone may make it seem forbidding. However, it's designed to be sensitive to a variety of business financial factors. Experiment with the interest rates, the percentage of sales increase, the cost of goods and operating expenses, and you'll see changes ripple through the model.

The model is particularly valuable in showing what happens with different percentages for receivables and payables. Remember that the figures used for cash, plus 30-, 60-, and 90-day receivables must add up to 100 percent. The same is true for the four categories of payables.

Figure 5-10 is a macro form of the model. In its construction, there's a new twist: when run, this macro prompts the user for data.

To enter the model, open a macro file and type the following instructions and save it under a macro filename:

Figure 5-10. CASHFLOW.XLM Macro

	A
1	CashBrus
2	=SELECT("R1C1")
3	=FORMULA("Cash Flow Analysis for Starflight, inc.")
4	=SELECT("R3C1")
5	=FORMULA("Assumptions:")
6	=SELECT("R5C1")
7	=FORMULA("For any month:")
8	=SELECT("R6C1")
9	=FORMULA(" Cash Sales")
10	=SELECT("R7C1")
11	=FORMULA(" 30-day collect")
12	=SELECT("R8C1")
13	=FORMULA(" 60-day Collect")
14	=SELECT("R9C1")
15	=FORMULA(" 90-day Collect")
16	=SELECT("R11C1")
17	=FORMULA(" Payable Issued.")
18	=SELECT("R12C1")
19	=FORMULA(" 30-day Payable")
20	=SELECT("R13C1")
21	=FORMULA(" 60-day Payable")
22	=SELECT("R14C1")
23	=FORMULA(" 90-day Payable")
24	=SELECT("R17C1")
25	=FORMULA("Sales")
26	=SELECT("R5C3")
27	=FORMULA("% of Sales")
28	=SELECT("R16C4")
29	=FORMULA("1/1/1988")
30	=FORMAT.NUMBER("mmm-yy")
31	=SELECT("R16C5")
32	=FORMULA("2/1/1988")
33	=FORMAT.NUMBER("mmm-yy")
34	=SELECT("R16C6")
35	=FORMULA("3/1/1988")
36	=FORMAT.NUMBER("mmm-yy")
37	=SELECT("R16C7")
38	=FORMULA("4/1/1988")
39	=FORMAT.NUMBER("mmm-yy")
40	=SELECT("R16C8")
41	=FORMULA("5/1/1988")
42	=FORMAT.NUMBER("mmm-yy")
43	=SELECT("R16C9")

44	=FORMULA("6/1/1988")
45	=FORMAT.NUMBER("mmmm-yy")
46	=SELECT("R16C10")
47	=FORMULA("7/1/1988")
48	=FORMAT.NUMBER("mmmm-yy")
49	=SELECT("R16C11")
50	=FORMULA("8/1/1988")
51	=FORMAT.NUMBER("R16C12")
52	=SELECT("R16C12")
53	=FORMULA("9/1/1988")
54	=FORMAT.NUMBER("mmmm-yy")
55	=SELECT("R16C13")
56	=FORMULA("10/1/1988")
57	=FORMAT.NUMBER("mmmm-yy")
58	=SELECT("R16C14")
59	=FORMULA("11/1/1988")
60	=FORMAT.NUMBER("mmmm-yy")
61	=SELECT("R16C15")
62	=FORMULA("12/1/1988")
63	=FORMAT.NUMBER("mmmm-yy")
64	=SELECT("R4C5")
65	=FORMULA("For")
66	=SELECT("R5C5")
67	=FORMULA("Prior Month")
68	=SELECT("R4C7")
69	=FORMULA("Sales")
70	=SELECT("R5C7")
71	=FORMULA("Increase")
72	=SELECT("R6C7")
73	=FORMULA("Per Month")
74	=SELECT("R7C7")
75	=FORMULA("(3)")
76	=SELECT("R7C7")
77	=ALIGNMENT(3)
78	=SELECT("R9C7")
79	=FORMULA("Minimum")
80	=SELECT("R10C7")
81	=FORMULA("Cash Bal.")
82	=SELECT("R12C7")
83	=FORMULA("Maximum")
84	=SELECT("R13C7")
85	=FORMULA("Credit")
86	=SELECT("R14C7")

	A
87	=FORMULA("Limit")
88	=SELECT("R5C9")
89	=FORMULA("Cost of")
90	=SELECT("R6C9")
91	=FORMULA("Goods (%)")
92	=SELECT("R7C9")
93	=FORMULA("of Sales)")
94	=SELECT("R10C9")
95	=FORMULA("Operating")
96	=SELECT("R11C9")
97	=FORMULA("Expenses")
98	=SELECT("R12C9")
99	=FORMULA("(% Sales)")
100	=HLINE(-8)
101	=SELECT("R18C1:R18C15")
102	=BORDER(FALSE,FALSE,FALSE,FALSE,FALSE,TRUE)
103	=SELECT("R19C1")
104	=FORMULA("Cash")
105	=SELECT("R20C1")
106	=FORMULA("Receivables")
107	=SELECT("R21C4:R21C15")
108	=BORDER(FALSE,FALSE,FALSE,FALSE,FALSE,FALSE)
109	=HLINE(-11)
110	=DISPLAY(FALSE,FALSE,TRUE,TRUE,0)
111	=VLINE(17)
112	=SELECT("R22C1")
113	=FORMULA("Total Cash Receipts")
114	=SELECT("R21C4:R21C15")
115	=BORDER(FALSE,FALSE,FALSE,FALSE,TRUE,FALSE)
116	=HLINE(-10)
117	=SELECT("R25C1")
118	=FORMULA("Cash Disbursements")
119	=SELECT("R26C1:R26C2")
120	=BORDER(FALSE,FALSE,FALSE,FALSE,FALSE,TRUE)
121	=SELECT("R27C1")
122	=FORMULA("Cost of Goods")
123	=SELECT("R28C1")
124	=FORMULA("Operating Expenses")
125	=SELECT("R29C1")
126	=FORMULA("Payment on Long Term Debt")
127	=SELECT("R30C1")
128	=FORMULA("Short Term Int. Rate (%)")
129	=SELECT("R31C1")

```
130 =FORMULA("Interest on Credit Line")
131 =SELECT("R32C1")
132 =FORMULA("Income Taxes")
133 =SELECT("R33C1")
134 =FORMULA("Other")
135 =SELECT("R35C1")
136 =FORMULA("Total Cash Disbursements")
137 =SELECT("R36C1:R36C15")
138 =BORDER(FALSE,FALSE,FALSE,FALSE,TRUE)
139 =FORMULA("Beginning Cash Balance")
140 =SELECT("R37C1")
141 =SELECT("R38C1")
142 =FORMULA("Net Cash this Period")
143 =SELECT("R40C1")
144 =FORMULA("Balance before Loan")
145 =SELECT("R41C1")
146 =FORMULA("Amt. under Min. Balance")
147 =SELECT("R43C1")
148 =FORMULA("Borrowing This Month")
149 =SELECT("R44C1")
150 =FORMULA("Current Credit Line Used")
151 =SELECT("R46C1")
152 =FORMULA("Ending Cash Balance")
153 =SELECT("R47C1:R47C15")
154 =BORDER(FALSE,FALSE,FALSE,FALSE,TRUE)
155 =HLINE(-12)
156 =SELECT("R48C1")
157 =FORMULA("Net Balances")
158 =SELECT("R50C1")
159 =FORMULA("Cash")
160 =SELECT("R51C1")
161 =FORMULA("Accounts Receivable")
162 =SELECT("R53C1")
163 =FORMULA("Accounts Payable")
164 =SELECT("R54C1")
165 =FORMULA("Credit Line Available")
166 =SELECT("R56C1")
167 =FORMULA("Working Capital Available")
168 =SELECT("R17C5")
169 =FORMULA("=RC(-1)+(RC(-1)*R6C8/100)")
170 =COPY()
171 =SELECT("R17C6:R17C15")
172 =PASTE()
```

```
173  =SELECT("R19C4")
174  =FORMULA("=R[-2]C*R6C3/100")
175  =COPY()
176  =SELECT("R19C5:R19C15")
177  =PASTE()
178  =SELECT("R20C4")
179  =CANCEL.COPY()
180  =FORMULA("=R[-13]C[1]+R[-12]C[1]+R[-11]C[1]")
181  =SELECT("R20C5")
182  =FORMULA("=(R[-3]C[-1]*R7C3/100)+R[-12]C+R[-11]C")
183  =SELECT("R20C6")
184  =FORMULA("=(R[-3]C[-1]*R7C3/100)+(R[-3]C[-2]*R8C3/100)+R[-11]C[-1]")
185  =SELECT("R20C7")
186  =FORMULA("=(R[-3]C[-1]*R7C3/100)+(R[-3]C[-2]*R8C3/100)+(R[-3]C[-3]*R9C3/100)")
187  =SELECT("R20C7")
188  =COPY()
189  =SELECT("R20C8:R20C15")
190  =PASTE()
191  =SELECT("R22C4")
192  =CANCEL.COPY()
193  =FORMULA("=SUM(R[-3]C:R[-2]C)")
194  =COPY()
195  =SELECT("R22C5:R22C15")
196  =PASTE()
197  =SELECT("R27C4")
198  =CANCEL.COPY()
199  =FORMULA("=R[-20]C[6]*(R[-16]C[1]+R[-15]C[1]+R[-14]C[1]+R[-13]C[1])/100")
200  =SELECT("R27C5")
201  =FORMULA("=R11C3/100*(R7C10/100*R[-10]C[-1])+R12C3/100*(R7C10/100*R[-10]C[-1])+R13C3/100*(R7C10/100*R[-10]C[-1])+R14C3/100*(R7C10/100*R[-10]C[-1])")
202  =SELECT("R27C6")
203  =FORMULA("=R11C3/100*(R7C10/100*R[-10]C[-1])+R12C3/100*(R7C10/100*R[-10]C[-1])+R13C3/100*(R7C10/100*R[-10]C[-1])+R14C3/100*(R7C10/100*R[-10]C[-2])")
204  =SELECT("R27C7")
205  =FORMULA("=R11C3/100*(R7C10/100*R[-10]C[-1])+R12C3/100*(R7C10/100*R[-10]C[-2])+R13C3/100*(R7C10/100*R[-10]C[-2])+R14C3/100*(R7C10/100*R[-10]C[-3])")
206  =COPY()
207  =SELECT("R27C8:R27C15")
208  =PASTE()
209  =SELECT("R28C4")
210  =CANCEL.COPY()
211  =FORMULA("=R[-11]C*(R[-16]C10/100)")
212  =COPY()
213  =SELECT("R28C5:R28C15")
214  =PASTE()
215  =SELECT("R31C4")
```

189

216	=CANCEL.COPY()
217	=FORMULA("=IF((R[6]C+R[-9]C-R[-4]C-R[-3]C-R[-2]C)>R10C8,0,((R[-11C/100)/12)*ABS(R10C8-(R(6)C+R[-9]C-R[-4]C-R[-3]C-R[-2]C)))")
218	=FORMAT.NUMBER("0")
219	=FORMULA("=IF((R[6]C+R[-9]C-R[-4]C-R[-3]C-R[-2]C)>R10C8,0,((R[-11C/100)/12)*ABS(R10C8-(R(6)C+R[-9]C-R[-4]C-R[-3]C-R[-2]C)))")
220	=COPY()
221	=SELECT("R31C5:R31C15")
222	=PASTE()
223	=SELECT("R32C4")
224	=CANCEL.COPY()
225	=FORMULA("=(R[-15]C-R[-5]C-R[-4]C-R[-3]C-R[-1]C)/2")
226	=COPY()
227	=SELECT("R32C5:R32C15")
228	=PASTE()
229	=SELECT("R35C4")
230	=CANCEL.COPY()
231	=FORMULA("=R[-8]C+R[-7]C+R[-6]C+R[-4]C+R[-3]C+R[-2]C")
232	=SELECT("R35C5:R35C15")
233	=SELECT("R35C5:R35C15")
234	=PASTE()
235	=SELECT("R37C5")
236	=CANCEL.COPY()
237	=FORMULA("=R[9]C[-1]")
238	=COPY()
239	=SELECT("R37C6:R37C15")
240	=PASTE()
241	=SELECT("R38C4")
242	=CANCEL.COPY()
243	=FORMULA("=R[-16]C-R[-3]C")
244	=COPY()
245	=SELECT("R38C5:R38C15")
246	=PASTE()
247	=SELECT("R40C4")
248	=CANCEL.COPY()
249	=FORMULA("=R[-3]C-R[-2]C")
250	=COPY()
251	=SELECT("R40C5:R40C15")
252	=PASTE()
253	=SELECT("R41C4")
254	=CANCEL.COPY()
255	=FORMULA("=IF(R[-1]C>=R10C8,0,R10C8-R[-1]C)")
256	=SELECT("R41C4")
257	=COPY()
258	=SELECT("R41C5:R41C15")

	A
259	=PASTE()
260	=SELECT("R43C4")
261	=CANCEL.COPY()
262	=FORMULA("=R[-2]C")
263	=COPY()
264	=SELECT("R43C5:R43C15")
265	=PASTE()
266	=SELECT("R44C4")
267	=CANCEL.COPY()
268	=FORMULA("=R[-1]C")
269	=SELECT("R44C5")
270	=FORMULA("=RC[-1]+R[-1]C")
271	=COPY()
272	=SELECT("R44C6:R44C15")
273	=PASTE()
274	=SELECT("R46C4")
275	=CANCEL.COPY()
276	=FORMULA("=R[-6]C+R[-3]C")
277	=COPY()
278	=SELECT("R46C5:R46C15")
279	=PASTE()
280	=SELECT("R50C4")
281	=CANCEL.COPY()
282	=FORMULA("=R[-10]C")
283	=COPY()
284	=SELECT("R50C5:R50C15")
285	=PASTE()
286	=SELECT("R51C4")
287	=CANCEL.COPY()
288	=FORMULA("=R[-34]C-(R6C3/100*R[-34]C)")
289	=COPY()
290	=SELECT("R51C5:R51C15")
291	=PASTE()
292	=SELECT("R53C4")
293	=FORMULA("=R[-41]C[1]+R[-40]C[1]+R[-39]C[1]")
294	=SELECT("R53C5")
295	=FORMULA("=R[-26]C-(R11C3/100*R7C10/100*R17C5)")
296	=COPY()
297	=SELECT("R53C6:R53C15")
298	=PASTE()
299	=SELECT("R54C4")
300	=HLINE(1)
301	=CANCEL.COPY()

	A
302	=FORMULA("=R[-42]C[1]+R[-41]C[1]+R[-40]C[1]")
303	=SELECT("R54C5")
304	=FORMULA("=R[-27]C-(R11C3/100*R7C10/100*R17C5)")
305	=COPY()
306	=SELECT("R54c6:R54C15")
307	=PASTE()
308	=SELECT("R56C4")
309	=CANCEL.COPY()
310	=FORMULA("=R[-6]C+R[-5]C-R[-3]C+R[-2]C")
311	=COPY()
312	=SELECT("R56C5:R56C15")
313	=PASTE()
314	=HLINE(-13)
315	=SELECT("R6C1")
316	=CANCEL.COPY()
317	=SELECT("R6C3")
318	=FORMULA(INPUT("Enter Percentage of Cash Sales",1,"Prompt"))
319	=SELECT("R7C3")
320	=FORMULA(INPUT("Enter Percentage of 30-day sales:",1,"Prompt"))
321	=SELECT("R8C3")
322	=FORMULA(INPUT("Enter Percentage of 60-day sales:",1,"Prompt"))
323	=SELECT("R9C3")
324	=FORMULA(INPUT("Enter Percentage of 90-day sales:",1,"Prompt"))
325	=SELECT("R10C3")
326	=FORMULA("=R[-4]C+R[-3]C-R[-2]C-R[-1]C")
327	=IF(ACTIVE.CELL()=100,GOTO(A328),GOTO(A317))
328	=CLEAR(1)
329	=SELECT("R12C3")
330	=FORMULA(INPUT("Enter Percentage of 30 day payable",1,"Prompt"))
331	=SELECT("R13C3")
332	=FORMULA(INPUT("Enter Percentage of 60 day payable",1,"Prompt"))
333	=SELECT("R14C3")
334	=FORMULA(INPUT("Enter Percentage of 90 day payable",1,"Prompt"))
335	=SELECT("R10C3")
336	=FORMULA("=R[2]C+R[3]C+R(4)C")
337	=IF(ACTIVE.CELL()=100,GOTO(A338),GOTO(A329))
338	=CLEAR(1)
339	=SELECT("R6C5")
340	=FORMULA(INPUT("Enter Cash Sales for last month",1,"Prompt"))
341	=SELECT("R7C5")
342	=FORMULA(INPUT("Enter 30-day sales for last month:",1,"Prompt"))
343	=SELECT("R8C5")
344	=FORMULA(INPUT("Enter 60-day sales for last month:",1,"Prompt"))

	A
345	=SELECT("R9C5")
346	=FORMULA(INPUT("Enter 90-day sales for last month:",1,"Prompt"))
347	=SELECT("R12C5")
348	=FORMULA(INPUT("Enter 30-day payable for last month:",1,"Prompt"))
349	=SELECT("R13C5")
350	=FORMULA(INPUT("Enter 60-day payable for last month:",1,"Prompt"))
351	=SELECT("R14C5")
352	=FORMULA(INPUT("Enter 90-day payable for last month:",1,"Prompt"))
353	=SELECT("R6C8")
354	=FORMULA(INPUT("Sales increase per month(%):",1,"Prompt"))
355	=SELECT("R10C8")
356	=FORMULA(INPUT("Minimum cash Balance=",1,"Prompt"))
357	=SELECT("R14C8")
358	=FORMULA(INPUT("Maximum Credit Limit:",1,"Prompt"))
359	=SELECT("R7C10")
360	=FORMULA(INPUT("Cost of Goods (% of sales):",1,"Prompt"))
361	=SELECT("R12C10")
362	=FORMULA(INPUT("Operating Expenses (% of sales):",1,"Prompt"))
363	=SELECT("R17C4")
364	=FORMULA(INPUT("Sales in January:",1,"Prompt"))
365	=SELECT("R29C4")
366	=CANCEL.COPY()
367	=FORMULA(INPUT("Payment on long term debt for January:",1,"prompt"))
368	=SELECT("R29C5")
369	=FORMULA(INPUT("Payment on long term debt for February:",1,"prompt"))
370	=SELECT("R29C6")
371	=FORMULA(INPUT("Payment on long term debt for March:",1,"prompt"))
372	=SELECT("R29C7")
373	=FORMULA(INPUT("Payment on long term debt for April:",1,"prompt"))
374	=SELECT("R29C8")
375	=FORMULA(INPUT("Payment on long term debt for May:",1,"prompt"))
376	=SELECT("R29C9")
377	=FORMULA(INPUT("Payment on long term debt for June:",1,"prompt"))
378	=SELECT("R29C10")
379	=FORMULA(INPUT("Payment on long term debt for July:",1,"prompt"))
380	=SELECT("R29C11")
381	=FORMULA(INPUT("Payment on long term debt for August:",1,"prompt"))
382	=SELECT("R29C12")
383	=FORMULA(INPUT("Payment on long term debt for September:",1,"prompt"))
384	=SELECT("R29C13")
385	=FORMULA(INPUT("Payment on long term debt for October:",1,"prompt"))
386	=SELECT("R29C14")
387	=FORMULA(INPUT("Payment on long term debt for November:",1,"prompt"))

	A
388	=SELECT("R29C15")
389	=FORMULA(INPUT("Payment on long term debt for December:",1,"prompt"))
390	=SELECT("R30C4")
391	=FORMULA(INPUT("Short term interest rate for January (%):",1,"Prompt"))
392	=SELECT("R30C5")
393	=FORMULA(INPUT("Short term interest rate for February (%):",1,"Prompt"))
394	=SELECT("R30C6")
395	=FORMULA(INPUT("Short term interest rate for March (%):",1,"Prompt"))
396	=SELECT("R30C7")
397	=FORMULA(INPUT("Short term interest rate for April (%):",1,"Prompt"))
398	=SELECT("R30C8")
399	=FORMULA(INPUT("Short term interest rate for May (%):",1,"Prompt"))
400	=SELECT("R30C9")
401	=FORMULA(INPUT("Short term interest rate for June (%):",1,"Prompt"))
402	=SELECT("R30C10")
403	=FORMULA(INPUT("Short term interest rate for July (%):",1,"Prompt"))
404	=SELECT("R30C11")
405	=FORMULA(INPUT("Short term interest rate for August (%):",1,"Prompt"))
406	=SELECT("R30C12")
407	=FORMULA(INPUT("Short term interest rate for September (%):",1,"Prompt"))
408	=SELECT("R30C13")
409	=FORMULA(INPUT("Short term interest rate for October (%):",1,"Prompt"))
410	=SELECT("R30C14")
411	=FORMULA(INPUT("Short term interest rate for November (%):",1,"Prompt"))
412	=SELECT("R30C15")
413	=FORMULA(INPUT("Short term interest rate for December (%):",1,"Prompt"))
414	=SELECT("R33C4:R33C15","R33C15")
415	=FORMAT.NUMBER("0.00")
416	=SELECT("R33C4")
417	=FORMULA(INPUT("Other January Disbursements:",1,"Promt"))
418	=SELECT("R33C5")
419	=FORMULA(INPUT("Other February Disbursements:",1,"Promt"))
420	=SELECT("R33C6")
421	=FORMULA(INPUT("Other March Disbursements:",1,"Promt"))
422	=SELECT("R33C7")
423	=FORMULA(INPUT("Other April Disbursements:",1,"Promt"))
424	=SELECT("R33C8")
425	=FORMULA(INPUT("Other May Disbursements:",1,"Promt"))
426	=SELECT("R33C9")
427	=FORMULA(INPUT("Other June Disbursements:",1,"Promt"))
428	=SELECT("R33C10")
429	=FORMULA(INPUT("Other July Disbursements:",1,"Promt"))
430	=SELECT("R33C11")

	A
431	=FORMULA(INPUT("Other August Disbursements:",1,"Prompt"))
432	=SELECT("R33C12")
433	=FORMULA(INPUT("Other September Disbursements:",1,"Prompt"))
434	=SELECT("R33C13")
435	=FORMULA(INPUT("Other October Disbursements:",1,"Prompt"))
436	=SELECT("R33C14")
437	=FORMULA(INPUT("Other November Disbursements:",1,"Prompt"))
438	=SELECT("R33C15")
439	=FORMULA(INPUT("Other December Disbursements:",1,"Prompt"))
440	=SELECT("R47C4:R55C15","R55C15")
441	=FORMAT.NUMBER("0")
442	=SELECT("R30C4:R45C15","R45C4")
443	=FORMAT.NUMBER("0")
444	=SELECT("R17C4:R28C15","R28C15")
445	=FORMAT.NUMBER("0")
446	=RETURN()

To run the model, open the macro file and a blank work-sheet; then use the Macro Run command. The macro will set up the labels and formulas and format the cells appropriately; then prompt the user for data. When data has been entered, it will show the totals.

Figure 5-11. Opening Screen when Cash Flow Macro is Run

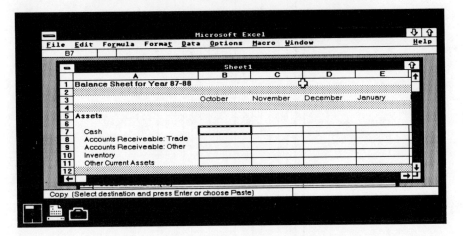

Chapter 6

Some Accounting Solutions

Accounting spreadsheets help you keep track of what you owe and what you're scheduled to pay, and how you're doing relative to a budget. In this chapter you'll see how to set up an accounts receivable worksheet, an accounts payable worksheet, and a worksheet for comparing actual expenses against budgeted expenses. You'll also see a worksheet for allocating overhead costs, such as insurance, advertising, plant, and equipment—among all departments—as a cost item.

Accounts Receivable

A simple Accounts Receivable worksheet is shown below. It lists individual accounts by name and shows the amounts due for the current month. The worksheet also shows accounts past due 30 to 60 days, and over 60 days.

Figure 6-1. Accounts Receivable Worksheet

	A	B	C	D	E	F	G
1	Accounts Receivable:			30-Jun-88			
2							
3	The Yuppie Toy Store						
4							
5	Individual Charge Accounts						
6				Current			
7	Customer Name			(Under 30 Days)	30 to 60 Days	Over 60 Days	Total
8	Aurlius, Marc			$623.23	$97.64	$0.00	$720.87
9	Brandoff, Bruski			$75.84	$92.45	$24.12	$192.41
10	Cala, Robert			$346.60	$6.00	$82.29	$434.89
11	Daniels, Jack					$935.63	$935.63
12	Edwards, Scott				$543.66	$634.63	$1,178.29
13	Foxworthy, Mike			$128.83	$82.77	$101.89	$313.49
14	Getswind, Micheal			$123.44		$643.44	$766.88
15	Hardesty, Jennifer				$334.00		$334.00
16	Iago, William S.			$4,333.44		$1,443.22	$5,776.66
17	de Bois, Jaques				$567.54		$567.54
18	Kirkby, David			$956.83		$113.44	$1,070.27
19	Martext, Oliver			$322.00			$322.00
20	TOTALS			$6,910.21	$1,724.06	$3,978.66	$12,612.93

This model is mostly labels and data, and uses formulas only in the last row (here, row 20) and in column G. To set up the model, enter the labels as shown:

Figure 6-2. Accounts Receivable Labels

	A	B	C	D	E	F	G
1	Accounts Receivable:			30-Jun-88			
2							
3	The Yuppie Toy Store						
4							
5	Individual Charge Accounts						
6				Current			
7	Customer Name			(Under 30 Days)	30 to 60 Days	Over 60 Days	Total
8							0
9							0
10							0
11							0
12							0
13							0
14							0
15							0
16							0
17							0
18							0
19							0
20	TOTALS			0	0	0	0

Note that we've left out the names in column A. This is where you enter your own, or if you wish to replicate Figure 6-1, enter the names shown. To enter a summary line after the last row of names, select the cells in that row, use the Format Border command, and choose the Bottom option. Use the same command to draw a line under the column titles in row 7.

The date at the top of the worksheet should be the last day of an accounting period (here, the last day of June), or the day you generate the accounts receivable report. A date was entered and formatted with the Format Number command using the m/d/yy option. If you want to use today's date, use the formula =NOW( ) and the same formatting; this retrieves the serial number for today's date and displays the integer portion as a date.

Enter formulas as follows:

G8   =D8+E8+F8 (use the Fill Down command to copy this formula into the appropriate cells in column G)

D20   =SUM(D8:D19) (copy this formula into E20 and F20. You can also use the same formula in G20)

To maintain this form of an accounts receivable worksheet, simply insert new rows for new accounts, and delete rows when the account is completely paid. The worksheet shown in Figure 6-1 contains a blank entry for a fictional customer, Scott Edwards. In order to restrict the report to current accounts only, you'd delete that row. If, on the other hand, you wanted to keep track of customers who had accounts, paid or otherwise, you wouldn't want to delete names of paid accounts.

This worksheet can easily be expanded to do more for you. For instance, if you want to add invoice numbers to the report, simply insert a column for invoice numbers. Then list the invoices for each customer.

You may also want to assign each customer a number, so you can link the accounts receivable to any other file, such as ones showing customer names, addresses, and phone numbers, or marketing profiles showing types of merchandise purchased.

While the example in Figure 6-1 shows customer accounts by name and when payments are due, you may have customers who operate on invoicing procedures such as *2% 10 net 30*, which means they get a two percent discount if they pay within 10 days of the date of the invoice; otherwise the entire amount is due in 30 days. You may also have a policy of a 1.5 percent per month finance charge to be added to all invoices unpaid after 30 days. You can modify the model to include automatic calculations for these, by inserting columns showing invoice date, type of term, or whether the finance charge applies.

We've also provided a macro version of the same spreadsheet model (Figure 6-3). Type in the listing shown below and store it as a macro file.

Figure 6-3. ACCTSREC.XLM Spreadsheet Macro

	A
1	Accounts_Receivable
2	=SELECT("R1C1:R20C7")
3	=COLUMN.WIDTH(12)
4	=SELECT("R1C4")
5	=COLUMN.WIDTH(15)
6	=SELECT("R1C1")
7	=FORMULA("Accounts Receivable:")
8	=SELECT("R3C1")
9	=FORMULA("The Yuppie Toy Store")
10	=SELECT("R5C1")
11	=FORMULA("Individual Charge Accounts")
12	=SELECT("R7C1")
13	=FORMULA("Customer Name")
14	=SELECT("R8C1")
15	=FORMULA("Aurlius, Marc")
16	=SELECT("R9C1")
17	=FORMULA("Brandoff, Bruski")
18	=SELECT("R10C1")
19	=FORMULA("Cala, Robert")
20	=SELECT("R11C1")
21	=FORMULA("Daniels, Jack")
22	=SELECT("R12C1")
23	=FORMULA("Edwards, Scott")
24	=SELECT("R13C1")
25	=FORMULA("Foxworthy, Mike")
26	=SELECT("R14C1")
27	=FORMULA("Getswind, Micheal")
28	=SELECT("R15C1")
29	=FORMULA("Hardesty, Jennifer")
30	=SELECT("R16C1")
31	=FORMULA("Iago, William S.")
32	=SELECT("R17C1")
33	=FORMULA("de Bois, Jaques")
34	=SELECT("R18C1")
35	=FORMULA("Kirkby, David")
36	=SELECT("R19C1")
37	=FORMULA("Martext, Oliver")
38	=SELECT("R20C1")
39	=FORMULA("TOTALS")
40	=SELECT("R1C4")
41	=FORMULA("June 30, 1988")
42	=FORMAT.NUMBER("d-mmm-yy")
43	=SELECT("R6C4")
44	=FORMULA("Current")
45	=SELECT("R7C4")
46	=FORMULA(" (Under 30 Days)")
47	=SELECT("R7C5")
48	=FORMULA("30 to 60 Days")
49	=SELECT("R7C6")
50	=FORMULA("Over 60 Days")
51	=SELECT("R7C7")
52	=FORMULA("Total")
53	=SELECT("R8C7")
54	=FORMULA("=RC[-3]+RC[-2]+RC[-1]")
55	=SELECT("R9C7")
56	=FORMULA("=RC[-3]+RC[-2]+RC[-1]")
57	=SELECT("R10C7")
58	=FORMULA("=RC[-3]+RC[-2]+RC[-1]")
59	=SELECT("R11C7")
60	=FORMULA("=RC[-3]+RC[-2]+RC[-1]")

	A
61	=SELECT("R12C7")
62	=FORMULA("=RC[-3]+RC[-2]+RC[-1]")
63	=SELECT("R13C7")
64	=FORMULA("=RC[-3]+RC[-2]+RC[-1]")
65	=SELECT("R14C7")
66	=FORMULA("=RC[-3]+RC[-2]+RC[-1]")
67	=SELECT("R15C7")
68	=FORMULA("=RC[-3]+RC[-2]+RC[-1]")
69	=SELECT("R16C7")
70	=FORMULA("=RC[-3]+RC[-2]+RC[-1]")
71	=SELECT("R17C7")
72	=FORMULA("=RC[-3]+RC[-2]+RC[-1]")
73	=SELECT("R18C7")
74	=FORMULA("=RC[-3]+RC[-2]+RC[-1]")
75	=SELECT("R19C7")
76	=FORMULA("=RC[-3]+RC[-2]+RC[-1]")
77	=SELECT("R20C4")
78	=FORMULA("=SUM(R[-12]C:R[-1]C)")
79	=COPY()
80	=SELECT("R20C5:R20C7")
81	=COPY()
82	=SELECT("R20C4")
83	=COPY()
84	=SELECT("R20C5:R20C7")
85	=PASTE()
86	=SELECT("R20C1:R20C7")
87	=BORDER(FALSE,FALSE,FALSE,FALSE,TRUE,FALSE,FALSE)
88	=SELECT("R7C1:R7C7")
89	=BORDER(FALSE,FALSE,FALSE,FALSE,TRUE,FALSE)
90	=SELECT("R1C1")
91	=DISPLAY(FALSE,FALSE,TRUE,TRUE,0)
92	=SELECT("R8C4")
93	=RETURN()

When you want to run it, open it as well as a blank worksheet file; then choose the Macro Run command and select the filename you've given it.

The macro sets up the worksheet as shown in Figure 6-4.

Figure 6-4. Accounts Receivable Macro Run on a Worksheet

	A	B	C	D	E	F	G
1	Accounts Receivable:			30-Jun-88			
2							
3	The Yuppie Toy Store						
4							
5	Individual Charge Accounts						
6				Current			
7	Customer Name			(Under 30 Days)	30 to 60 Days	Over 60 Days	Total
8	Aurlius, Marc						0
9	Brandoff, Bruski						0
10	Cala, Robert						0
11	Daniels, Jack						0
12	Edwards, Scott						0
13	Foxworthy, Mike						0
14	Getswind, Micheal						0
15	Hardesty, Jennifer						0
16	Iago, William S.						0
17	de Bois, Jaques						0
18	Kirkby, David						0
19	Martext, Oliver						0
20	TOTALS			0	0	0	0

Notice that today's date is automatically placed at the top of the worksheet. The names of the individual accounts are listed in column A, and summary formulas are listed in column G. All you have to do is add data for columns D, E, and F, and the formula in column G automatically computes the total for each account.

It's an easy matter to replace the name of the entity, as well as the names of individual customers, if you want to tailor this model to your own situation. Use the F2 key to edit each macro statement containing a name you want to replace, and type the name you want instead of the one shown. If you have more names than are shown, repeat the sequence of instructions on lines 34 and 35 of the macro, changing the cell references to include the new account names as well as the TOTAL line.

Accounts Payable

Accounts payable are bills you owe, pure and simple. What makes them less than simple is the terms under which you are to pay. Some accounts insist on payment upon receipt; others offer discounts for early payment, but expect payment in full within a specified time if you don't take advantage of the discount. Still, others have other terms, or no terms at all.

Many companies assign an *aging policy* to bills, indicating that they are to be paid in 30, 45, 60, or even 90 days. Keeping track of each bill relative to its due date can be a major headache. The model shown here keeps you aware of the invoice terms for a bill, as well as whether it's due now or past due.

In addition, this model lets you assign an account number under which each invoice will be paid. The account number can be part of your overall accounting system, and anytime a bill is paid you can copy the relevant information to an expense file and store it under the correct account.

Enter the labels and headings as shown in Figure 6-5.

Figure 6-5. Accounts Payable Worksheet with Labels

	A	B	C	D	E	F	G	H	I	J
1	ACCOUNTS PAYABLE			For:			8/22/88			
2	The Yuppie Toy Store									
3										
4					Date	Invoice	Days			
5	Account #	Invoice #	Company	Date of Invoice	Due	Terms	till Due	Due Today?	Past Due?	Amount Due

In cell F1, type the formula

= NOW( )

and format the cell using the Format Number command and the m/d/yy option. The NOW function retrieves the current day/time serial number stored in your computer, and the format converts the serial number to today's date.

Use one of the date options on the Format Number command for Column D and Column E from Row 6 down, to reflect the type of date format you'd like to use for invoice dates. Enter formulas as follows:

G6 = INT(E6) − INT(D6) (copy this formula down column F as many rows as you need)

H6 = IF((D6 + F6) = INT(NOW( )), "YES","NO") (copy this formula down column G as many rows as you've used in column F)

I6 = IF((D6 + F6)<INT(NOW( )), "YES","NO") (copy this formula down column H as many rows as you've used in column F)

Once the formulas have been entered, enter the data for your bills, including account number, invoice number (if any), company, date of invoice, invoice terms, and amount due. The worksheet computes the other information.

You can sort data with this worksheet, producing a list of past-due accounts and those due today or in the near future. Using the Data menu, select all of the invoices, from A6 to the end of the data in column I, as the database. With the Data Sort command, specify the First Key as $I$6. Then specify either ascending or descending order.

The results appear sorted within the existing worksheet on your screen. If you've specified ascending order, the oldest records appear at the top of the list. You can then print all or part of the worksheet, and save it with the File Save As command under a different filename than the regular Accounts Payable file.

One such example is shown in Figure 6-6.

Figure 6-6. Sorted Accounts Payable Records

	A	B	C	D	E	F	G	H	I	J
1	ACCOUNTS PAYABLE			For:						
2	The Yuppie Toy Store									
3							8/26/88			
4										
5	Account #	Invoice #	Company	Date of Invoice	Date Due	Invoice Terms	Days till Due	Due Today?	Past Due?	Amount Due
6	68101	C3278206	Jones & Jones, Ltd.	30-Jun-88	30-Jul-88	2%10 net 30	30	NO	YES	$433.80
7	68102	114931	Cobb Engineering	1-Jul-88	15-Jul-88	net 14	14	NO	YES	$105.50
8	67101		Payroll	2-Jul-88	2-Jul-88	total of payro	0	NO	YES	$21,573.47
9	67103		Sales Commissions	2-Jul-88	2-Jul-88	total of sales	0	NO	YES	$28,102.79
10	70101	T32-76203	Siladi Office Supplies	4-Jul-88	20-Jul-88	net 16	16	NO	YES	$446.52
11	67102		U.S Internal Revenue Se	9-Jul-88	9-Jul-88		0	NO	YES	$1,095.23
12	67102		California Revenue Serv	9-Jul-88	9-Jul-88		0	NO	YES	$302.87
13	68101	C3719931	Jones & Jones, Ltd.	14-Jul-88	13-Aug-88	2%10 net30	30	NO	YES	$364.58
14	70104		U. S. Postal Service	15-Jul-88	15-Jul-88		0	NO	YES	$150.00
15	72101		Dougherty Marketing Con	17-Jul-88	7-Aug-88	2%7 net 21	21	NO	YES	$2,195.48
16	64302		Consolidated Holdings	22-Jul-88	6-Aug-88	net 15	15	NO	YES	$3,854.87
17	64308	M04578	Midas Muffler	28-Jul-88	4-Aug-88	net 7	7	NO	YES	$602.27
18	71201	45-G9831	Stanford Shopping Cente	29-Jul-88	15-Aug-88	net 15	17	NO	YES	$7,350.00
19							0	NO	YES	
20										

Budgeted Versus Actual Costs

One of the ongoing tasks in good financial management is budgeting. An annual budget is an attempt to predict what expenses and income are going to be. When they're broken down into monthly increments, they give the manager benchmarks by which financial performance can be measured so corrective action can be taken quickly.

The model shown here uses two worksheet files, the annual budget with its monthly increments, and one of a series of monthly budgets. Some of the figures from the previous month's budget are used in the subsequent month's budget. The summary for the year, which simply draws on the annual budget and the individual month budgeted and actual figures, can show deviations from projected figures on a month-by-month basis.

This model's use of other files is a good example of how *Excel* can use external references to other files in a currently active worksheet. You'll see how when we get to the point where formulas are entered.

To set up the model, enter the labels as shown in Figure 6-7. Assume the account numbers will appear on all worksheets, whether they're annual or monthly. (In real life, it's difficult to accurately predict which row labels will be needed for the entire year. If a general enough description, you can add notes each month with the Formula Note command to identify any monthly interpretations or subaccounts.)

Figure 6-7. Budget Worksheet with Labels

	A	B/C/D	E June Real	F June Budget	G June Diff.	H YTD Real	I YTD Budget	J YTD Diff.	K Annual Budget
1	The Yuppie Toy Store								
2									
3	Budgeted vs. Actual Expenses for: June, 1988								
4			June	June	June	YTD	YTD	YTD	Annual
5			Real	Budget	Diff.	Real	Budget	Diff.	Budget
6	Account #	Account Name/Description							
7	Employee Costs/ Benefits								
8	67101	Salaries/Wages							
9	67102	Payroll Taxes							
10	67103	Sales Commisions							
11	67104	Employee Benefits							
12									
13	Outside Labor & Services								
14	68101	Marketing research							
15	68102	Outside Labor							
16									
17	Supplies								
18	70101	Office Supplies							
19	70102	Office Equipment & Furniture							
20	70103	Mailing							
21	70104	Printing							
22									
23	Facilities & Service								
24	71201	Store Rent							
25	71202	Telephone							
26	71203	Utilities							
27									
28	Advertising & Promotion								
29	72101	Newspaper/ Media Ads							
30	72102	In-House Advertising							
31	72103	Outside Copy Preparation							
32	72104	Other Advertising							
33									
34	Warehouse & Stocking								
35	64302	Warehouse Rent & Expenses							
36	64303	Purchasing/ Consumer Goods							
37	64304	Purchasing/ Personal Goods							
38	64305	Purchasing/ Electronics							
39	64306	Purchasing/ Other							
40	64307	Vehicle Expenses							
41	64308	Vehicle Maint & Repair							
42	64309	Shipping Expenses							
43									
44	Other								
45	77801	Misc. Admin.							
46	77802	Misc. Sales							
47	77803	Misc. Warehousing							
48	Total Expenses								

Next, construct a sample annual budget, showing monthly expenditures for each category. Figure 6-8 shows the numbers we used.

Save the file under the name *BUDG1988.XLS.*

To construct a monthly budget, you'll use the same row titles, but you'll need to label the columns as follows:

E	F	G	H	I	J	K
June	**June**	**June**	**YTD**	**YTD**	**YTD**	**Annual**
Actual	**Budget**	**Diff.**	**Actual**	**Budget**	**Diff.**	**Budget**

Use the Format Alignment command to center the labels, if you wish. Also use the Format Column Width command to increase the column width to 10 (or more, if you want to use a number format that includes the $ sign and two decimal places).

Enter the June Actual figures and summary formula as shown below:

E8	23072.88
E9	1477.23
E10	27814.73
E11	4155.62
E14	1262.71
E15	322.83
E18	541.87
E19	371.52
E20	477.67
E21	102.72
E24	7350.00
E25	401.45
E26	303.65
E29	167.74
E30	217.73
E31	83.35
E32	41.63
E35	3854.87
E36	56255.67
E37	51731.64
E38	76126.79
E39	13135.62
E40	473.73
E41	814.63

Figure 6-8. Annual Budget Worksheet

	A	B	C	D	E	F	G	H	I
1					January	February	March	April	May
2	Account #	Account Name/Description			Budget	Budget	Budget	Budget	Budget
3	Employee Costs/ Benefits								
4	67101	Salaries/Wages			$19,000.00	$20,500.00	$21,000.00	$21,000.00	$22,000.00
5	67102	Payroll Taxes			$1,250.00	$1,300.00	$1,325.00	$1,325.00	$1,360.00
6	67103	Sales Commisions			$25,000.00	$26,500.00	$27,500.00	$28,000.00	$28,500.00
7	67104	Employee Benefits			$4,000.00	$4,000.00	$4,000.00	$4,000.00	$4,250.00
8									
9	Outside Labor & Services								
10	68101	Marketing Research			$750.00	$500.00	$800.00	$900.00	$1,000.00
11	68102	Outside Labor			$575.00	$300.00	$300.00	$300.00	$300.00
12									
13	Supplies								
14	70101	Office Supplies			$375.00	$250.00	$250.00	$250.00	$300.00
15	70102	Office Equipment & Furniture			$500.00	$300.00	$300.00	$300.00	$300.00
16	70103	Mailing			$500.00	$500.00	$300.00	$300.00	$300.00
17	70104	Printing			$125.00	$50.00	$50.00	$75.00	$175.00
18									
19	Facilities & Service								
20	71201	Store Rent			$7,200.00	$7,200.00	$7,200.00	$7,200.00	$7,200.00
21	71202	Telephone			$600.00	$300.00	$300.00	$300.00	$400.00
22	71203	Utilities			$420.00	$390.00	$360.00	$350.00	$330.00
23									
24	Advertising & Promotion								
25	72101	Newspaper/ Media Ads			$100.00	$100.00	$100.00	$100.00	$100.00
26	72102	In-House Advertising			$200.00	$175.00	$175.00	$200.00	$200.00
27	72103	Outside Copy Preparation			$100.00	$75.00	$75.00	$75.00	$75.00
28	72104	Other Advertising			$50.00	$40.00	$40.00	$40.00	$50.00
29									
30	Warehouse & Stocking								
31	64302	Warehouse Rent & Expenses			$3,800.00	$3,800.00	$3,800.00	$3,800.00	$3,800.00
32	64303	Purchasing/ Consumer Goods			$80,000.00	$50,000.00	$50,000.00	$50,000.00	$55,000.00
33	64304	Purchasing/ Personal Goods			$40,000.00	$35,000.00	$37,500.00	$37,500.00	$45,000.00
34	64305	Purchasing/ Electronics			$57,500.00	$57,500.00	$60,000.00	$62,500.00	$67,500.00
35	64306	Purchasing/ Other			$11,500.00	$11,000.00	$11,000.00	$11,500.00	$12,000.00
36	64307	Vehicle Expenses			$400.00	$300.00	$300.00	$300.00	$350.00
37	64308	Vehicle Maint & Repair			$400.00	$200.00	$200.00	$200.00	$200.00
38	64309	Shipping Expenses			$350.00	$225.00	$225.00	$225.00	$250.00
39									
40	Other								
41	77801	Misc. Admin.			$150.00	$150.00	$150.00	$150.00	$150.00
42	77802	Misc. Sales			$250.00	$250.00	$250.00	$250.00	$250.00
43	77803	Misc. Warehousing			$400.00	$400.00	$400.00	$400.00	$400.00
44	Total Expenses				$255,495.00	$221,305.00	$227,900.00	$231,540.00	$251,740.00

E42	407.66
E45	302.15
E46	277.49
E47	521.35
E48	=SUM(E8:E47)

The other numbers will be entered only after it's been determined whether you can use already existing data. Start with the Annual Budget column. Those figures already exist in the rightmost column of the file BUDG1988.XLS. How can you use them here?

	J	K	L	M	N	O	P	Q	R
	June	July	August	September	October	November	December	Annual	
1	Budget	Budget	Budget	Budget	Budget	Budget	Budget	Budget	
2									
3									
4	$23,500.00	$24,750.00	$25,500.00	$25,500.00	$26,000.00	$30,750.00	$40,500.00	$300,000.00	$300,000.00
5	$1,400.00	$1,540.00	$1,625.00	$1,625.00	$1,700.00	$2,150.00	$3,400.00	$20,000.00	
6	$29,000.00	$30,000.00	$37,000.00	$30,000.00	$32,500.00	$37,000.00	$76,000.00	$400,000.00	$400,000.00
7	$4,500.00	$4,750.00	$4,750.00	$4,250.00	$4,250.00	$4,500.00	$7,250.00	$54,500.00	
8									
9									
10	$1,000.00	$1,000.00	$1,100.00	$1,000.00	$1,000.00	$1,450.00	$2,000.00	$12,500.00	$12,500.00
11	$400.00	$500.00	$500.00	$400.00	$600.00	$900.00	$925.00	$6,000.00	$6,000.00
12									
13									
14	$300.00	$325.00	$325.00	$300.00	$300.00	$400.00	$625.00	$4,000.00	
15	$400.00	$400.00	$450.00	$400.00	$500.00	$600.00	$550.00	$5,000.00	$5,000.00
16	$400.00	$400.00	$400.00	$350.00	$350.00	$600.00	$850.00	$5,250.00	
17	$100.00	$125.00	$125.00	$100.00	$100.00	$350.00	$425.00	$1,800.00	$1,800.00
18									
19									
20	$7,200.00	$7,200.00	$7,200.00	$7,200.00	$7,200.00	$7,200.00	$7,200.00	$86,400.00	$86,400.00
21	$450.00	$500.00	$550.00	$500.00	$400.00	$600.00	$800.00	$5,700.00	
22	$330.00	$330.00	$330.00	$350.00	$375.00	$395.00	$440.00	$4,400.00	
23									
24									
25	$150.00	$200.00	$200.00	$150.00	$175.00	$250.00	$375.00	$2,000.00	$2,000.00
26	$225.00	$300.00	$300.00	$225.00	$275.00	$350.00	$375.00	$3,000.00	$3,000.00
27	$100.00	$125.00	$125.00	$100.00	$100.00	$200.00	$200.00	$1,350.00	$1,350.00
28	$55.00	$70.00	$70.00	$55.00	$55.00	$80.00	$145.00	$750.00	$750.00
29									
30									
31	$3,800.00	$3,800.00	$3,800.00	$3,800.00	$3,800.00	$3,800.00	$3,800.00	$45,600.00	
32	$60,000.00	$65,000.00	$65,000.00	$60,000.00	$65,000.00	$85,000.00	$90,000.00	$775,000.00	$775,000.00
33	$50,000.00	$57,000.00	$60,000.00	$48,000.00	$55,000.00	$75,000.00	$85,000.00	$625,000.00	$625,000.00
34	$75,000.00	$80,000.00	$80,000.00	$70,000.00	$70,000.00	$120,000.00	$150,000.00	$950,000.00	$950,000.00
35	$12,500.00	$14,000.00	$13,750.00	$12,750.00	$12,500.00	$16,000.00	$18,500.00	$157,000.00	
36	$400.00	$450.00	$450.00	$375.00	$375.00	$550.00	$750.00	$5,000.00	$5,000.00
37	$200.00	$250.00	$250.00	$225.00	$225.00	$275.00	$375.00	$3,000.00	
38	$300.00	$325.00	$325.00	$300.00	$300.00	$575.00	$1,100.00	$4,500.00	$4,500.00
39									
40									
41	$150.00	$150.00	$150.00	$150.00	$150.00	$150.00	$250.00	$1,900.00	$1,900.00
42	$250.00	$250.00	$250.00	$250.00	$250.00	$250.00	$500.00	$3,250.00	$3,250.00
43	$400.00	$400.00	$400.00	$400.00	$400.00	$400.00	$600.00	$5,000.00	$5,000.00
44	$272,510.00	$294,140.00	$297,925.00	$268,755.00	$283,880.00	$389,775.00	$492,935.00	$3,487,900.00	$3,188,450.00

Make sure BUDG1988.XLS is also an open file. (Check the files listed under the Windows menu. If it's shown there, it's open. If not, open it.) On BUDG1988.XLS, select the annual figures in column K, from K8:K48, and choose the Edit Copy command. Then on the Window menu, choose the filename of your monthly budget worksheet to make it the active window. Position the active cell in K8 on this worksheet, and choose the Edit Paste Link command. This not only copies the data into K8:K48 on the monthly budget, but it also copies the external reference for each cell. You can verify this by scrolling down column K on the monthly worksheet and watching the formula bar, which will contain an external reference, including filename and absolute cell reference, for each cell in the range used.

Figure 6-9 is an example of what you'll see:

Figure 6-9. Cell Containing External Reference

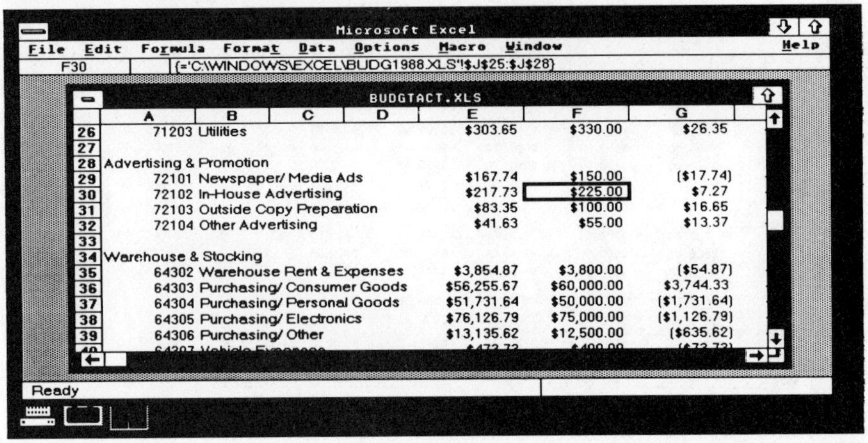

Are there any other figures you can get from the annual budget? You can use the budget figures for the current month (in this case, June). Copy them from the annual budget window in the same way you copied the annual figures.

Note that you can also use a different application of the Edit Copy command to copy the figures from the annual budget to the monthly report. If you use Edit Copy and simply press the Enter key when you get to the proper cell on the monthly report, only the figures will be copied, not the external cell references. The difference in effect between using the normal Paste (or Enter key) approach and using the Paste Link approach is that the normal Paste approach simply takes a snapshot of the figures at the time you copy them, and uses that snapshot in the destination worksheet. However, the Paste Link approach establishes a pathway so *Excel* can always check the source worksheet for data (which may have changed since the link was established) and use the most current figures.

Let's turn back to our June budget report. You still need the June Actual, and YTD Actual, and Budget figures. You can't get what you need by copying any more figures from the annual budget. You could derive the YTD Budget figures by adding the monthly budgets through June in the annual budget, but there's a simpler way.

Let's assume you created the previous month's budget report, a May file, using the same row and column headings as the June file. You could use the YTD Actual and YTD Budget figures for May, which show the accumulated actual and budgeted expenses through May. You can use those with the June actual and budget figures to derive the June YTD figures. You can also copy the formulas (they subtract the Actual figure from the Budget figure for each row) from the May Diff. and YTD Diff. columns into the corresponding June columns.

Assuming the May file is as accessible as the annual file, copying the figures you need from the May file works the same way as copying the figures from the annual file: Select the cell range containing the figures you want, choose the Edit Copy command, go to the June budget window, position the active cell where you want to use the figures, and either press the Enter key or choose the Paste Link command. When you copy the formulas from the May Diff. column into the June Diff. column, the formulas will work with the data in the June budget. The difference between E8 and F8, for instance, would be reported in G8. To create this on your current worksheet, in G8 type the formula

$$= E8 - F8$$

and use the Edit Fill Down command to copy the formula down column G to row 47. The same formula could be copied to column J, from J8:J47.

Now you're left with the YTD Actual and YTD Budget columns. The June YTD Actual figure for any row is going to be the sum of the June Actual and May YTD Actual figures. And the June YTD Budget figure for any row is going to be the sum of the June Budget and May YTD Actual figures.

Here's a way to get them quickly. The Edit Paste Special command shows you a dialog box that lets you manipulate data you're copying:

Figure 6-10. Edit Paste Special Dialog Box

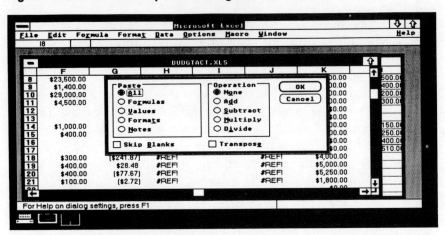

If you choose the Add button in the Operation box, whatever is copied will be added to the contents of the corresponding
destination cell. That means, for instance, that if you already
have the Salaries/Wages figure for June in H8 on your currently
active worksheet, when you use the Edit Paste Special command
and turn on the Add button, data copied from H8 (the equivalent YTD Actual figure) in the May budget file will be added to
the figure already there.

Doing this takes three steps:

Step 1. Copy the June Actual and June Budget columns of figures to columns H and I, respectively.

Step 2. Go to the May worksheet. Select H8:I47 and choose Edit
copy.

Step 3. Return to the June worksheet. Position the active cell in
H8, choose Edit Paste Special, and in the dialog box, turn on
the Add button. Then press the Enter key or choose the OK
bar.

Excel automatically adds the figures it has copied to the figures already in the equivalent cells.

Because the formula for calculating the difference between
YTD Actual and YTD Budget has already been copied to column
J, as soon as the YTD figures are there, the differences are calcu-
lated and displayed in column J.

Now you have a completed June budget report that resem-
bles the spreadsheet shown in 6-11.

Figure 6-11. June Budget Versus Actual

The Yuppie Toy Store

Budgeted vs. Actual Expenses for: June, 1988

Account #	Account Name/Description	June Real	June Budget	June Diff.	YTD Real	YTD Budget	YTD Diff.	Annual Budget
	Employee Costs/ Benefits							
67101	Salaries/Wages	$23,072.88	$23,500.00	$427.12	#REF!	#REF!	#REF!	$300,000.00
67102	Payroll Taxes	$1,477.23	$1,400.00	($77.23)	#REF!	#REF!	#REF!	$20,000.00
67103	Sales Commisions	$27,814.73	$29,000.00	$1,185.27	#REF!	#REF!	#REF!	$400,000.00
67104	Employee Benefits	$4,155.62	$4,500.00	$344.38	#REF!	#REF!	#REF!	$54,500.00
	Outside Labor & Services							
68101	Marketing research	$1,262.71	$1,000.00	($262.71)	#REF!	#REF!	#REF!	$12,500.00
68102	Outside Labor	$322.83	$400.00	$77.17	#REF!	#REF!	#REF!	$6,000.00
	Supplies							
70101	Office Supplies	$541.87	$300.00	($241.87)	#REF!	#REF!	#REF!	$4,000.00
70102	Office Equipment & Furniture	$371.52	$400.00	$28.48	#REF!	#REF!	#REF!	$5,000.00
70103	Mailing	$477.67	$400.00	($77.67)	#REF!	#REF!	#REF!	$5,250.00
70104	Printing	$102.72	$100.00	($2.72)	#REF!	#REF!	#REF!	$1,800.00
	Facilities & Service							
71201	Store Rent	$7,350.00	$7,200.00	($150.00)	#REF!	#REF!	#REF!	$86,400.00
71202	Telephone	$401.45	$450.00	$48.55	#REF!	#REF!	#REF!	$5,700.00
71203	Utilities	$303.65	$330.00	$26.35	#REF!	#REF!	#REF!	$4,400.00
	Advertising & Promotion							
72101	Newspaper/ Media Ads	$167.74	$150.00	($17.74)	#REF!	#REF!	#REF!	$2,000.00
72102	In-House Advertising	$217.73	$225.00	$7.27	#REF!	#REF!	#REF!	$3,000.00
72103	Outside Copy Preperation	$83.35	$100.00	$16.65	#REF!	#REF!	#REF!	$1,350.00
72104	Other Advertising	$41.63	$55.00	$13.37	#REF!	#REF!	#REF!	$750.00
	Warehouse & Stocking							
64302	Warehouse Rent & Expenses	$3,854.87	$3,800.00	($54.87)	#REF!	#REF!	#REF!	$45,600.00
64303	Purchasing/ Consumer Goods	$56,255.67	$60,000.00	$3,744.33	#REF!	#REF!	#REF!	$775,000.00
64304	Purchasing/ Personal Goods	$51,731.64	$50,000.00	($1,731.64)	#REF!	#REF!	#REF!	$625,000.00
64305	Purchasing/ Electronics	$76,126.79	$75,000.00	($1,126.79)	#REF!	#REF!	#REF!	$950,000.00
64306	Purchasing/ Other	$13,135.62	$12,500.00	($635.62)	#REF!	#REF!	#REF!	$157,000.00
64307	Vehicle Expenses	$473.73	$400.00	($73.73)	#REF!	#REF!	#REF!	$5,000.00
64308	Vehicle Maint & Repair	$814.63	$200.00	($614.63)	#REF!	#REF!	#REF!	$3,000.00
64309	Shipping Expenses	$407.66	$300.00	($107.66)	#REF!	#REF!	#REF!	$4,500.00
	Other							
77801	Misc. Admin.	$302.15	$150.00	($152.15)	#REF!	#REF!	#REF!	$1,900.00
77802	Misc. Sales	$277.49	$250.00	($27.49)	#REF!	#REF!	#REF!	$3,250.00
77803	Misc. Warehousing	$521.35	$400.00	($121.35)	#REF!	#REF!	#REF!	$5,000.00
	Total Expenses	$272,066.93	$272,510.00	$443.07	#REF!	#REF!	#REF!	$3,487,900.00

This model can also be used as a macro that fetches the related files and prompts you for the current month's actual expenses. The macro instructions are shown in Figure 6-12.

Figure 6-12. BUDACTBB.XLM Macro

	A
1	BudActBB
2	=DISPLAY(FALSE,FALSE,TRUE,TRUE,0)
3	=SELECT("R1C5:R1C11")
4	=COLUMN.WIDTH(12)
5	=SELECT("R1C1")
6	=FORMULA("The Yuppie Toy Store")
7	=SELECT("R3C1")
8	=FORMULA("Budgeted vs. Actual Expenses for: ")
9	=SELECT("R1C1")
10	=COLUMN.WIDTH(11)
11	=SELECT("R3C4")
12	=FORMULA("June, 1988")
13	=SELECT("R6C1")
14	=FORMULA("Account #")
15	=SELECT("R6C2")
16	=FORMULA("Account Name/Description")
17	=SELECT("R6C1:R6C11")
18	=BORDER(FALSE,FALSE,FALSE,FALSE,TRUE,FALSE)
19	=SELECT("R5C5")
20	=FORMULA("June")
21	=SELECT("R6C6")
22	=FORMULA("Budget")
23	=SELECT("R6C5")
24	=FORMULA("Real")
25	=SELECT("R5C6")
26	=FORMULA("June")
27	=SELECT("R5C7")
28	=FORMULA("June")
29	=SELECT("R6C7")
30	=FORMULA("Diff.")
31	=SELECT("R6C8")
32	=FORMULA("Real")
33	=SELECT("R5C8")
34	=FORMULA("YTD")
35	=SELECT("R5C9")
36	=FORMULA("YTD")
37	=SELECT("R6C9")
38	=FORMULA("Budget")
39	=SELECT("R6C10")
40	=FORMULA("Diff.")
41	=SELECT("R5C10")
42	=FORMULA("YTD")
43	=SELECT("R5C11")

	A
44	=FORMULA("Annual")
45	=SELECT("R6C11")
46	=FORMULA("Budget")
47	=SELECT("R5C5:R6C11","R6C11")
48	=ALIGNMENT(3)
49	=SELECT("R7C1")
50	=FORMULA("Employee Cost/ Benefits")
51	=SELECT("R8C1")
52	=FORMULA("67101")
53	=SELECT("R9C1")
54	=FORMULA("67102")
55	=SELECT("R10C1")
56	=FORMULA("67103")
57	=SELECT("R11C1")
58	=FORMULA("67104")
59	=SELECT("R8C2")
60	=FORMULA("Salaries/Wages")
61	=SELECT("R9C2")
62	=FORMULA("Payroll Taxes")
63	=SELECT("R10C2")
64	=FORMULA("Sales Commisions")
65	=SELECT("R11C2")
66	=FORMULA("Employee Benefits")
67	=SELECT("R13C1")
68	=FORMULA("Outside Labor & Services")
69	=SELECT("R14C1")
70	=FORMULA("68101")
71	=SELECT("R15C1")
72	=FORMULA("68102")
73	=SELECT("R14C2")
74	=FORMULA("Marketing Research")
75	=SELECT("R15C2")
76	=FORMULA("Outside Labor")
77	=SELECT("R17C1")
78	=FORMULA("Supplies")
79	=SELECT("R18C1")
80	=FORMULA("70101")
81	=SELECT("R19C1")
82	=FORMULA("70102")
83	=SELECT("R20C1")
84	=FORMULA("70103")
85	=SELECT("R21C1")
86	=FORMULA("70104")

	A
87	=SELECT("R18C2")
88	=FORMULA("Office Supplies")
89	=SELECT("R19C2")
90	=FORMULA("Office Equipment & Furniture")
91	=SELECT("R20C2")
92	=FORMULA("Mailing")
93	=SELECT("R21C2")
94	=FORMULA("Printing")
95	=SELECT("R23C1")
96	=FORMULA("Facilities & Service")
97	=SELECT("R24C1")
98	=FORMULA("71201")
99	=SELECT("R25C1")
100	=FORMULA("71202")
101	=SELECT("R26C1")
102	=FORMULA("71203")
103	=SELECT("R24C2")
104	=FORMULA("Store Rent")
105	=SELECT("R25C2")
106	=FORMULA("Telephone")
107	=SELECT("R26C2")
108	=FORMULA("Utilities")
109	=SELECT("R28C1")
110	=FORMULA("Advertising & Promotion")
111	=SELECT("R29C1")
112	=FORMULA("72101")
113	=SELECT("R30C1")
114	=FORMULA("72102")
115	=SELECT("R31C1")
116	=FORMULA("72103")
117	=SELECT("R32C1")
118	=FORMULA("72104")
119	=SELECT("R29C2")
120	=FORMULA("Newspaper/ Media Ads")
121	=SELECT("R30C2")
122	=FORMULA("In-House Advertising")
123	=SELECT("R31C2")
124	=FORMULA("Outside Copy Preperation")
125	=SELECT("R32C2")
126	=FORMULA("Other Advertising")
127	=SELECT("R34C1")
128	=FORMULA("Warehouse & Stocking")
129	=SELECT("R35C1")

	A
130	=FORMULA("64302")
131	=SELECT("R36C1")
132	=FORMULA("64303")
133	=SELECT("R37C1")
134	=FORMULA("64304")
135	=SELECT("R38C1")
136	=FORMULA("64305")
137	=SELECT("R39C1")
138	=FORMULA("64306")
139	=SELECT("R40C1")
140	=FORMULA("64307")
141	=SELECT("R41C1")
142	=FORMULA("64308")
143	=SELECT("R42C1")
144	=FORMULA("64309")
145	=SELECT("R35C2")
146	=FORMULA("Warehouse Rent & Expenses")
147	=SELECT("R36C2")
148	=FORMULA("Purchasing/ Consumer Goods")
149	=SELECT("R37C2")
150	=FORMULA("Purchasing/ Personal Goods")
151	=SELECT("R38C2")
152	=FORMULA("Purchasing/ Electronics")
153	=SELECT("R39C2")
154	=FORMULA("Purchasing/ Other")
155	=SELECT("R40C2")
156	=FORMULA("Vehicle Expenses")
157	=SELECT("R41C2")
158	=FORMULA("Vehicle Maint & Repair")
159	=SELECT("R42C2")
160	=FORMULA("Shipping Expenses")
161	=SELECT("R44C1")
162	=FORMULA("Other")
163	=SELECT("R45C1")
164	=FORMULA("77801")
165	=SELECT("R46C1")
166	=FORMULA("77802")
167	=SELECT("R47C1")
168	=FORMULA("77803")
169	=SELECT("R45C2")
170	=FORMULA("Misc. Admin.")
171	=SELECT("R46C2")
172	=FORMULA("Misc. Sales")

	A
173	=SELECT("R47C2")
174	=FORMULA("Misc. Warehousing")
175	=SELECT("R48C1")
176	=FORMULA("Total Expenses")
177	=OPEN("budg1988.xls")
178	=ACTIVATE("BUDG1988.XLS")
179	=SELECT("R4C10:R7C10")
180	=COPY()
181	=ACTIVATE("Sheet1")
182	=SELECT("R8C6:R11C6")
183	=PASTE.LINK()
184	=ACTIVATE("BUDG1988.XLS")
185	=SELECT("R10C10:R11C10")
186	=COPY()
187	=ACTIVATE("Sheet1")
188	=SELECT("R14C6:R15C6")
189	=PASTE.LINK()
190	=ACTIVATE("BUDG1988.XLS")
191	=SELECT("R14C10:R17C10")
192	=COPY()
193	=ACTIVATE("Sheet1")
194	=SELECT("R18C6:R21C6")
195	=PASTE.LINK()
196	=ACTIVATE("BUDG1988.XLS")
197	=SELECT("R20C10:R22C10")
198	=COPY()
199	=ACTIVATE("Sheet1")
200	=SELECT("R24C6:R26C6")
201	=PASTE.LINK()
202	=VLINE(21)
203	=ACTIVATE("BUDG1988.XLS")
204	=VLINE(21)
205	=SELECT("R25C10:R28C10")
206	=COPY()
207	=ACTIVATE("Sheet1")
208	=SELECT("R29C6:R32C6")
209	=PASTE.LINK()
210	=ACTIVATE("BUDG1988.XLS")
211	=SELECT("R31C10:R38C10")
212	=COPY()
213	=ACTIVATE("Sheet1")
214	=SELECT("R35C6:R42C6")
215	=PASTE.LINK()

	A
216	=ACTIVATE("BUDG1988.XLS")
217	=SELECT("R41C10:R44C10")
218	=COPY()
219	=ACTIVATE("Sheet1")
220	=SELECT("R45C6:R48C6")
221	=PASTE.LINK()
222	=SELECT("R8C7")
223	=CANCEL.COPY()
224	=FORMULA("=RC[-1]-RC[-2]")
225	=COPY()
226	=SELECT("R9C7:R11C7,R14C7:R15C7,R18C7:R21C7,R24C7:R26C7","R24C7")
227	=VLINE(19)
228	=SELECT("R9C7:R11C7,R14C7:R15C7,R18C7:R21C7,R24C7:R26C7,R29C7:R32C7,R35C7:R42C7,R45C7:R47C7","R45C7")
229	=PASTE()
230	=OPEN("may88bta.xls")
231	=ACTIVATE("MAY88BTA.XLS")
232	=SELECT("R8C8")
233	=COPY()
234	=ACTIVATE("Sheet1")
235	=SELECT("R8C8")
236	=PASTE.LINK()
237	=CANCEL.COPY()
238	=FORMULA("=MAY88BTA.XLS!RC8+RC[-3]")
239	=COPY()
240	=SELECT("R9C8:R11C8,R14C8:R15C8,R18C8:R21C8,R24C8:R26C8,R29C8:R32C8,R35C8:R42C8,R45C8:R47C8,R45C8:R48C8","R45C8")
241	=PASTE()
242	=SELECT("R8C9")
243	=FORMULA("=MAY88BTA.XLS!RC+RC[-3]")
244	=COPY()
245	=SELECT("R9C9:R11C9")
246	=PASTE()
247	=SELECT("R14C9:R15C9")
248	=PASTE()
249	=SELECT("R18C9:R21C9")
250	=PASTE()
251	=SELECT("R24C9:R26C9")
252	=PASTE()
253	=SELECT("R29C9:R32C9")
254	=PASTE()
255	=SELECT("R35C9:R42C9")
256	=PASTE()
257	=SELECT("R45C9:R47C9")
258	=PASTE()

A
259 =SELECT("R7C5:R48C11","R48C11")
260 =FORMAT.NUMBER("0")
261 =SELECT("R8C10")
262 =CANCEL.COPY()
263 =FORMULA("=RC[-1]-RC[-2]")
264 =COPY()
265 =SELECT("R9C10")
266 =HLINE(-1)
267 =SELECT("R9C10:R11C10,R14C10:R15C10,R18C10:R21C10,R24C10:R26C10,R29C10:R32C10,R35C10:R42C10,R45C10:R47C10","R45C10")
268 =PASTE()
269 =ACTIVATE("BUDG1988.XLS")
270 =SELECT("R4C17:R7C17")
271 =COPY()
272 =ACTIVATE("Sheet1")
273 =SELECT("R8C11:R11C11")
274 =PASTE.LINK()
275 =ACTIVATE("BUDG1988.XLS")
276 =SELECT("R10C17:R11C17")
277 =COPY()
278 =ACTIVATE("Sheet1")
279 =SELECT("R14C11:R15C11")
280 =PASTE.LINK()
281 =ACTIVATE("BUDG1988.XLS")
282 =SELECT("R14C17:R17C17")
283 =COPY()
284 =ACTIVATE("Sheet1")
285 =SELECT("R18C11:R21C11")
286 =PASTE.LINK()
287 =ACTIVATE("BUDG1988.XLS")
288 =SELECT("R20C17:R22C17")
289 =COPY()
290 =ACTIVATE("Sheet1")
291 =SELECT("R24C11:R26C11")
292 =PASTE.LINK()
293 =ACTIVATE("BUDG1988.XLS")
294 =SELECT("R25C17:R28C17")
295 =COPY()
296 =ACTIVATE("Sheet1")
297 =SELECT("R29C11:R32C11")
298 =PASTE.LINK()
299 =ACTIVATE("BUDG1988.XLS")
300 =SELECT("R31C17:R38C17")
301 =COPY()

	A
302	=ACTIVATE("Sheet1")
303	=SELECT("R35C11:R42C11")
304	=PASTE.LINK()
305	=ACTIVATE("BUDG1988.XLS")
306	=SELECT("R41C17:R43C17")
307	=COPY()
308	=ACTIVATE("Sheet1")
309	=SELECT("R45C11:R47C11")
310	=PASTE.LINK()
311	=ACTIVATE("BUDG1988.XLS")
312	=SELECT("R44C17")
313	=COPY()
314	=ACTIVATE("Sheet1")
315	=SELECT("R48C11")
316	=PASTE.LINK()
317	=SELECT("R48C10")
318	=CANCEL.COPY()
319	=FORMULA("=SUM(R[-40]C:R[-1]C)")
320	=SELECT("R48C9")
321	=FORMULA("=SUM(R[-40]C:R[-1]C)")
322	=SELECT("R48C7")
323	=FORMULA("=SUM(R[-40]C:R[-1]C)")
324	=SELECT("R48C5")
325	=FORMULA("=SUM(R[-40]C:R[-1]C)")
326	=SELECT("R47C1:R47C11")
327	=BORDER(FALSE,FALSE,FALSE,FALSE,TRUE,FALSE)
328	=SELECT("R50C3")
329	=FORMULA(INPUT("You must now enter the values for June actual. Please enter yes if you understand",2,"Prompt"))
330	=IF(ACTIVE.CELL()="yes",GOTO(A331),GOTO(A329))
331	=CLEAR(1)
332	=RETURN()

To run the macro, open the macro file and use the Window menu to return to the blank worksheet named SHEET1.XLS. (This becomes very important to the running of the macro, because of several functions that need to work with the default worksheet file SHEET1.XLS.)

The macro looks for the annual budget (named BUDG1988.XLS) and the previous month's file (named MAY88BTA.XLS) on drive C:. If you wish to use other filenames, edit the macro instructions that look for these specific filenames.

When finished, the model looks like the one shown in Figure 6-13.

Figure 6-13. The Finished Model

The Yuppie Toy Store

Budgeted vs. Actual Expenses fo May, 1988

Account #	Account Name/Description	May Real	May Budget	May Diff.	YTD Real	YTD Budget	YTD Diff.	Annual Budget
	Employee Costs/ Benefits							
67101	Salaries/Wages	$21,712.63	$23,500.00	$1,787.37	$110,338.74	$140,000.00	$29,661.26	$300,000.00
67102	Payroll Taxes	$1,273.66	$1,400.00	$126.34	$14,861.39	$14,000.00	($861.39)	$20,000.00
67103	Sales Commisions	$24,652.82	$29,000.00	$4,347.18	$149,500.11	$180,000.00	$30,499.89	$400,000.00
67104	Employee Benefits	$5,011.29	$4,500.00	($511.29)	$24,028.12	$27,000.00	$2,971.88	$54,500.00
								$0.00
	Outside Labor & Services							
68101	Marketing research	$791.34	$1,000.00	$208.66	$3,926.70	$5,400.00	$1,473.30	$12,500.00
68102	Outside Labor	$589.34	$400.00	($189.34)	$2,854.81	$2,500.00	($354.81)	$6,000.00
								$0.00
	Supplies							
70101	Office Supplies	$302.20	$300.00	($2.20)	$1,473.94	$1,800.00	$326.06	$4,000.00
70102	Office Equipment & Furniture	$226.74	$400.00	$173.26	$2,017.20	$2,400.00	$382.80	$5,000.00
70103	Mailing	$391.74	$400.00	$8.26	$2,245.96	$2,500.00	$254.04	$5,250.00
70104	Printing	$115.77	$100.00	($15.77)	$710.04	$750.00	$39.96	$1,800.00
								$0.00
	Facilities & Service							
71201	Store Rent	$7,350.00	$7,200.00	($150.00)	$36,450.00	$43,200.00	$6,750.00	$86,400.00
71202	Telephone	$338.83	$450.00	$111.17	$2,626.01	$2,900.00	$273.99	$5,700.00
71203	Utilities	$311.26	$330.00	$18.74	$1,851.07	$2,000.00	$148.93	$4,400.00
								$0.00
	Advertising & Promotion							
72101	Newspaper/ Media Ads	$206.12	$150.00	($56.12)	$1,047.90	$1,000.00	($47.90)	$2,000.00
72102	In-House Advertising	$188.50	$225.00	$36.50	$1,333.95	$1,400.00	$66.05	$3,000.00
72103	Outside Copy Preparation	$56.90	$100.00	$43.10	$594.30	$600.00	$5.70	$1,350.00
72104	Other Advertising	$63.69	$55.00	($8.69)	$336.01	$350.00	$13.99	$750.00
								$0.00
	Warehouse & Stocking							
64302	Warehouse Rent & Expenses	$3,812.54	$3,800.00	($12.54)	$18,722.64	$22,750.00	$4,027.36	$45,600.00
64303	Purchasing/ Consumer Goods	$58,287.17	$60,000.00	$1,712.83	$325,912.17	$375,000.00	$49,087.83	$775,000.00
64304	Purchasing/ Personal Goods	$46,156.83	$50,000.00	$3,843.17	$266,007.89	$310,000.00	$43,992.11	$625,000.00
64305	Purchasing/ Electronics	$73,915.73	$75,000.00	$1,084.27	$393,031.96	$475,000.00	$81,968.04	$950,000.00
64306	Purchasing/ Other	$12,165.16	$12,500.00	$334.84	$53,131.70	$70,000.00	$16,868.30	$157,000.00
64307	Vehicle Expenses	$404.72	$400.00	($4.72)	$1,205.08	$2,500.00	$1,294.92	$5,000.00
64308	Vehicle Maint & Repair	$31.61	$200.00	$168.39	$151.99	$1,200.00	$1,048.01	$3,000.00
64309	Shipping Expenses	$277.63	$300.00	$22.37	$1,204.17	$2,000.00	$795.83	$4,500.00
								$0.00
	Other							
77801	Misc. Admin.	$107.67	$150.00	$42.33	$286.26	$900.00	$613.74	$1,900.00
77802	Misc. Sales	$32.83	$250.00	$217.17	$212.02	$1,500.00	$1,287.98	$3,250.00
77803	Misc. Warehousing	$173.61	$400.00	$226.39	$699.22	$2,400.00	$1,700.78	$5,000.00
	Total Expenses	$258,948.33	$272,510.00	$13,561.67	$1,416,761.35	$1,691,050.00	$274,288.65	$3,487,900.00

The macro sets up the same worksheet as shown above in Figure 6-12. However, in order to run, it needs to use the same external files, here named BUDG1988.XLS and MAY88BTA.XLS, and it expects to find them on drive C:. You also must have the default opening worksheet named SHEET1.XLS as the active window.

The macro takes several minutes to run. While it's running you'll be prompted for several pieces of information. When asked about updating references to unopened documents, answer Yes. When asked about opening files, answer OK. When the macro prompts you about entering the June Actual figures, type the word Yes (not just the letter *y*) if you intend to enter the June figures.

When the macro finishes running, you'll see the June Budget figures in the appropriate column, but the adjacent Difference column will show negative values. This happens because you haven't yet entered the June Actual figures, and the formulas in the Difference column reflect that. Once you enter the Actual figures, you'll see the Difference column reflect the action of the formula.

Allocating Overhead Costs

How do you handle those costs common to all segments of a business, but which can't be classed as a direct cost of making a product or service? If you make a product in the same building that houses the telemarketing staff and also houses the service people, how do you allocate the rent and utilities associated with that building? And where should you put the cost of advertising? How about the cost of the administrative and finance staff?

Granted, some budgets simply allocate costs that can't be associated with a particular business segment into a category sometimes called *overhead* or *administration*. This model attempts to show you other ways of assigning overhead costs to various departments. The result is a figure that can then be plugged into monthly financial reports for the departments.

The top part of the worksheet is a projected budget for the components of overhead costs. If you want to use this as a financial report using actual figures, you can use the same model and just change the figures. If there are more items that should be included in the overhead costs, insert rows to list them. The allocation formula as shown works only with the total of those

Figure 6-14. Allocation of Overhead Costs

	A	B	C	D	E	F	G
1	ALLOCATION OF OVERHEAD COSTS				Fiscal Year		1987-1988
2	The Yuppie Toy Store						
3							
4	Overhead		June	July	August	September	October
5							
6	Site Rent		2100	2100	2100	2100	2100
7	Utilities		300	350	350	350	400
8	Phone Service		250	250	250	250	250
9	Advertising		3700	3800	2600	2100	2200
10	Security (shared)		250	250	250	250	250
11	Salaries		6700	6700	6700	7500	7500
12	Totals		13300	13450	12250	12550	12700
13							
14							
15	Groups Sharing Overhead						
16							
17		%	Monthly Allocation				
18	Product A	67%	8911	9012	8208	8409	8509
19	Product B	11%	1463	1480	1348	1381	1397
20	Marketing	15%	1995	2018	1838	1883	1905
21	Service	7%	931	942	858	879	889

expenses. (You can change this if you want to weight some of the costs more heavily.)

The bottom part of the model determines a flat figure to be used as the department's share of the overhead costs. In column B, notice the percentages that determine how the overhead costs are distributed. These numbers are entered as decimal fractions, but formatted to display percentages.

The monthly share of overhead costs is determined by multiplying this percentage by the total for the month shown in row 12. Once you've typed the formula in C18, you can use the Edit Fill Down command to copy it into rows 19 through 21. However, you should then edit the formulas so the reference to B18, B19, B20, and B21 are absolute rather than relative:

C8   =$B$18*C$12
C9   =$B$19*C$12
C10   =$B$20*C$12
C11   =$B$21*C$12

If the above formulas are copied into the rest of the respective rows from column D through column O with the Edit Fill Right command, the only part of the formula that will be adjusted is the column identifier.

The finished allocation chart looks like the spreadsheet in Figure 6-14.

	H	I	J	K	L	M	N	O
1								
2								
3								
4	November	December	January	February	March	April	May	Total
5								
6	2100	2100	2100	2100	2100	2100	2100	25200
7	450	450	450	425	400	375	350	4650
8	250	250	250	250	250	250	250	3000
9	4200	4500	1700	2100	2400	2200	2700	34200
10	250	250	250	250	250	250	250	3000
11	8200	9700	8000	8500	8500	8500	9100	95600
12	15450	17250	12750	13625	13900	13675	14750	165650
13								
14								
15								
16								
17								
18	10352	11558	8543	9129	9313	9162	9883	110986
19	1700	1898	1403	1499	1529	1504	1623	18222
20	2318	2588	1913	2044	2085	2051	2213	24848
21	1082	1208	893	954	973	957	1033	11596

You can experiment with this model to see what happens with different percentages. As currently set up, however, it uses one percentage to determine a share of overhead costs for the entire year. You may wish to change this, editing the formulas to reflect different allocation percentages for different periods during the year. If you do this, be sure you either add rows to the bottom to show what percentages are in effect, or add notes to the cells where you've edited the original formula.

Chapter 7

Some Finance Solutions

Beyond the income-and-expense studies of how money is used by a business, a manager needs to pay attention to some details within financial statements. If a particular project is given financing based on an ability to turn a profit within a specified period of time, it falls to the manager to pay close attention to start-up money, the amount of borrowing allowed and the costs associated with borrowing, lumped expenses for items that can be used over a period of time, and the value that major purchases such as equipment can contribute either to the business entity itself or to the parent entity, in the form of depreciable assets.

In addition, there are conditions within the financial marketplace that can influence business borrowing and business performance. Conditions such as rapidly rising inflation make planning difficult. An unexpected shortage of critical parts, such as the DRAM (Dynamic Random Access Memory) chips in 1987 and 1988, can slow down production lines and drive up prices of end products. What happens to a planned capital outlay if suddenly there's an investment capital shortage because of investor fears related to some world condition?

Spreadsheets are a particularly useful tool for fine-tuning assumptions about business performance, because you can change one assumption and watch its effect on the rest of the worksheet. Once you have correctly taken into account all of the variables in your plan, it's a simple matter to print the resulting worksheet and/or share the file with others.

While there are a number of financial applications for which spreadsheets and macros can provide help, we show you three in this chapter. (More macros that fall into the category of investment analysis are presented in Chapter 9: Investment Solutions.)

Cash Flow Projections for a Project

There are a number of factors that can influence a cash flow projection. Earlier, in Chapter 5, we developed a Cash Flow Statement that assumed a linear growth in sales, at a fixed percentage per month. Rarely does sales growth work that way. A number of factors can influence that:

- Introduction of a new product or a new version of an existing product can hamper sales of current products for several months. Frequently, when buyers hear of a new version of an existing product, they'll wait to see the new version rather than buy the existing model.
- Seasonal factors, such as the Christmas buying season or the back-to-school rush, can have considerable impact on sales. If your product is being sold to retailers, the buying/stocking cycles of retailers will have a strong influence on your sales pattern. If you sell patio furniture, sales will be low during the winter, and revive in the spring and summer. Obviously the opposite would be true of ski equipment.
- Economic conditions affecting consumers can have a profound impact on retail sales, and hence on businesses that sell to the retailers. High mortgage rates have a domino effect on building materials and on products sold for home improvements.
- Local factors play a part, too. If you sell locally, and local industry is destroyed by competition from overseas, demand for your product will dry up because local income levels will drop.
- Product acceptance is cyclical. If yours is the first product of its kind, you may have a tougher time getting people to buy it than if you're riding the second or third wave of product development in an area. Consider the proliferation of personal computers: The first ones, introduced in the late 1970s, were not widely accepted. Customer acceptance grew during the next decade, to be sure, but makers of computer equipment aimed at the consumer marketplace led less than totally predictable lives in the early 1980s.

Because of factors like these, a spreadsheet's ability to recalculate quickly makes it a highly useful tool in coming up with more reliable business plans.

The cash flow projection shown below takes a number of factors into account. However, once it's set up and running, you should review the assumptions and formulas on which it's based, fine tuning them to include corrections or conditions that could have an effect.

To set up the cash flow model used below, enter row and column labels as shown in Figure 7-1.

Enter formulas and data as follows:

C3	= NOW( ) (this puts today's date on the report)
E5	30000
E7	13.25
C11	35000
D11	= C11 + (0.25*C11) (copy this formula into E11 through N11)
C12	35000
D12	= 0.35*C15 (copy this formula into E12 through N12)
C13	20000
D13	= 0.2*C15 (copy this formula into E13 through N13)
C14	10000
D14	= 0.1*C15 (copy this formula into E14 through N14)
C15	= SUM(C11:C14) (copy this formula into D15 through N15)
C16	= 0.08*C15 (copy this formula into D16 through N16)
C17	= 0.05*C15 (copy this formula into D17 through N17)
C18	= C15 − C16 − C17 (copy this formula into D18 through N18)
C21	56000
D21	= 2000 + C21 (copy this formula into E21 through N21)
C22	24000
D22	= 2000 + C22 (copy this formula into E22 through N22)
C23	14500
D23	14500
E23	= 1500 + C23
F23	= 1500 + D23 (copy the above two formulas into G23 and H23, and repeat this process for subsequent pairs of cells)
C24	12000
D24	= 2000 + C24(copy this formula into E24 through N24)
C25	21000 (copy this value into D25 and E25, then increase the value by $3000 every three months)
C26	8000 (copy this value into D26 and E26, then increase the value by $2000 every three months)
C27	= SUM(C21:C26)
C29	= C18 − C27
C31	0

Figure 7-1. Cash Flow Projection Labels

	A	B	C	D	E	F	G	H	I	J	K	L	M	N
1	Project:		Berry Flakes											
2	Person Responsible:		Sara Pereira											
3	Date of this report:													
4														
5			Minimum cash balance				Assumption:							
6														
7			Beg. interest rate:											
8														
9														
10			1-Jan-89	1-Feb-89	1-Mar-89	1-Apr-89	1-May-89	1-Jun-89	1-Jul-89	1-Aug-89	1-Sep-89	1-Oct-89	1-Nov-89	1-Dec-89
11	Cash Sales													
12	Receivables pmts: 30													
13	: 60													
14	: 90													
15	Total Sales													
16	less commissions													
17	less returns													
18	Net Sales													
19														
20	Expenses													
21	Grain purchases													
22	Processing													
23	Printing, pkging.													
24	Marketing													
25	Distribution													
26	Administration													
27	Total expenses													
28														
29	Net Income													
30														
31	Pmt. on Debt													
32														
33	Net Inc. w/debt pmt.													
34														
35	Borrowing this mo.													
36														
37	Current balance													

D31	= ($E$8/12)/100*C35 + IF(C350,C35,0))
C33	= C29 − C31
D33	= IF(C33<0, − C33 + $E$6,IF(C33< $E$6,$E$6 − C33,0))
C35	100000
C37	C33 + C35

Format C3 as a date, using the m/d/yy format. Format the range C11:N37 with the Format Number command, using the 0 option. Draw summary lines in rows 14, 17, 26, 31, and 35 with the Format Border command, using the Bottom option.

With these formulas and data properly entered, your initial cash flow projection should look like Figure 7.2.

The original cash flow projection has some assumptions built into the formulas:

- Cash sales increase 25 percent per month. Accounts receivable for sales in the 30-day, 60-day, and 90-day categories are 35 percent, 20 percent, and 10 percent respectively of the previous month's total sales.
- Commissions are 8 percent of total sales, and returns are 5 percent of total sales.
- Grain purchases and processing costs increase $2000 a month, each.
- Printing costs increase $1500 every two months, and marketing costs increase $2000 a month.
- Distribution costs increase $3000 a quarter, and administrative costs increase $2000 a quarter.
- Any borrowing is paid back the next month, if possible. The minimum cash balance of $30,000 is respected, even if it means borrowing more. One month's interest (the current rate here is 13.25 percent) is paid on the full amount of the previous month's borrowing, regardless of whether the borrowing was paid off in the current month.

Notice that with these assumptions, and initial sales, expenses, and borrowing figures as shown, the business goes into the black in September, with all loans paid back.

Figure 7-2. Cash Flow Projections for Berry Flakes

	1-Jan-89	1-Feb-89	1-Mar-89	1-Apr-89	1-May-89	1-Jun-89	1-Jul-89	1-Aug-89	1-Sep-89	1-Oct-89	1-Nov-89	1-Dec-89
Project: Berry Flakes												
Person Responsible: Sara Pereira												
Date of this report: 26-Aug-88												
Assumptions:												
Minimum cash balance			30000		Assumption:							
Beg. interest rate:			13.25									
Cash Sales	35000	43750	54688	68359	85449	106812	133514	166893	208616	260770	325963	407454
Receivables pmts: 30	35000	35000	38063	43881	52449	63999	78983	98069	122158	152418	190341	237809
: 60	20000	20000	21750	25075	29971	36571	45133	56040	69804	87096	108766	135891
: 90	10000	10000	10875	12538	14985	18285	22567	28020	34902	43548	54383	67945
Total Sales	100000	108750	125375	149853	182854	225666	280198	349021	435480	543832	679454	849099
less commissions	8000	8700	10030	11988	14628	18053	22416	27922	34838	43507	54356	67928
less returns	5000	5438	6269	7493	9143	11283	14010	17451	21774	27192	33973	42455
Net Sales	87000	94613	109076	130372	159083	196330	243772	303649	378868	473134	591125	738716
Expenses												
Grain purchases	56000	58000	60000	62000	64000	66000	68000	70000	72000	74000	76000	78000
Processing	24000	26000	28000	30000	32000	34000	36000	38000	40000	42000	44000	46000
Printing, pkging.	14500	14500	16000	16000	17500	17500	19000	19000	20500	20500	22000	22000
Marketing	12000	14000	16000	18000	20000	22000	24000	26000	30000	32000	34000	36000
Distribution	21000	21000	21000	25000	25000	25000	29000	29000	29000	33000	33000	33000
Administration	8000	8000	8000	10000	10000	10000	12000	12000	12000	14000	14000	14000
Total expenses	135500	141500	149000	161000	168500	174500	188000	194000	203500	215500	223000	229000
Net Income	-48500	-46888	-39924	-30628	-9417	21830	55772	109649	175368	257634	368125	509716
Pmt. on Debt	0	101104	127888	169665	202504	214262	194557	140317	31007	0	0	0
Net Inc. w/debt pmt.	-48500	-96492	-137812	-170293	-181922	-162432	-108785	-668	174361	431995	800120	1309836
Borrowing this mo.	100000	126492	167812	200293	211922	192432	138785	30668	0	0	0	0
Current balance	51500	30000	30000	30000	30000	30000	30000	30000	174361	431995	800120	1309836

However, notice that the assumptions are, for the most part, linear: Sales and expenses grow by a certain percentage or a certain amount every period. In real life, that doesn't happen often. With this as a basis, however, you can change figures and formulas until you have a financial picture with which you can live.

For instance, what would happen if a marketing campaign with print and video ads started in May, resulting in a 10 percent increase in sales per month? In the example below, it's assumed that this campaign results in $15000 more marketing expenses in May, with marketing expenses in general rising by $2000 a month after that (Figure 7-3).

You might wish to make adjustments in the amounts spent for grain purchases, processing, and printing since, after all, more product is being sold.

What would happen if in addition to the above there were an international event raising gas prices starting in April? Distribution costs would go up, regardless of whether you were using your own vehicles or paying others to truck your product (Figure 7-4).

What if there were a drought that ruined much of the existing grain crop, driving up the price of grain? Both the cost of grain and the cost of processing would go up. In the example below, these events are assumed to have happened in June, and grain becomes increasingly expensive during the rest of the year (Figure 7-5).

Since both the price of grain and the cost of processing for any particular month is controlled by a formula, simple editing of the formula for one or more months will help you tinker with the effects.

In each of the modified examples above, the assumptions in effect were listed at the top of the spreadsheet. Another way to show your assumptions on a modified existing spreadsheet is to use the Formula Add Note command. However, unlike the examples above, the notes wouldn't be visible unless you specifically requested to see them.

Figure 7-3. Cost Projections, Berry Flakes, Marketing Campaign

		1-Jan-89	1-Feb-89	1-Mar-89	1-Apr-89	1-May-89	1-Jun-89	1-Jul-89	1-Aug-89	1-Sep-89	1-Oct-89	1-Nov-89	1-Dec-89
Project:	Berry Flakes												
Person Responsible:	Sara Pereira												
Date of this report:	26-Aug-88												
Assumptions:													
Minimum cash balance	30000			Assumption:									
				Marketing campaign starts in May, 10% more sales/mo.									
Beg. interest rate:	13.25												
Cash Sales		35000	43750	54688	68359	92285	124585	168190	227056	306526	413810	558643	754168
Receivables pmts: 30		35000	35000	38063	43881	52449	66391	86759	115260	154389	207637	279797	377393
: 60		20000	20000	21750	25075	29971	37938	49577	65863	88222	118649	159884	215653
: 90		10000	10000	10875	12538	14985	18969	24788	32931	44111	59325	79942	107827
Total Sales		100000	108750	125375	149853	189690	247883	329314	441110	593247	799420	1078266	1455041
less commissions		8000	8700	10030	11988	15175	19831	26345	35289	47460	63954	86261	116403
less returns		5000	5438	6269	7493	9484	12394	16466	22056	29662	39971	53913	72752
Net Sales		87000	94613	109076	130372	165030	215658	286503	383766	516125	695496	938092	1265886
Expenses													
Grain purchases		56000	58000	60000	62000	64000	66000	68000	70000	72000	74000	76000	78000
Processing		24000	26000	28000	30000	32000	34000	36000	38000	40000	42000	44000	46000
Printing, pkging.		14500	14500	16000	16000	17500	17500	19000	19000	20500	20500	22000	22000
Marketing		12000	14000	16000	18000	35000	37000	39000	41000	43000	45000	47000	49000
Distribution		21000	21000	21000	25000	25000	25000	29000	29000	29000	33000	33000	33000
Administration		8000	8000	8000	10000	10000	10000	12000	12000	12000	14000	14000	14000
Total expenses		135500	141500	149000	161000	183500	189500	203000	209000	216500	228500	236000	242000
Net Income		-48500	-46888	-39924	-30628	-18470	26158	83503	174766	299625	466996	702092	1023886
Pmt. on Debt		0	101104	127888	169665	202504	223414	199434	117211	0	0	0	0
Net Inc. w/debt pmt.		-48500	-96492	-137812	-170293	-190974	-167256	-85931	87555	387180	854176	1556268	2580154
Borrowing this mo.		100000	126492	167812	200293	220974	197256	115931	0	0	0	0	0
Current balance		51500	30000	30000	30000	30000	30000	30000	87555	387180	854176	1556268	2580154

Figure 7-4. Cost Projections, Berry Flakes, Gas Rate Hike

	A	B	C	D	E	F	G	H	I	J	K	L	M	N
1	Project:		Berry Flakes											
2	Person Responsible:		Sara Pereira											
3	Date of this report:		26-Aug-88											
4	Asssumptions:													
5														
6		Minimum cash balance			30000		Assumption:							
7							Marketing campaign starts in May, 10% more sales/mo.							
8		Beg. interest rate:			13.25		Gas price hike in April forces distribution costs up							
9														
10			1-Jan-89	1-Feb-89	1-Mar-89	1-Apr-89	1-May-89	1-Jun-89	1-Jul-89	1-Aug-89	1-Sep-89	1-Oct-89	1-Nov-89	1-Dec-89
11	Cash Sales		35000	43750	54688	68359	92285	124585	168190	227056	306526	413810	558643	754168
12	Receivables pmts: 30		35000	35000	38063	43881	52449	66391	86759	115260	154389	207637	279797	377393
13	: 60		20000	20000	21750	25075	29971	37938	49577	65863	88222	118649	159884	215653
14	: 90		10000	10000	10875	12538	14985	18969	24788	32931	44111	59325	79942	107827
15	Total Sales		100000	108750	125375	149853	189690	247883	329314	441110	593247	799420	1078266	1455041
16	less commissions		8000	8700	10030	11968	15175	19831	26345	35289	47460	63954	86261	116403
17	less returns		5000	5438	6269	7493	9484	12394	16466	22056	29662	39971	53913	72752
18	Net Sales		87000	94613	109076	130372	165030	215658	286503	383766	516125	695496	938092	1265886
19														
20	Expenses													
21	Grain purchases		56000	58000	60000	62000	64000	66000	68000	70000	72000	74000	76000	78000
22	Processing		24000	26000	28000	30000	32000	34000	36000	38000	40000	42000	44000	46000
23	Printing, pkging.		14500	14500	16000	16000	17500	17500	19000	19000	20500	20500	22000	22000
24	Marketing		12000	14000	16000	18000	35000	37000	39000	41000	43000	45000	47000	49000
25	Distribution		21000	21000	21000	27000	28000	29000	33000	34000	35000	39000	40000	41000
26	Administration		8000	8000	8000	10000	10000	10000	12000	12000	12000	14000	14000	14000
27	Total expenses		135500	141500	149000	163000	186500	193500	207000	214000	222500	234500	243000	250000
28														
29	Net Income		-48500	-46888	-39924	-32628	-21470	22158	79503	169766	293625	460996	695092	1015886
30														
31	Pmt. on Debt		0	101104	127888	169665	204526	228492	208612	130534	0	0	0	0
32														
33	Net Inc. w/debt pmt.		-48500	-96492	-137812	-172293	-195996	-176333	-99109	69232	362857	823852	1518944	2534830
34														
35	Borrowing this mo.		100000	126492	167812	202293	225996	206333	129109	0	0	0	0	0
36														
37	Current balance		51500	30000	30000	30000	30000	30000	30000	69232	362857	823852	1518944	2534830

Figure 7-5. Cost Projections, Berry Flakes, Drought Impact

	A	B	C	D	E	F	G	H	I	J	K	L	M	N
1	Project:		Berry Flakes											
2	Person Responsible:		Sara Pereira											
3	Date of this report:		26-Aug-88											
4	Assumptions:													
5														
6	Minimum cash balance				30000		Assumption:							
7							Marketing campaign starts in May, 10% more sales/mo.							
8	Beg. interest rate:				13.25		Gas price hike in April forces distribution costs up							
9							Drought cause grain, processing prices up starting in June							
10			1-Jan-89	1-Feb-89	1-Mar-89	1-Apr-89	1-May-89	1-Jun-89	1-Jul-89	1-Aug-89	1-Sep-89	1-Oct-89	1-Nov-89	1-Dec-89
11	Cash Sales		35000	43750	54688	68359	92285	124585	168190	227056	306526	413810	558643	754168
12	Receivables pmts: 30		35000	35000	38063	43881	52449	66391	86759	115260	154389	207637	279797	377393
13	: 60		20000	20000	21750	25075	29971	37938	49577	65863	88222	118649	159884	215653
14	: 90		10000	10000	10875	12538	14985	18969	24788	32931	44111	59325	79942	107827
15	Total Sales		100000	108750	123375	149853	189690	247883	329314	441110	593247	799420	1078266	1455041
16	less commissions		8000	8700	10030	11988	15175	19831	26345	35289	47460	63954	86261	116403
17	less returns		5000	5438	6269	7493	9484	12394	16466	22056	29662	39971	53913	72752
18	Net Sales		87000	94613	109076	130372	165030	215658	286503	383766	516125	695496	938092	1265886
19														
20	Expenses													
21	Grain purchases		56000	58000	60000	62000	64000	69000	75000	82000	90000	99000	101000	103000
22	Processing		24000	26000	28000	30000	32000	38000	46000	54000	64000	74000	84000	90000
23	Printing, pkging.		14500	14500	16000	16000	17500	17500	19000	19000	20500	20500	22000	22000
24	Marketing		12000	14000	16000	18000	35000	37000	39000	41000	43000	45000	47000	49000
25	Distribution		21000	21000	21000	27000	28000	29000	33000	34000	35000	39000	40000	41000
26	Administration		8000	8000	8000	10000	10000	10000	12000	12000	12000	14000	14000	14000
27	Total expenses		135500	141500	149000	163000	186500	200500	224000	242000	264500	291500	308000	319000
28														
29	Net Income		-48500	-46888	-39924	-32628	-21470	15158	62503	141766	251625	403996	630092	946886
30														
31	Pmt. on Debt		0	101104	127888	169665	204526	228492	215689	154877	13256	0	0	0
32														
33	Net Inc. w/debt pmt.		-48500	-96492	-137812	-172293	-195996	-183333	-123186	16888	268369	672365	1302456	2249342
34														
35	Borrowing this mo.		100000	126492	167812	202293	225996	213333	153186	13112	0	0	0	0
36														
37	Current balance		51500	30000	30000	30000	30000	30000	30000	30000	268369	672365	1302456	2249342

Using Depreciation

When you buy something for a business, you can count on
either using it, or having it outlive its usefulness. When you buy
a box of envelopes, you can usually count on using them up,
thus having the value of your purchase (the amount you paid for
the box of envelopes) reduced each time you use an envelope.
The same principle applies to a piece of equipment: As equipment is used, its useful life is reduced by some amount, however
large or small that amount may be.

Depreciation assigns a percentage of decline in value from
the purchase price as a result of equipment use over a year.
When the useful life is over, you'll probably sell the equipment
for some salvage value, much as you would sell cardboard, alu-
minum, and paper waste to a recycler.

There are three standard methods of depreciation in use:
straight line, double declining balance, and sum of the years'
digits. With straight line depreciation, you allocate the same percentage of depreciation for each year of the item's useful life.
With the other two methods, more depreciation is allowed in the
early years of an item's useful life, and less is allowed in later
years.

Choosing the appropriate method of depreciation is something that should be done with a tax consultant. What we show
you here is how to calculate depreciation with all three methods.

The original model looks like Figure 7-6.

Figure 7-6. Depreciation Comparison

	A	B	C	D	E	F	G
1		Comparison of Depreciation Methods					
2							
3		Description of Item:					
4		Original cost:		10			
5		Useful life (in yrs.)		10			
6		Salvage value:		0			
7				Double		Sum of	
8		Straight	Cumulative	Declining	Cumulative	the Years	Cumulative
9	Year	Line	Percentage	Balance	Percentage	Digits	Percentage
10	1	1	10.00%	2	20.00%	2	18.18%
11	2	1	20.00%	2	36.00%	2	34.55%
12	3	1	30.00%	1	48.80%	1	49.09%
13	4	1	40.00%	1	59.04%	1	61.82%
14	5	1	50.00%	1	67.23%	1	72.73%
15	6	1	60.00%	1	73.79%	1	81.82%
16	7	1	70.00%	1	79.03%	1	89.09%
17	8	1	80.00%	0	83.22%	1	94.55%
18	9	1	90.00%	0	86.58%	0	98.18%
19	10	1	100.00%	0	89.26%	0	100.00%

To set up the model, type the row and column labels as shown in column B, and in rows 7, 8, and 9. Enter the numbers 1 through 10 in column A, starting with A10. Enter the value 10 in D4 and D5, and 0 in D6 so the cells containing formulas will show data rather than error messages. (You'll change these values later.)

Enter formulas as follows:

B10 = SLN($D$4,$D$6,$D$5) (copy this formula into B11 through B19)

C10 = (B10/$D$4)

D10 = DDB($D$4,$D$6,$D$5,A10) (copy this formula into D11 through D19)

E10 = (D10/$D$4)

F10 = SYD($D$4,$D$6,$D$5,A10) (copy this formula into F11 through F19)

G10 = (F10/$D$4)

C11 = (B11/$D$4) + C10 (copy this formula into C12 through C19)

E11 = (D11/$D$4) + E10 (copy this formula into E12 through E19)

G11 = (F11/$D$4) + G10 (copy this formula into G12 through G19)

Now the worksheet is ready for you to enter some real data, and watch the results. For instance, we've moved some of the text around in the top few rows, added some borders, and cleared rows 17, 18 and 19 for the worksheet shown below. But basically it's the same worksheet:

Figure 7-7. Desktop Publishing System Depreciation Comparison

	A	B	C	D	E	F	G	H	I	J
1	Silicon Gulch Computer Fair					Purchase Date:		Jun-88		
2		Depreciation Comparison				System Components:		IBM PC-AT with enhancements		
3	Description of Item:			Desktop Publishing System				HP LaserJet		
4	Purchase Cost::			6576				Ethernet connection		
5	Lifetime (in yrs.):			7						
6	Salvage Value at end of Lifetime:			500						
7				Double		Sum of				
8		Straight	Cumulative	Declining	Cumulative	the Years	Cumulative			
9	Year	Line	Percentage	Balance	Percentage	Digits	Percentage			
10	1	868	13.20%	1879	28.57%	1519	23.10%			
11	2	868	26.40%	1342	48.98%	1302	42.90%			
12	3	868	39.60%	959	63.56%	1085	59.40%			
13	4	868	52.80%	685	73.97%	868	72.60%			
14	5	868	66.00%	489	81.41%	651	82.50%			
15	6	868	79.20%	349	86.72%	434	89.10%			
16	7	868	92.40%	250	90.51%	217	92.40%			

This worksheet lets you make an informed decision about how to depreciate equipment when you prepare a balance sheet or a tax return.

We've turned the above spreadsheet into a macro that uses the data you provide to construct a line chart:

Figure 7-8. DEPCHART.XLM Macro

	A
1	charting
2	=SELECT("R13C2:R19C2,R13C4:R19C4,R13C6:R19C6","R13C6")
3	=NEW(2)
4	=GALLERY.LINE(5,TRUE)
5	=RETURN()

When run with the preceding spreadsheet on your screen, the macro produces a chart like Figure 7-9.

Figure 7-9. Depreciation Chart

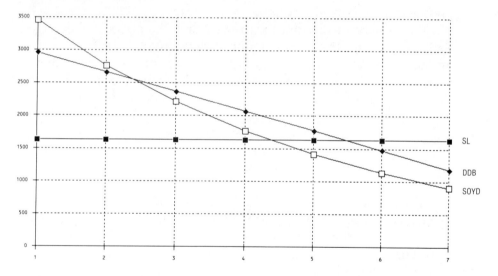

If you looked quickly while the macro was running, you saw a bar chart as the first form of the graph, which was replaced by the line graph as the final form. Once the graph is on the screen, you can choose any of the other forms *Excel* offers. The point of the chart form of your data is to get a graphic comparison of the figures. Pick the form that's most appropriate for your purposes.

Working with a Line of Credit

Businesses pay interest on borrowed funds everyday. Normally, the interest rate charged on short-term borrowing for operation of a business is higher than that charged for longer-term borrowing or for secured loans. Thus it makes sense for the manager to monitor when money needs to be borrowed, and to make sure it's borrowed for as short a term as possible. The problem is knowing when to borrow money and when to pay it back.

The model shown here helps you keep track of short-term borrowing. At the beginning of the month, enter the maximum amount of credit you can use. Each day, start with the previous night's balance of borrowed funds. You then decide whether you need new credit, or if you can pay off some or all of the borrowing. Enter the amount of new credit and/or payment on existing credit, along with today's interest rate. The model computes the costs of borrowing on the balance for today, and tells you the ending balance, including today's interest.

At the end of the month, the last line computes the average daily borrowing, the total amount of new credit used, the total amount paid back, the average interest rate for the month, the total amount of interest paid (which is also reported at the top of the model, in F5), and the average ending balance for the month.

To set up the model, type the text as shown in the first eight lines of the model. Format E8 using the Format Number command, mmm-yy option, and type the month and year you want to use.

Format column A, rows 9 through 39, with the Format Number command, dd-mmm option. Format columns B, C, D, F, and G with the $#,##0.00 option, and column E with the 0.00% option. For the summary line in row 39, use the Format Border command, Bottom option.

Type in formulas and data as shown below:

F5   = F40 (the total interest shown for column F)
B9   (enter your beginning balance for the month)
C9   (enter any credit you need to use)
D9   (enter any payment you'll make today)
E9   (enter today's interest rate)
F9   = (E9/365)*(B9 + C9 − D9) (copy this formula into rows 10 through 39)

Figure 7-10. Line of Credit

	A	B	C	D	E	F	G
1	Silicon Gulch Computer Fair						
2							
3	Credit Line Useage			For:	June, 1988		
4							
5	Maximum Line of Credit:		$250,000	Total Interest This Month:		$530.02	
6							
7		Beginning	New		Interest	Interest	Ending
8	Day	Balance	Credit	Payment	Rate	Cost	Balance
9	1-Jun	$102,756.32	$0.00	$65,000.00	14.25%	$14.74	$37,771.06
10	2-Jun	$37,771.06	$0.00	$0.00	14.25%	$14.75	$37,785.81
11	3-Jun	$37,785.81	$0.00	$0.00	14.25%	$14.75	$37,800.56
12	4-Jun	$37,800.56	$35,000.00	$0.00	14.25%	$28.42	$72,828.98
13	5-Jun	$72,828.98	$0.00	$0.00	14.25%	$28.43	$72,857.41
14	6-Jun	$72,857.41	$0.00	$0.00	14.25%	$28.44	$72,885.86
15	7-Jun	$72,885.86	$0.00	$0.00	14.25%	$28.46	$72,914.31
16	8-Jun	$72,914.31	$0.00	$0.00	14.25%	$28.47	$72,942.78
17	9-Jun	$72,942.78	$0.00	$42,000.00	14.50%	$12.29	$30,955.07
18	10-Jun	$30,955.07	$18,000.00	$0.00	14.50%	$19.45	$48,974.52
19	11-Jun	$48,974.52	$0.00	$0.00	14.50%	$19.46	$48,993.98
20	12-Jun	$48,993.98	$0.00	$0.00	14.50%	$19.46	$49,013.44
21	13-Jun	$49,013.44	$0.00	$0.00	14.50%	$19.47	$49,032.91
22	14-Jun	$49,032.91	$0.00	$10,000.00	14.50%	$15.51	$39,048.42
23	15-Jun	$39,048.42	$0.00	$0.00	14.50%	$15.51	$39,063.93
24	16-Jun	$39,063.93	$0.00	$0.00	14.50%	$15.52	$39,079.45
25	17-Jun	$39,079.45	$0.00	$0.00	14.50%	$15.52	$39,094.97
26	18-Jun	$39,094.97	$19,000.00	$0.00	14.50%	$23.08	$58,118.05
27	19-Jun	$58,118.05	$0.00	$0.00	14.50%	$23.09	$58,141.14
28	20-Jun	$58,141.14	$0.00	$0.00	14.50%	$23.10	$58,164.24
29	21-Jun	$58,164.24	$0.00	$0.00	14.50%	$23.11	$58,187.34
30	22-Jun	$58,187.34	$0.00	$47,000.00	14.50%	$4.44	$11,191.79
31	23-Jun	$11,191.79	$0.00	$0.00	14.50%	$4.45	$11,196.23
32	24-Jun	$11,196.23	$38,000.00	$0.00	14.75%	$19.88	$49,216.11
33	25-Jun	$49,216.11	$0.00	$0.00	14.75%	$19.89	$49,236.00
34	26-Jun	$49,236.00	$0.00	$0.00	14.75%	$19.90	$49,255.90
35	27-Jun	$49,255.90	$0.00	$35,000.00	14.75%	$5.76	$14,261.66
36	28-Jun	$14,261.66	$0.00	$0.00	14.75%	$5.76	$14,267.42
37	29-Jun	$14,267.42	$0.00	$0.00	14.75%	$5.77	$14,273.19
38	30-Jun	$14,273.19	$0.00	$0.00	14.75%	$5.77	$14,278.96
39	1-Jul	$14,278.96	$4,000.00	$0.00	14.75%	$7.39	$18,286.34
40		$45,922.19	$114,000.00	$199,000.00	14.50%	$530.02	$43,197.35

G9 = B9 + C9 − D9 + F9 (copy this formula into rows 10 through 39)

A10 = A9 + 1 (this adds one day to the serial number for the previous date)

B10 = G9 (copy this formula into rows 11 through 39)

B40 = AVERAGE(B9:B39)

C40 = SUM(C9:C39)

D40 = SUM(D9:D39)

E40 = AVERAGE(E9:E39)

F40 = SUM(F9:F39)

G40 = AVERAGE(G9:G39)

At any time during the month, the totals in line 40 will show you cumulative figures to date. Note, however, that the model does not automatically check to see if the credit used exceeds the maximum indicated in C5. That's something you'll have to do.

Chapter 8

Managing Your Resources

Whether you're working in a service business, a wholesale or retail environment, or in manufacturing, your major concern must be how you'll manage your resources. Whether those resources are people, time, money, components, or shelf space, you need to have certain kinds of information at your fingertips.

Record-keeping within a manufacturing environment frequently involves keeping track of a large number of parts, suppliers, and factors contributing to predicted need. Since inventory resting on a shelf is money spent but not earning income, economical use of inventory requires careful, consistent monitoring in several areas, namely cost, volume, and quality of components and goods in various states of completion.

Further, though unsold inventory is considered an asset on a balance sheet, if it sits too long it's increasingly likely that it will have to be written off as a loss.

Excel's ability to use records from external files quickly and easily makes working with manufacturing applications a breeze. In this chapter you'll find an inventory model that tracks the cost of inventory.

Another common problem is controlling the quality of items bought from different suppliers. The quality-control model takes as an example the production of gourmet ice cream and fruit sherbets. The quality concerns of this ice cream maker are common to those involved in making many kinds of products.

Another example of resource management is tracking the amount of time employees spend on different projects, and vacation and sick time earned and used. The human resource management model shown can be used in conjunction with such files as payroll accounts, vacation schedules, employee files, and project billing.

Value of Inventory

This model tracks the number of items that move in and out of inventory in a month and computes the current value of the inventory remaining.

In this case, the business is a producer of gourmet ice cream and sherbet. Since it's summer, the business has sold an enormous volume and the future looks even brighter.

Figure 8-1. Inventory Count

	A	B	C	D	E	F	G
1	Inventory Count::		30-Apr-88				
2							
3			.	Last Mo.	This Mo.	Stock	Current
4	Unit #	Description	Size	Count	Used	Added	Count
5	12177	French Vanilla	pint	1203	1189	974	988
6	13019	Chocolate	quart	8912	8017	8500	9395
7	12177	Rum Raisin	pint	1217	934	1000	1283
8	12186	Strawberry	quart	7411	7501	7400	7310
9	13104	Vanilla	quart	9505	8993	8000	8512
10	13284	Chocolate Chocolate Mint	quart	9071	10273	8772	7570
11	13207	Coffee	quart	10224	7208	6000	9016
12	12381	Espresso	pint	1495	1302	1200	1393
13	13277	Pecan Praline	quart	8423	6213	8000	10210
14	13288	Fudge Brownie	quart	9323	9104	9008	9227
15	13202	Creamy Carmel & Nuts	quart	9012	8341	7560	8231
16	13022	Rocky Road	quart	7185	10235	7521	4471
17	12984	Almond Fudge	pint	1194	1057	1050	1187

Use the Format Column Width command to change column B's width to 25 characters. Enter the unit numbers, description, and size as text in columns A, B, and C. Enter the inventory in columns D, E, and F. In cell G5, enter the formula

$$=D5-E5+F5$$

and copy the formula down row G as many rows as you have product units.

The values in columns H, I, J, and K work with the inventory numbers to determine a current value of inventory remaining at the end of the month. Column H, Value of Previous Inventory, uses the values from column K for the previous month's worksheet. Use an appropriate external reference formula for each cell from row 5 on down, such as

$$=JUNINVCT.XLS!K5$$

which copies the contents of cell K5 on the June Inventory Count file to H5 on the current Inventory Count file. Copy the formula down the rest of column H.

Enter the dollar value of the cost to produce one item of the size shown for each product in column I. Then enter formulas in these cells:

J5	= F5*I5
K5	= H5 + J5

and copy the formulas down their respective columns.

While the unit number is entered simply as text, you can use it to indicate information about a product. For instance, in the example shown here, unit numbers starting with 12 indicate gourmet products, and unit numbers starting with 13 indicate products sold to chain stores for repackaging under store labels. These unit numbers can be sorted and processed with one or more of the text functions, such as FIND, LEFT, or VALUE.

Supplier Comparison

When you buy components to make a product, you depend on your suppliers to provide you with items of acceptable quality. If several of your suppliers consistently provide goods of poor quality, you can't afford to do business with them. But how do you know who's delivering acceptable ingredients and who isn't?

The model shown in Figure 8-2 provides one way of answering that question.

Jan & Berry's Gourmet Ice Creams need to monitor the quality of the fruits used in their ice cream and sherbet. The fruit comes from different suppliers, and is tracked through product numbers that relate to the suppliers' invoices.

Jan & Berry's maintains certain standards of acceptability regarding damaged and spoiled goods. These are stated as percentages at the top of the model.

The receiving dock does a spot-check of the fruit as it comes in, and reports how many fruits were hand-inspected. This number is reflected in column F. Items that were damaged or spoiled are also counted, and this value is reported in columns G and H.

The model computes the percent of damaged or spoiled goods for each supplier for the month, and compares this percentage against the standards at the top. If the percentage damaged or spoiled is less than the standard, the supplier is consid-

Figure 8-2. Supplier Comparison

	A	B	C	D	E
1	Jan & Berry's Gourmet Ice Creams				
2		Month of:	Jul-88		
3	Supplier Comparison				
4					
5	Supplier	Supplier Location	Product	Product #	# Delivered
6	Knight Enterprises	Gainesville, FL	Lemons	731283	300 gross
7	Almaden Valley Growers Coop	San Jose, CA	Peaches	1472	200 cases
8	Imperial Valley Farms, Inc.	Los Angeles, CA	Peaches	P18923	1000 cartons
9	Jensen Agricultural	Yakima, WA	Apples	MN16334	85 pallets
10	Almaden Valley Growers Coop	San Jose, CA	Apples	3314	110 cases
11	Jensen Agricultural	Yakima, WA	Pears	D171847	320 gross
12	Golden State Growers	San Diego, CA	Apples	67-G518	1800 dozen
13	Golden State Growers	San Diego, CA	Oranges	38-N817	1200 gross
14	Austine Agro-products	San Francisco, CA	Oranges	63482	1350 cartons
15	Gavello & Assoc.	Fremont, CA	Pears	5H7325	5200 dozen

ered acceptable. A higher percentage marks the supplier as not acceptable.

To set up the model, format

Column A	30 characters wide
Column B	17 characters wide
Column C	12 characters wide
Column D	12 characters wide
Column E	12 characters wide
Column F	10 characters wide
Column G	10 characters wide
Column H	10 characters wide
Column I	10 characters wide
Column J	10 characters wide
Column K	17 characters wide

You could use a two-row label for column K, like this:

Acceptable

Supplier

and reduce the column width; however, if you intend to use this worksheet as a database, the label must be in the single cell above the data, so a two-row label won't work. Enter the text into a single cell.

Enter the percentages you wish to use in G2 and G3. Enter data as text in columns A through E. Enter the numbers checked, damaged, and spoiled in columns F, G, and H. Enter formulas as follows:

	F	G	H	I	J	K
1	Acceptable Standards					
2	Damage	9.25%				
3	Spoilage	7.50%				
4						
5	#Checked	#Damaged	#Spoiled	%Damaged	%Spoiled	Acceptable Supplier
6	841	42	38	4.99%	4.52%	YES
7	1027	78	63	7.59%	6.13%	YES
8	1877	206	117	10.97%	6.23%	NO
9	653	47	33	7.20%	5.05%	YES
10	447	17	12	3.80%	2.68%	YES
11	502	36	21	7.17%	4.18%	YES
12	736	84	69	11.41%	9.38%	NO
13	91	7	6	7.69%	6.59%	YES
14	138	2	6	1.45%	4.35%	YES
15	348	28	17	8.05%	4.89%	YES

I6	= G6/F6
J6	= H6/F6
K6	= IF(AND(I6<$G$2,J6<$G$3),"YES","NO")

Copy all three formulas as far down their respective columns as necessary.

The formula in column K requires that a supplier meet both damage and spoilage criteria in order to be judged acceptable. If you wish to have a supplier meet either criterion (but not necessarily both) to be considered acceptable, substitute OR for AND in the formula.

If you wanted to modify the spreadsheet to take volume into account, you might change the way the value is entered in column E, # Delivered, substituting a number. By inserting a column, you could then use the number delivered and the number in column F to calculate the percent of items spot- checked.

The calculation can be accomplished with the macro shown in Figure 8-3. It uses the data you enter for the suppliers, and determines acceptability.

Figure 8-3. SUPPCOMP.XLM Macro

	A
1	Suppliercomparison
2	=SELECT("R5C9")
3	=CANCEL.COPY()
4	=FORMULA("%Damaged")
5	=SELECT("R5C10")
6	=FORMULA("%Spoiled")
7	=SELECT("R5C11")
8	=FORMULA("Acceptable
9	=SELECT("R6C9")
10	=FORMULA("=RC[-2]/RC
11	=SELECT("R6C10")
12	=FORMULA("=RC[-2]/RC
13	=SELECT("R6C11")
14	=FORMULA("=IF(AND(RC
15	=SELECT(,"r[+1]c[-3]
16	=IF(ACTIVE.CELL()=""
17	=SELECT("R[-1]C[+1]:
18	=COPY()
19	=SELECT("R[+1]C:RC[+
20	=PASTE()
21	=SELECT("R[+1]C[+2]"
22	=SELECT(,"r[+1]c[-3]
23	=IF(ACTIVE.CELL()=""
24	=SELECT("R6C9:R16C10
25	=FORMAT.NUMBER("0.00
26	=SELECT("R6C11:R15C1
27	=ALIGNMENT(3)
28	=RETURN()

This macro has to be run with the worksheet form of the Supplier Comparison on the screen. With the worksheet on your screen and the macro file open, choose the Macro Run command, and select SUPPCOMP.XLM as the macro to run.

Tracking Employee Hours

Most businesses allow their employees sick time and vacation time. Sometimes there's a formula for determining this, and sometimes there isn't. This model gives you one way of allocating sick time and vacation time as a function of hours worked.

The model can be copied from period to period, with the hours shown as cumulative hours. Then it's easy to create a small report for each employee to be distributed monthly or at some regular interval, showing accrued sick and vacation time.

Figure 8-4. Vacation Tracking Worksheet

Vacation Tracking Worksheet for: Jan 1 through Mar. 31

Paid Sick Leave: 1 hour per 20
Paid Vacation: 1 hour per 16

Name	Employee #	Hours Worked	Vacation Hours Earned	Sick Leave Hours Earned	Vacation Hours Used	Sick Leave Hours Used	Vacation Hours Remaining	Sick Leave Hours Remaining
Aldridge, Kent	507-11-9123	519	32.44	25.95	13.00	15.00	19.44	10.95
Brandoff, Bruce	547-12-3456	504	31.50	25.20	24.00	3.00	7.50	22.20
Cala, Charles	581-41-5422	606	37.88	30.30	0.00	8.00	37.88	22.30
Davidson, Rita	592-43-5732	252	15.75	12.60	8.00	3.75	7.75	8.85
Edwards, Scott	571-28-4835	493	30.81	24.65	15.00	8.00	15.81	16.65
Fitzgerald, Penny	566-88-3342	512	32.00	25.60	32.00	24.00	0.00	1.60
Gerrold, Dave	592-44-5391	578	36.13	28.90	0.00	3.00	36.13	25.90
Hardy, Pamela	581-43-3542	525	32.81	26.25	8.00	4.50	24.81	21.75
Ingrams, Roberta	595-45-5723	501	31.31	25.05 .	16.00	7.50	15.31	17.55
Jones, Angela	557-35-5387	677	42.31	33.85	40.00	16.00	2.31	17.85

To set up the worksheet, format column A as 15 characters wide, column B as 11 characters wide, and the remaining columns as 10 characters wide. Enter the labels shown in Figure 8-4. However, the criteria at the top are not entered as text. In B3 and B5, enter the numbers to use as a ratio for sick leave, and in C3 and C5, enter the numbers to use as a ratio for vacation time.

In columns A and B, enter the employee name and identifying number. In column C, enter the accumulated hours worked to date. In D8 and E8 enter the following formulas:

D8	$= C8/\$D\$4*\$B\$4$
E8	$= C8/\$D\$3*\$B\$3$

Copy these formulas down columns D and E as far as necessary.

In columns F and G, enter the cumulative number of hours of vacation time and sick leave used. In H8 and I8 enter the following formulas:

H8	$= D8 - F8$
I8	$= E8 - G8$

and copy the formulas down their respective columns.

Some companies use allocations like these to cover all forms of vacation, including national holidays and discretionary holidays such as the day after Thanksgiving, or Christmas week. Any holiday is thus considered vacation time used.

By varying the ratio used for sick leave and vacation time, you can control the amount of time off an employee can earn. The lower the ratio, the longer it will take an employee to earn a full day off.

Figure 8-5. TIMELOG.XLM Macro

	A
1	TimLogBB
2	=DISPLAY(FALSE,FALSE,TRUE,TRUE,0)
3	=SELECT("R1C1")
4	=FORMULA("Vacation Tracking Worksheet for:")
5	=COLUMN.WIDTH(20)
6	=SELECT("R1C2")
7	=COLUMN.WIDTH(11)
8	=SELECT("R1C3:R1C9")
9	=COLUMN.WIDTH(10)
10	=SELECT("R3C1")
11	=FORMULA("Paid Sick Leave:")
12	=SELECT("R4C1")
13	=FORMULA("Paid Vacation:")
14	=SELECT("R7C1")
15	=FORMULA("Name")
16	=SELECT("R7C2")
17	=FORMULA("Employee #")
18	=SELECT("R1C3")
19	=FORMULA("Jan 1 through Mar. 31")
20	=SELECT("R3C3")
21	=FORMULA("hour per")
22	=SELECT("R4C3")
23	=FORMULA("hour per")
24	=SELECT("R3C2")
25	=CANCEL.COPY()
26	=FORMULA("1")
27	=SELECT("R4C2")
28	=FORMULA("1")
29	=SELECT("R3C4:R4C4")
30	=ALIGNMENT(2)
31	=SELECT("R6C3")
32	=FORMULA("Hours")
33	=SELECT("R7C3")
34	=FORMULA("Worked")
35	=SELECT("R5C4")
36	=FORMULA("Vacation")
37	=SELECT("R6C4")
38	=FORMULA("Hours")
39	=SELECT("R7C4")
40	=FORMULA("Earned")
41	=SELECT("R5C5")
42	=FORMULA("Sick Leave")
43	=SELECT("R6C5")
44	=FORMULA("Hours")
45	=SELECT("R7C5")
46	=FORMULA("Earned")
47	=SELECT("R5C6")
48	=FORMULA("Vacation")
49	=SELECT("R6C6")
50	=FORMULA("Hours")
51	=SELECT("R7C6")
52	=FORMULA("Used")
53	=SELECT("R5C7")
54	=FORMULA("Sick Leave")
55	=SELECT("R6C7")
56	=FORMULA("Hours")
57	=SELECT("R7C7")
58	=FORMULA("Used")
59	=SELECT("R5C8")
60	=FORMULA("Vacation")
61	=SELECT("R6C8")
62	=FORMULA("Hours")
63	=SELECT("R7C8")

You can use different copies of the same model, each with different ratios, to cover different classifications of employees: hourly versus salaried; those with different levels of responsibility; those with different levels of seniority. Each copy, however, must be stored as a separate file.

This model can easily be turned into a macro, too. Type in

	A
64	=FORMULA("Remaining")
65	=SELECT("R5C9")
66	=FORMULA("Sick Leave")
67	=SELECT("R6C9")
68	=FORMULA("Hours")
69	=SELECT("R7C9")
70	=FORMULA("Remaining")
71	=SELECT("R7C9")
72	=SELECT("R5C3:R7C9","R7C9")
73	=ALIGNMENT(4)
74	=HLINE(5)
75	=SELECT("R7C1:R7C9","R7C9")
76	=BORDER(FALSE,FALSE,FALSE,FALSE,TRUE,FALSE)
77	=SELECT("R8C4")
78	=FORMULA("=RC[-1]/R4C4")
79	=SELECT("R8C5")
80	=FORMULA("=RC[-2]/R3C4*R3C2")
81	=SELECT("R8C8")
82	=FORMULA("=RC[-4]-RC[-2]")
83	=SELECT("R8C8")
84	=COPY()
85	=SELECT("R8C9")
86	=PASTE()
87	=SELECT("R3C4")
88	=FORMULA(INPUT("Please enter hours needed to earn an hour of paid sick leave",1,"Prompt"))
89	=SELECT("R4C4")
90	=FORMULA(INPUT("Please enter hours needed to earn an hour of paid vacation",1,"Prompt"))
91	=SELECT("R8C1")
92	=FORMULA(INPUT("Please enter employee name",2,"Prompt"))
93	=SELECT("R8C2")
94	=FORMULA(INPUT("Please enter employee number",2,"Prompt"))
95	=SELECT("R8C3")
96	=FORMULA(INPUT("Please enter hours worked",1,"Prompt"))
97	=SELECT("R8C6")
98	=FORMULA(INPUT("Please enter hours of vacation used",1,"Prompt"))
99	=SELECT("R8C7")
100	=FORMULA(INPUT("Please enter hours of sick leave used",1,"Prompt"))
101	=SELECT("R8C10")
102	=FORMULA(INPUT("If you wish to continue entering names type yes. If not enter no",2,"Prompt"))
103	=IF(ACTIVE.CELL()="yes",GOTO(A104),GOTO(A125))
104	=CLEAR(1)
105	=SELECT("R8C1:R8C9")
106	=INSERT(2)
107	=SELECT("R9C4")
108	=COPY()
109	=SELECT("R8C4")
110	=PASTE()
111	=SELECT("R9C5")
112	=COPY()
113	=SELECT("R8C5")
114	=PASTE()
115	=SELECT("R9C8")
116	=COPY()
117	=SELECT("R8C8")
118	=PASTE()
119	=SELECT("R9C9")
120	=COPY()
121	=SELECT("R8C9")
122	=PASTE()
123	=SELECT("R8C10")
124	=GOTO(A91)
125	=CLEAR(1)
126	=RETURN()

the instructions shown in Figure 8-5 to create a macro file. Then open the macro file and use the Window menu to use a blank worksheet as the currently active window.

The macro prompts for the ratios for sick time and vacation time, and then for employee name, employee number, hours worked, vacation time used, and sick time used. It then computes the hours earned of sick time and vacation time, and the amount remaining in each category.

If you want to enter another employee's records into this worksheet, it inserts a new row, and goes through the prompting and calculations again.

When you have a completed worksheet, you can very easily use the Data Sort command to sort the information. In Figure 8-6, we show you the results of employee data as it was entered.

Figure 8-6. TIMLGJAN.XLS

	A	B	C	D	E	F	G	H	I
1	Vacation Tracking Worksheet for:		Jan 1 through Mar. 31						
2									
3	Paid Sick Leave:		1 hour per	20					
4	Paid Vacation:		1 hour per	13					
5					Vacation	Sick Leave	Vacation	Sick Leave	Vacation	Sick Leave
6				Hours	Hours	Hours	Hours	Hours	Hours	Hours
7	Name	Employee #		Worked	Earned	Earned	Used	Used	Remaining	Remaining
8	Chu, Marilyn	555-11-1357		525	40.38	26.25	16	16	24.38	10.25
9	Ito, Kenzo	555-10-2634		560	43.08	28.00	16	8	27.08	20.00
10	Figuero, Isabel	555-11-1423		520	40.00	26.00	16	40	24.00	-14.00
11	Christiansen, Dan	555-111-1333		510	39.23	25.50	24	8	15.23	17.50
12	Adams, John	555-12-1345		545	41.92	27.25	16	16	25.92	11.25
13	Nickels, Timothy	555-12-1210		520	40.00	26.00	16	24	24.00	2.00

By selecting the data from A8:I20 (in the example above) and choosing the Data Set Database command, you can then decide how to sort our data. If you wanted an alphabetical list of employees, you could use the Data Sort command. Leave the default options as they were but specify $A$8 as the cell reference for the first sort key. You'd get the listing shown in Figure 8-7.

Figure 8-7. Employee Records Sorted by Name

	A	B	C	D	E	F	G	H	I
1	Vacation Tracking Worksheet for:		Jan 1 through Mar. 31						
2									
3	Paid Sick Leave:		1 hour per	20					
4	Paid Vacation:		1 hour per	13					
5					Vacation	Sick Leave	Vacation	Sick Leave	Vacation	Sick Leave
6				Hours	Hours	Hours	Hours	Hours	Hours	Hours
7	Name	Employee #		Worked	Earned	Earned	Used	Used	Remaining	Remaining
8	Adams, John	555-12-1345		545	41.92	27.25	16	16	25.92	11.25
9	Christiansen, Dan	555-111-1333		510	39.23	25.50	24	8	15.23	17.50
10	Chu, Marilyn	555-11-1357		525	40.38	26.25	16	16	24.38	10.25
11	Figuero, Isabel	555-11-1423		520	40.00	26.00	16	40	24.00	-14.00
12	Ito, Kenzo	555-10-2634		560	43.08	28.00	16	8	27.08	20.00
13	Nickels, Timothy	555-12-1210		520	40.00	26.00	16	24	24.00	2.00

If you wanted the list sorted by the number of vacation hours remaining, select the same range as the database for the Data Set Database command. Then, with the Data Sort command, specify $H$8 as the first sort key, and turn on the Descending button for the first key. You would be presented with the report in Figure 8-8.

Figure 8-8. Employee Records Sorted by Vacation Hours Remaining

	A	B	C	D	E	F	G	H	I
1	Vacation Tracking Worksheet for:		Jan 1 through Mar. 31						
2									
3	Paid Sick Leave:		1 hour per	20					
4	Paid Vacation:		1 hour per	13					
5					Vacation	Sick Leave	Vacation	Sick Leave	Vacation	Sick Leave
6			Hours	Hours	Hours	Hours	Hours	Hours	Hours
7	Name	Employee #	Worked	Earned	Earned	Used	Used	Remaining	Remaining
8	Ito, Kenzo	555-10-2634	560	43.08	28.00	16	8	27.08	20.00
9	Adams, John	555-12-1345	545	41.92	27.25	16	16	25.92	11.25
10	Chu, Marilyn	555-11-1357	525	40.38	26.25	16	16	24.38	10.25
11	Figuero, Isabel	555-11-1423	520	40.00	26.00	16	40	24.00	-14.00
12	Nickels, Timothy	555-12-1210	520	40.00	26.00	16	24	24.00	2.00
13	Christiansen, Dan	555-111-1333	510	39.23	25.50	24	8	15.23	17.50

Chapter 9

Investment Solutions

The power of a spreadsheet's ability to handle speculative "what if?" recalculations is most obvious when you're dealing with the changing scenarios one might use in judging whether to invest in a project or business entity.

Whether you're making a long-term investment in real estate, considering playing the markets, or making a direct investment in a small company, putting your assumptions down in a spreadsheet helps you analyze how an investment could turn out.

Real Estate Projections

Real estate lends itself well to spreadsheet analysis. By varying interest rates by a tenth of a point, you can immediately see the effect in changed payments, and in some cases also in grossly altered overall profits.

Several examples of spreadsheet analysis in real estate have been included in this section. The first, a table that looks at factors involved in negotiating for a loan with which to buy a house, is shown in Figure 9-1.

In the top part of the model the purchase price and the maximum down payment were specified. The model calculates the loan balance, and tells you what percent of the price the loan will be.

The three tables in boxes (boxes are indicated by slightly heavier borders around regions A7:B16, D7:E16, and G6:H16) show the result of your estimates, with varying assumptions about loan terms, interest rates, and mortgage amounts.

Once the model is set up, enter an interest rate in B7, and the model automatically calculates monthly payments for the amount shown above as Loan Balance, based on varying number of years for the term. The variation was set at five years; you could change the variation to one year and use the same formulas to refine the calculation of monthly payments.

Figure 9-1. Loan Tables

	A	B	C	D	E	F	G	H
1	Purchase Price:	$256,000.00						
2	Max. Down Pmt.:	$52,500.00						
3	Loan Balance:	$203,500.00						
4								
5	Your loan would be	79.49%	percent of the purchase price					
6							Interest Rate:	12.75%
7	Interest Rate:	14.25%		Loan Duration	20		Loan Duration:	30
8								
9	Period in years	Monthly payments		Interest Rate	Monthly payments		Mortgage amount	Monthly payments
10								
11	5	$4,761.51		12.50%	$2,312.05		$183,500.00	$1,994.08
12	10	$3,190.33		13.00%	$2,384.16		$193,500.00	$2,102.75
13	15	$2,744.36		13.50%	$2,457.01		$202,500.00	$2,200.55
14	20	$2,567.60		14.00%	$2,530.56		$203,500.00	$2,211.42
15	25	$2,488.66		14.50%	$2,604.80		$208,500.00	$2,265.76
16	30	$2,451.54		15.00%	$2,679.67		$213,500.00	$2,320.09

The payments are calculated with the PMT function. The formula used below assumes monthly payments, so the interest rate is divided by 12 to produce a monthly interest rate, and the term is multiplied by 12 to produce the number of monthly payments. If you wish to use some other frequency of payments, adjust the formula appropriately. (If you want quarterly payments, for instance, divide the interest rate by four and multiply the term by four.)

The middle table (D7:E16) illustrates what happens when you fix a loan duration for the same loan amount with differing interest rates. Interest rates are shown with a 0.5 percent variation. You could use a smaller variation to see more precisely calculated monthly payments. This table also uses the PMT function to produce the payment figures.

The rightmost table (G6:H16) shows the effect of varying the down payment while holding the interest rate and loan term constant, resulting in different loan amounts. The amounts listed under Mortgage amount are calculated from the loan amount shown in B3, with the following variations (see Figure 9-2):

G11	−20000
G12	−10000
G13	−1000
G14	=B3
G15	+5000
G16	+10000

This table lets you see what would happen to your monthly payment if, for instance, you could borrow money from relatives to increase the amount of the down payment. Again, the calculation of monthly payments uses the PMT function.

To set up the model as shown, use the Format Column Width command to widen the columns as follows:

Column A	17 characters wide
Column B	16 characters wide
Column C	(default value)
Column D	12 characters wide
Column E	16 characters wide
Column F	15 characters wide
Column G	15 characters wide
Column H	16 characters wide

Figure 9-2. The Formulas that Produced Figure 9-1

	A	B	C	D
1	Purchase Price:	256000		
2	Max. Down Pmt.::	52500		
3	Loan Balance:	=B1-B2		
4			percent of the purch	
5	Your loan would be	=B3/B1		
6				Loan Duration
7	Interest Rate:	0.1425		
8				Interest Rate
9	Period in years	Monthly payments		
10	5	=-PMT($B$7/12,A11*12,$B$3)		0.125
11	10	=-PMT($B$7/12,A12*12,$B$3)		0.13
12	15	=-PMT($B$7/12,A13*12,$B$3)		0.135
13	20	=-PMT($B$7/12,A14*12,$B$3)		0.14
14	25	=-PMT($B$7/12,A15*12,$B$3)		0.145
15	30	=-PMT($B$7/12,A16*12,$B$3)		0.15

	E	F	G	H
1				
2				
3				
4				
5				
6			Interest Rate:	0.1275
7	20		Loan Duration:	30
8				
9	Monthly payments		Mortgage amount	Monthly payments
10				
11	=-PMT(D11/12,$E$7*12,$B$3)		=G14-20000	=-PMT($H$6/12,$H$7*12,G11)
12	=-PMT(D12/12,$E$7*12,$B$3)		=G14-10000	=-PMT($H$6/12,$H$7*12,G12)
13	=-PMT(D13/12,$E$7*12,$B$3)		=G14-1000	=-PMT($H$6/12,$H$7*12,G13)
14	=-PMT(D14/12,$E$7*12,$B$3)		=B3	=-PMT($H$6/12,$H$7*12,G14)
15	=-PMT(D15/12,$E$7*12,$B$3)		=G14+5000	=-PMT($H$6/12,$H$7*12,G15)
16	=-PMT(D16/12,$E$7*12,$B$3)		=G14+10000	=-PMT($H$6/12,$H$7*12,G16)

Next, set up labels as follows:

A1	Purchase Price:
B1	256000 (or use any number as the purchase price)
A2	Max. Down Pmt.:
B2	52500 (or use any number as the down payment)
A3	Loan Balance:
A5	Your loan would be
C5	percent of the purchase price
G6	Interest Rate
H6	0.1275 (or any other target interest rate)
A7	Interest Rate:
B7	14.25 (or any other target interest rate)
D7	Loan Duration
E7	20 (or any other number as the loan term in years)
G7	Loan Duration
H7	30 (or any other number as the loan term in years)
A9	Period in years
B9	Monthly payments
D9	Interest Rate
E9	Monthly payments
G9	Mortgage amount
H9	Monthly payments

Now enter the formulas:

B3	$= B1 - B2$
B5	$= B3/B1$
A11	$= 5$ (enter any range of years for A11 through A16)
A12	$= 10$
A13	$= 15$
A14	$= 20$
A15	$= 25$
A16	$= 30$
B11	$= PMT(\$B\$7/12,A11*12,\$B\$3)$ (copy this formula down from B12 through B16)
D11	$= 0.125$ (enter any range of percentages for D11 through D16; remember to use the Format Number command and the 0.00% option)
D12	$= 0.13$
D13	$= 0.135$
D14	$= 0.14$

D15	= 0.145
D16	= 0.15
E11	= PMT(D11/12,$E$7/12,$B$3) (copy this formula down from E12 to E16)
G11	= G14 − 20000
G12	= G14 − 10000 (these formulas set up a range of loan amounts to let you see the results of more or less amounts of a down payment; they use the loan balance in B3 as a reference)
G13	= G14 − 1000
G14	= B3
G15	= G14 + 5000
G16	= G14 + 10000
H11	= PMT($H$6/12,$H$7*12/G11) (copy this formula down from H12 to H16)

A Different Real Estate Application

Another application of spreadsheet capabilities is shown in the example below. Consider the following scenario:

You and some friends have an opportunity to purchase an undeveloped piece of land on Waterside Way in an area that's growing rapidly. The lot is underpriced for the market at $115,000.

It has one major problem: It's always too wet to pass a percolation test (the geological review required to determine whether the lot can support a septic system). After looking closely at the topography and noticing a number of thriving willows, you determine that the wetness is probably coming from several springs located on the lot uphill from the one you're considering.

One of your friends is a civil engineer. He knows of a technique called a "French drain" which would intercept the water and divert it through graded channels along the upper border and down the sides of the lot, where it would be directed into drainage gutters next to the road at the bottom of the lot.

He estimates that the engineering, plans, grading, and permits would run around $7500. If all goes well, the work could be completed in four months.

Your realtor says the lot would sell immediately once it passes the percolation test.

Would this lot be a good investment? A spreadsheet can help you look at the possibilities (Figure 9-3).

Figure 9-3. Waterside Way, Round 1

	A	B	C	D	E	F	G
1	PROJECTIONS			Property:	Unimproved lot,	Waterside Way	
2							
3	Purchase price:		115000		Market value, impr.		30000
4	Appreciation rate/yr:		17.50%		Sale price		153385
5	Loan amt. (% of price)		75.00%				
6	Loan terms: int. rate:		12.50%		Term:	10	years
7							
8			February	March	April	May	June
9	Down payment		28750				
10	Closing costs		1725				2301
11	Permits			865			135
12	Engineering				2500		545
13	Grading					2000	
14	Plans				1500		
15	Loan payments		1262	1262	1262	1262	1262
16	Commissions						9203
17	Totals		31737	2127	5262	3262	13446
18							
19	Profit	11299		%profit on investmen		20.24%	

The assumptions are listed in the upper part of the spread-sheet: the going rate of appreciation for lots in that area (17.5 percent), the percent of the purchase price you could borrow, the interest rate and term for that loan, and the cost of improvements.

Then there's an estimate of what it would cost to install the French drain, and to hold the property until it could be resold approximately five months later. The model calculates the profit and the percent profit on your investment over the life of the project.

To set up the model, enter labels as indicated. (Widen column A to 10 characters. The rest can use the default width.)

A1	PROJECTIONS
D1	Property: Unimproved lot, Waterside Way
A3	Purchase price:
E3	Market value, impr.
A4	Appreciation rate/yr:
E4	Sales price
A5	Loan amt. (% of price)
A6	Loan terms: int. rate:
E6	Term:
G6	years
C8	February
D8	March

E8	April
F8	May
G8	June
A9	Down payment
A10	Closing costs
A11	Permits
A12	Engineering
A13	Grading
A14	Plans
A15	Loan payments
A16	Commissions
A17	Totals
A19	Profit
C19	% profit on investment

Use the Format Number command, 0 option to format the following cells and ranges:

C3
G3:G4
E6
C9:G17
B19

Use the Format Number command, 0.00% option to format the following cells:

C4:C6
F19

Enter formulas as follows:

G4	$= C3 + (C4*(COUNTA(C8:Z8)/12)*C3) + G3$ (the COUNTA function counts the number of months (or other labels) you've used in row 8, allowing you to expand the model to column Z if necessary)
C9	$= C3 - (C5*C3)$
C10	$= 0.015*C3$ (this assumes 1.5 percent of the sales price was closing costs paid by the buyer)
G10	$= 0.015*G4$
C15	$= -PMT(\$C\$6/12,\$F\$6*12,\$C\$3-\$C\$9)$ (using the calculated loan amount, and specified interest rate and term, this calculates the monthly payment; copy this formula into D15 through G15)

G16	=0.06*G4 (the commission is six percent of the sale price)
C17	=SUM(C9:C16) (copy this formula into D17 through G17)
B19	=G4−(C3−C9+SUM(C17:G17))
F19	=B19/SUM(C17:G17)

For the model shown in Figure 9-3, we entered data as follows:

C3	115000
G3	30000
C4	0.175
C5	0.75
C6	0.125
F6	10
D11	865
F11	135
E12	2500
G12	545
F13	2000
E14	1500

To add some finishing touches, we changed the fonts for the labels in row 8 to Bold, and used the Format Border command to add underlines in B16:G16.

But what if things didn't go as planned, and you had to hold onto the lot for three more months before you could sell it? What would your profit picture look like then?

Given the existing model, it's a simple matter to extend it several columns to the right, either move or copy some of the formulas and figures, and change a couple of the formulas.

To see the new projections, add new month labels to row 8, columns H, I, and J. Move the closing costs and commission figures from their respective locations in column G to the same rows in column J. Copy the =SUM formula into H17 through J17. With these changes, the model should now look like Figure 9-4.

Figure 9-4. Extended Real Estate Projection

	A	B	C	D	E	F	G	H	I	J
1	PROJECTIONS				Property: Unimproved lot, Waterside Way					
2										
3	Purchase price:		115000		Market value, impr.		30000			
4	Appreciation rate/yr:		17.50%		Sale price		158417			
5	Loan amt. (% of price)		75.00%							
6	Loan terms: int. rate:		12.50%		Term:		10	years		
7										
8			February	March	April	May	June	July	August	Sept.
9	Down payment		28750							
10	Closing costs		1725							2376
11	Permits			865			135			
12	Engineering				2500		545			
13	Grading					2000				
14	Plans				1500					
15	Loan payments		1262	1262	1262	1262	1262	1262	1262	1262
16	Commissions									9505
17	Totals		31737	2127	5262	3262	17611	15669	14406	13144
18										
19	Profit	12165			%profit on investmen	20.28%				

But wait! The calculation of the sale price (in G4) uses the formula

$$= C3 + ((C4*COUNTA(C8:Z8)/12)*C3) + G3$$

It uses the initial purchase price (C3), computes the product of the appreciation rate (C4) times the fractional portion of a year the lot was held (COUNTA(C8:Z8)/12), multiplies that by the purchase price (C3), and then adds the market value of the improvements (G3).

The problem with that reasoning is that, once the improvements were made, they appreciated at the going rate, too. That means in July, the lot's appreciation was based on a value of $149,025. This means we should redo the formula for G4 to reflect the new improvements when they happened. That formula is:

$$= C3 + ((C4*COUNTA(C8:G8)/12)*C3) + G3 + ((C3 + G3)*(C4* COUNTA(H8:Z8)/12))$$

With this formula changed, the spreadsheet now looks like Figure 9-5.

Figure 9-5. Corrected Real Estate Projections

	A	B	C	D	E	F	G	H	I	J
1	PROJECTIONS			Property: Unimproved lot, Waterside Way						
2										
3	Purchase price:		115000		Market value, impr.		30000			
4	Appreciation rate/yr:		17.50%		Sale price		159729			
5	Loan amt. (% of price)		75.00%							
6	Loan terms: int. rate:		12.50%		Term:		10 years			
7										
8			February	March	April	May	June	July	August	Sept.
9	Down payment		28750							
10	Closing costs		1725							2396
11	Permits			865			135			
12	Engineering				2500		545			
13	Grading					2000				
14	Plans				1500					
15	Loan payments		1262	1262	1262	1262	1262	1262	1262	1262
16	Commissions									9584
17	Totals		31737	2127	5262	3262	17710	15767	14505	13242
18										
19	Profit	13380		%profit on investmen		22.26%				

This is the sort of analysis that helps you get past the seat-of-the-pants judgment call that sometimes leads to a bad investment. You could enter all this information in an hour or two, with your investor friends looking over your shoulder to fine-tune your assumptions.

Stock and Bond Portfolio

If you believe in spreading your risks among several types of investments, chances are good that you've invested in some stocks and/or bonds. If your money is invested in several places, how do you keep track?

This model, which tracks the performance of both stocks and bonds, makes use of several *Excel* functions to automatically compute your current position. For the sake of convenience, we've included both the stock and bond portfolios on the same model.

Stock portfolio. This model is concerned with stocks. When you buy a stock, you enter date of purchase and the number of shares and price per share in the model. It computes the total cost. If any dividends are issued while you're holding the shares, enter them in column I.

When you run the model, enter the current price per share. It uses the =NOW( ) function to compute the total dividends and yield on an annual basis, along with the gains or losses to date. It also computes the net portfolio value for the stocks shown, along with a net gain or loss.

To use the model, enter labels and data as shown in Figure 9-6, columns *A*, *B*, *C*, and *D*, rows 1–12 and column labels.

Change the column widths as follows:

Column A 25 characters
Column B 15 characters
Column C 10 characters
Column D 12 characters
Column E 13 characters
Column F 13 characters
Column G 12 characters
Column H 10 characters
Column I   10 characters
Column J   10 characters
Column K 12 characters

Format C2:C12 with the Format Number command, m/d/yy option. Format K5:K14 with the 0.00% option. Format D5:J14 and B16:B17 with the $#,##0.00 option.

Enter the labels as shown in Figure 9-6 above, and draw a line under the column headings with the Format Border command, Bottom option.

Enter formulas as follows:

C2	=NOW( )
E5	=B5*D5 (copy this formula into E6 through E12)
G5	=B5*F5 (copy this formula into G6 through G12)
H5	=G5−E5 (copy this formula into H6 through H12)
J5	=B5*I5 (copy this formula into J6 through J12)
K5	=((J5+H5)/((NOW( )−C5)365.25))/E5 (copy this formula into K6 through K12)
B14	=SUM(B5:B12) (copy this formula into E14, G14, H14, and J14)
K14	=J14/G14
B16	=H14+J14
B17	=G14

To run the model, enter the name of the stock, the number of shares, and the purchase price when you buy the stock. As dividends are paid, enter the dividend amount. On the day you check your stocks, simply enter the current price. The model calculates all the rest.

If you want to add more stocks, simply insert new rows before row 12. If you want the model to show cumulative activity, add two columns with the headings Sale Date and Sale Price.

Figure 9-6. Stock Portfolio

	A	B	C	D	E
1	Stock Portfoilo				
2		Calculated on:	8/25/88		
3	Name of	No. of	Purchase	Purchase	
4	Stock	Shares	Date	Price	Cost
5	Altos Computer Systems	1300	6/15/88	$9.00	$11,700.00
6	Apple Computer	1100	10/19/87	$20.50	$22,550.00
7	Corvus Systems	575	10/19/87	$12.75	$7,331.25
8	Eagle Computer	325	10/19/87	$9.00	$2,925.00
9	Hewlett-Packard	200	3/7/85	$40.50	$8,100.00
10	Plantronics	250	8/22/86	$22.38	$5,595.00
11	Seagate Technology	2150	10/20/87	$12.50	$26,875.00
12	Televideo Systems	600	11/2/87	$21.50	$12,900.00
13					
14	total	6,500			$97,976.25
15					
16	Net Gain/Loss:	$12,615.09			
17	Net Stock Portfolio Value:	$106,014.84			
18					
19					

Bond Portfolio. The bond portion of the model is a bit more complex. The column headings are used as follows:

Purchase Price	The amount of money actually paid for the bond at the time of purchase.
Par Value	The listed base value of the bond; equivalent to how much the bond was worth when it was issued.
Coupon Rate	The interest rate per annum listed on the bond.
Period of Bond (in years.)	The amount of time between the issue date of the bond and its date of maturity.
Total Yield	The total amount the bond will be worth when it matures, including money earned through interest and the original money invested in the bond.
Return on Investment	The yield on the bond minus the money invested to purchase the bond. If the bond was acquired when it was originally released, the return on investment will be the amount of interest income earned.
Purchase Date	The date you purchased the bond.
Issue Date	The date the bond was originally issued.
Current Value	The interest income earned on the bond from date of original issue to the current date.

268

	F	G	H	I	J	K
1						
2						
3	Current	Current	Gains/	Div./	Total	Yield
4	Price	Value	Losses	Share	Dividend	Percent
5	$9.38	$12,187.50	$487.50	$0.75	$975.00	63.76%
6	$42.75	$47,025.00	$24,475.00	$2.00	$2,200.00	138.66%
7	$0.16	$89.84	($7,241.41)	$0.00	$0.00	-115.78%
8	$12.25	$3,981.25	$1,056.25	$0.02	$6.50	42.59%
9	$50.25	$10,050.00	$1,950.00	$1.75	$350.00	8.18%
10	$19.75	$4,937.50	($657.50)	$1.00	$250.00	-3.62%
11	$12.63	$27,143.75	$268.75	$0.30	$645.00	4.00%
12	$1.00	$600.00	($12,300.00)	$0.25	$150.00	-115.59%
13						
14		$106,014.84	$8,038.59		$4,576.50	4.32%
15						
16						
17						
18						
19						

To enter the model, type the labels as shown in Figure 9-7.

Format B24:C33, F24:G33, and J24:J33 with the Format Number command, $#,##0.00 option. Format D24:D32 with the 0.00% option. Format E24:E32 with the 0 option. Format C20 and H24:I32 with the m/d/yy option.

Enter formulas as follows:

C20   =NOW( )

F24   =C24*((1+D24)^E24)+C24 (copy this formula to F25 through F32)

G24   =F24−B24 (copy this formula to G25 through G32)

J24   =C24*((1+D24)^((NOW( )−I24)/365.25)) (copy this formula to J25 through J32)

B33   =SUM(B24:B31) (copy this formula to C33, F33, G33 and J33)

When you purchase a bond, enter the name, purchase price, par value, coupon rate (enter as a decimal: for instance, 0.085), period, purchase date, and issue date. Because of the presence of the =NOW( ) function, every time you open the file, the figures in the Current Value column will be automatically updated.

Internal Rate of Return

The internal rate of return is a calculation performed in a situation where you have an initial investment and a series of steady cash flows over a period of time. The rate of return calculated

Figure 9-7. Bond Portfolio

	A	B	C	D	E
20	Bond Portfolio	Calculated on:	8/25/88		
21					
22	Name of	Purchase	Par	Coupon	Period of Bond
23	Bond	Price	Value	Rate	(in years)
24	Altos Computer Systems	$4,000.00	$4,000.00	8.50%	15
25	Apple Computer	$1,100.00	$1,250.00	7.75%	20
26	Corvus Systems	$600.00	$700.00	6.50%	15
27	Eagle Computer	$750.00	$800.00	7.00%	10
28	Hewlett-Packard	$1,000.00	$1,000.00	8.00%	25
29	Plantronics	$1,250.00	$1,500.00	9.00%	15
30	Seagate Technology	$2,150.00	$2,250.00	8.75%	15
31	Televideo Systems	$2,000.00	$2,000.00	9.25%	20
32					
33	total	$12,850.00	$13,500.00		

finds the discount rate that equates the present value of future cash flows to the cost of an investment.

The IRR function is one of *Excel*'s built-in functions. The general form of it is:

= IRR(*values,guess*)

where *guess* is an approximation of what the IRR will be, and *values* stands for either the actual values or the cell references where the cash flow values can be found.

The IRR function is one of the iterative calculation functions, which means it tries a series of attempts to narrow down the possible return rates until it reaches a satisfactory degree of accuracy, or has completed enough guesses that it gives up. Hence it's important that you specify in *guess* a value likely to be close to the calculated rate of return.

The values specified in *values* don't have to be the same, but they do have to be in a single range.

In the example shown here, the scenario is an investment in a small apartment building, with annual income and expense statements that take into consideration an approximation of tax payments. The owners want to know what the internal rate of return will be after they've held it for five years, including the down payment but not including any proceeds from a sale at the end of the holding period.

	F	G	H	I	J
20					
21					
22	Total	Return on	Purchase	Issue	Current
23	Yield	Investment	Date	Date	Value
24	$17,598.97	$13,598.97	7/20/88	7/20/88	$4,032.85
25	$6,812.32	$5,712.32	6/15/88	9/12/85	$1,558.26
26	$2,500.29	$1,900.29	12/30/86	5/7/80	$1,180.80
27	$2,373.72	$1,623.72	8/4/85	9/3/83	$1,120.46
28	$7,848.48	$6,848.48	7/3/83	9/18/75	$2,706.68
29	$6,963.72	$5,713.72	3/4/82	4/30/77	$3,979.79
30	$10,168.11	$8,018.11	1/17/82	7/14/73	$7,996.44
31	$13,734.35	$11,734.35	3/27/81	5/2/70	$10,111.85
32					
33	$67,999.95	$55,149.95			$32,687.13

To set up the model, widen column A to 20 characters, and enter the labels as shown. Enter the column labels in row 6. Enter formulas as follows:

E3	= IRR(B20:F20,E2)
B9	= B7 − B8 (copy this formula into C9 through F9)
B13	= B9 − B11 − B12 (copy this formula into C13 through F13)
B15	= B9 (copy this formula into C15 through F15)
B17	= B15 − B16 (copy this formula into C17 through F17)
B18	= 0.37*B17 (copy this formula into C18 through F18) (an approximate income tax rate of 37 percent was used; you may wish to use some other rate)
B19	= B17 − B18 (copy this formula into C19 though F19)
B20	= B19 − B4 (copy this formula into C20 through F20)

Figure 9-8. Internal Rate of Return

	A	B	C	D	E	F
1	Internal Rate of Return					
2				Guess:	0.2	
3				Calculated IRR:	0.24514161	
4	Down Payment:	35000				
5						
6		Year 1	Year 2	Year 3	Year 4	Year 5
7	Gross Income	32500	35150	37202	38812	40126
8	Operating Expenses	7500	7850	8016	8229	8432
9	Net Op. Income	25000	27300	29186	30583	31694
10						
11	Interest	11024	10693	10337	10198	9914
12	Depreciation	3216	3216	3216	3216	3216
13	Taxable Income	10760	13391	15633	17169	18564
14						
15	Net Op. Income	25000	27300	29186	30583	31694
16	Mortgage Pmts.	12400	12400	12400	12400	12400
17	Cash Flow Bef. Taxes	12600	14900	16786	18183	19294
18	Income Taxes	3981.2	4954.67	5784.21	6352.53	6868.68
19	Cash Flow Aft. Taxes	8618.8	9945.33	11001.79	11830.47	12425.32
20	Adjusted Cash Flow	-26381.2	9945.33	11001.79	11830.47	12425.32

Enter data for Guess, Down Payment, Gross Income, Operating Expenses, Interest, Depreciation, and Mortgage Payments. Use our figures, or others if you want to experiment.

Notice that the formula in row 20 subtracts the down payment. Because the formula is copied into other locations, any values in those columns in row 4 will be taken into consideration. This means, for instance, that if the owners want to make some capital improvements in the building during the holding period, the cost of the improvements can easily be included in the calculation simply by including the number in the appropriate location in row 4.

Both guess and the computed internal rate of return are expressed as decimal fractions. In the example above, for instance, that means the internal rate of return is actually 24.5142 percent.

Comparison of Common Business Ratios

The business ratios shown in this model are used commonly by analysts, stockbrokers, and bankers to determine how well a company is doing. They work with data taken from income statements and balance sheets, and are usually used to measure a company's financial health.

The ratios are computed as follows:

$$\text{Quick Ratio} = \frac{(\text{Current Assets} - \text{Inventory})}{\text{Current Liabilities}}$$

$$\text{Current Ratio} = \frac{\text{Current Assets}}{\text{Current Liabilities}}$$

$$\text{Current Liabilities as Percent of Net Worth} = \frac{\text{Current Liabilities}}{\text{Net Worth}}$$

$$\text{Current Liabilities as Percent of Inventory} = \frac{\text{Current Liabilities}}{\text{Inventory}}$$

$$\text{Total Liabilities as Percent of Net Worth} = \frac{\text{Total Liabilities}}{\text{Net Worth}}$$

$$\text{Fixed Assets Turnover} = \frac{\text{Sales}}{\text{Net Fixed Assets}}$$

$$\text{Total Assets Turnover} = \frac{\text{Sales}}{\text{Total Assets}}$$

$$\text{Inventory Turnover} = \frac{\text{Sales}}{\text{Inventory}}$$

$$\text{Return on Sales} = \frac{\text{Net Income}}{\text{Sales}}$$

$$\text{Return on Total Assets} = \frac{\text{Net Income}}{\text{Total Assets}}$$

$$\text{Return on Net Worth} = \frac{\text{Net Income}}{\text{Net Worth}}$$

$$\text{Debt to Total Assets} = \frac{\text{Total Debt}}{\text{Total Assets}}$$

$$\text{Times Interest Earned} = \frac{\text{Net Income Before Taxes}}{\text{Interest}}$$

$$\text{Price/Earnings Ratio} = \frac{\text{Stock Price}}{\text{Earnings per Share}}$$

The data shown in the model below is for an income statement and balance sheet. To make things clearer, the cells are named after the variables used in the formulas. For instance, the cell containing the Sales figure is called SALES and the cell containing the Net Income calculation is called NET_INCOME. Thus the formula for calculating Total Sales in cell C6 is expressed thus:

=SALES – COST_OF_GOODS

Note that an underline can be used to join together into one word variable names made up of several words.

The ratios are all the bottom, starting in A33. Note that in E35:I36 we've stated the current market value of the shares, so they can be used to compute the Price/Earnings ratio on rows 49 and 50. To set up the model, use the following column widths:

Column A	15
Column B	default value
Column C	12
Column D	4
Column E	20
Column F	default
Column H	12

Type the labels as shown in columns A and E. In G27:G28 and G35:G36 type the text *shares @*, and in I27:I28 and I35:I36 type the text per share.

Format C5:C21, G5:G26, F27:F28, G29:G32, and F35:F36 with the Format Number command, #,##0 option. Format H27:H28 and H35:H36 with the $#,##0.00 option. Format C36:C39 with the #,##0.00% option. Format F34 and B49:B50 with the m/d/yy option.

Figure 9-9. Business Ratio Model

	A	B	C	D	E	F	G	H	I
1	INCOME STATEMENT				BALANCE SHEET				
2	1987-88				1987-88				
3									
4	Income				Assets				
5	Sales		1,250,428		Cash		35,112		
6	Cost of goods sold		467,886		Accounts Receivable		453,224		
7	Net Sales		782,542		Inventory		97,231		
8					Prepaid Expenses		15,223		
9	Expenses				Total Current Assets		600,790		
10	Operating Expenses								
11	Marketing/Sales		232,523		Fixed Assets		53,119		
12	Research & Develop.		156,944		less Depreciation		23,155		
13	Administration		80,223		Good Will		11,533		
14	Facility		48,112		Other Assets		32,554		
15	Other Op. Expenses		37,325		Total Assets		721,151		
16	Total Op. Expenses		555,127						
17	Depreciation		23,155		Liabilities				
18	Interest expense		33,700		Accounts Payable		156,344		
19	Net Inc. Before Taxes		170,560		Notes Payable		65,000		
20	Taxes @	23.00%	39,229		Other Current Liabilities		33,476		
21	Net Inc. After Taxes		131,331		Total Current Liabilities		254,820		
22					Long-term Debt		220,000		
23					Total Liabilities		474,820		
24									
25					Shareholders' Equity				
26					Common Stock		115,000		
27					Class A (book)	2,000	shares @	$20.00	per share
28					Class B (book)	5,000	shares @	$15.00	per share
29					Retained Earnings		131,331		
30					Total Shareholders' Equity		246,331		
31									
32					Total Liabilities + Equity		721,151		
33	Quick Ratio		1.98						
34	Current Ratio		2.36		Market Value, shares	8/29/88			
35	Current Liabilities as				Class A	2,000	shares @	$63.50	per share
36	% of Net Worth		103.45%		Class B	5,000	shares @	$61.25	per share
37	% of Inventory		262.08%						
38	Total Liabilities as								
39	% of Net Worth		192.76%						
40	Fixed Assets Turnover		14.73						
41	Total Assets Turnover		1.09						
42	Inventory Turnover		8.05						
43	Return on Sales		0.17						
44	Return on Total Assets		0.18						
45	Return on Net Worth		0.53						
46	Debt to Total Assets		0.40						
47	Times Interest Earned		0.53						
48	Price/Earnings Ratio								
49	Class A	8/29/88	3.38						
50	Class B	8/29/88	3.26						

Use the Format Border command, Bottom option to create underlines in C6, G8, G14, C15, C18, C20, G20, G22, and G29.

Use the Formula Define Names command to create the names. When entering from the list below, position the active cell in the location specified, choose the Formula Define Name command, and type the corresponding name in the box.

Location	Name
C5	Sales
C6	Cost__of__Goods
C7	Net__Sales
G7	Inventory
C9	Current__Assets
G11	Fixed__Assets
G15	Total__Assets
C17	Depreciation
C19	NIBT
G19	Notes
B20	Tax__Rate
C20	Taxes
C21	NIAT
G21	Current__Liabilities
G22	Long__Term__Debt
G23	Total__Liabilities
G29	Earnings
G30	Total__Equity

As you enter these names, the corresponding absolute cell references will be recorded in the Name table associated with this worksheet file.

Enter formulas as follows:

C7	= Sales − Cost__of__Goods
G9	= SUM(G5:G8)
G15	= SUM(G9:G14)
C16	= SUM(C11:C15)
C19	= Net__Sales − SUM(C16:C18)
C20	= Tax__Rate*NIBT
C21	= Taxes − NIBT
G21	= SUM(G18:G20)
G23	= G21 + G22
G26	= (F27*H27) + (F28*H28)

G29	= NIAT
G30	= G26 + EARNINGS
G32	= Total_Liabilities + Total_Equity
C33	= (Current_Assets − Inventory)/Current_Liabilities
C34	= Current_Assets/Current_Liabilities
F34	= NOW( )
C36	= Current_Liabilities/(Total_Assets − Total_Liabilities)
C37	= Current_Liabilities/Inventory
C39	= Total_Liabilities/(Total_Assets − Total_Liabilities)
C40	= Net_Sales/Fixed_Assets
C41	= Net_Sales/Total_Assets
C42	= Net_Sales/Inventory
C43	= NIAT/Net_Sales
C44	= NIAT/Total_Assets
C45	= NIAT/(Total_Assets − Total_Liabilities)
C46	= (Notes + Long_Term_Debt)/Total_Assets
C47	= NIAT/(Total_Assets − Total_Liabilities)
B49	= NOW( )
C49	= H35/(Earnings/(F35 + F36))
B50	= NOW( )
C50	= H36/(Earnings/(F35 + F36))

Enter data as it's shown, or make up your own. Note, however, that the book value of your stock may not be the same as the current market value; the book value is entered in rows 27 and 28, and the market value is entered in rows 35 and 36.

Additionally, make sure the balance sheet really balances; the figure in Total_Assets must equal Total_Liabilities + Total_Equity.

Chapter 10

Using Statistical Analysis

The spreadsheet functions built into *Excel* help you handle statistical operations that might otherwise take a lot of time and computer memory. The functions were presented in Chapter 3, along with a few examples to show how the functions work.

This chapter will demonstrate several applications of statistical analysis, using *Excel*'s capabilities.

Linear Regression

One of the most commonly used statistical functions is the linear regression. This formula uses a series of data as the basis for projecting a straight line of datapoints.

Each data point is computed using the formula

y = ax + b

where *a* is the slope of the line, usually expressed as a decimal, *b* is the constant by which the initial datapoint is offset from the starting point, usually (but not necessarily) 0, *x* is the independent variable, and *y* is the dependent variable. In the example below, the independent variable *(x)* is sales and the dependent variable *(y)* is the quarter.

Most linear regression lines, in attempting to predict a trend over time, are inclined upward toward the right if the values in the range are increasing, and inclined downward toward the right if the values in the range are decreasing (see Figure 10-2).

To set up the worksheet in Figure 10-1, enter the labels as shown in rows 1 and 2, and the column labels for columns A though F and I. Also enter the column labels in G6 and G7.

Figure 10-1. Linear Regression

	A	B	C	D	E	F	G	H	I
1	Linear Regression								
2		Formula: Predicted Sales =(slope*quarter) + intercept							
3			Y= AX + B						
4									
5	Data								Trended
6	Quarter	Sales	X^2	Y^2	X*Y	N	Slope =	2.98	Datapoint
7	1	622	1	386884	622		Intercept	625.70	629
8	2	624	4	389376	1248				632
9	3	652	9	425104	1956				635
10	4	643	16	413449	2572				638
11	5	638	25	407044	3190				641
12	6	649	36	421201	3894				644
13	7	654	49	427716	4578				647
14	8	628	64	394384	5024				650
15	9	644	81	414736	5796				653
16	10	661	100	436921	6610				656
17	11	659	121	434281	7249				659
18	12	667	144	444889	8004				661
19	78	7741	650	4995985	50743	12			

Enter data as shown in columns A and B, from row 7 through row 18. Enter formulas as follows:

C7	= A7^2 (copy this formula to C8 through C18)
D7	= B7^2 (copy this formula to D8 through D18)
E7	= A7*B7 (copy this formula to E8 through E18)
H6	= ((F19*E19) − (B19*A19))/(F19*C19)(A19*A19))
H7	= (B19*F19) − (H6*A19)/F19
I7	= ($H$6*A7) + $H$7 (copy this formula to I8 through I18)
A19	= SUM(A8:A18) (copy this formula to B19 through E19)
F19	= COUNT(A7:A18)

Note that the formula in F19 uses the statistical function COUNT, which counts the number of numeric values in the range specified.

You may wish to add borders, such as summary lines in row 18, or outlines around the slope and intercept formulas and around the trended data, as shown in the figure.

Once you have the worksheet constructed, you may wish to plot the information on a chart. To illustrate the line produced by a linear regression formula, the trended data was charted as well in Figure 10-2.

Figure 10-2. Chart of Linear Regression Data

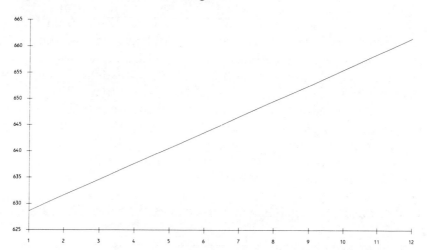

To compare the original data to the trended data, select both B7:B18 and I7:I18. The result is shown in Figure 10-3.

Figure 10-3. Chart of Original Versus Trended Data

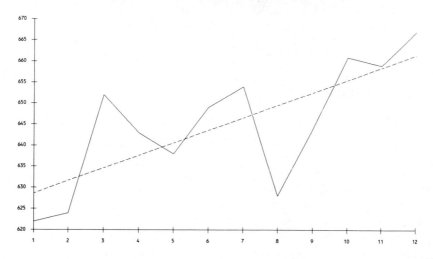

For the next example *Excel*'s built-in TREND function was used to predict a future population.

In this instance, actual census data was used for seven zip codes, and the purpose of the study is to look for the appropriate place to locate a new upscale day care center. The two data items we were looking for were a rising population of children under six years of age and a high percentage of families with incomes over $75,000 (or, as it's shown in the spreadsheet, a low incidence of families with incomes equal to or less than $75,000). The census data used is made up of actual counts for 1980, data updated from a sample in 1987, and projected to 1992.

The probable population of young people in this income category was charted using the census data, producing the table in Figure 10-4.

Figure 10-4. Projected Population of Preschoolers, Selected Zip Codes

	A	B	C	D	E	F	G
1	Population ages 0 to 5 yrs of age by zip code and income						
2							
3				Percent			
4				w/income	1980	1987	1992
5			Percent	=<75,000	Number	Estimate	Projection
6	94306		4.80%	2.10%	24	155	289
7	94301		4.00%	5.11%	48	119	168
8	94025		5.40%	9.60%	121	693	974
9	94043		7.70%	0.80%	14	88	247
10	94041		5.50%	0.40%	5	23	67
11	94040		4.90%	1.70%	19	124	238
12	94022		5.10%	12.50%	149	755	996

The macro in Figure 10-5 predicts future population trends using the trended data for any year.

Figure 10-5. POPTREND.XLM

	A
1	Trendedpop
2	=SELECT("R4C8")
3	=CANCEL.COPY()
4	=FORMULA(INPUT("Please enter year to trend to:",1,"Prompt"))
5	=SELECT("R5C8")
6	=FORMULA("Trended")
7	=SELECT("R6C8")
8	=FORMULA("=TREND(RC[-3]:RC[-1],R4C[-3]:R4C[-1],R4C)")
9	=COPY()
10	=SELECT("R7C8:R12C8")
11	=PASTE()
12	=SELECT("R6C9")
13	=SELECT("R6C8:R12C8")
14	=FORMAT.NUMBER("0")
15	=SELECT("r5c5")
16	=RETURN()

To run the macro, have the worksheet shown in Figure 10-4 on your screen, and select the macro. It will prompt you for the year for which you want a projection; then it will compute the figures. Figure 10-6 shows what happened when the macro was asked to supply 1997 figures.

Figure 10-6. 1997 Projections

	A	B	C	D	E	F	G	H
1	Population ages 0 to 5 yrs of age by zip code and income							
2								
3				Percent				
4				w/income	1980	1987	1992	1997
5			Percent	=<75,000	Number	Estimate	Projection	Trended
6	94306		4.80%	2.10%	24	155	289	389
7	94301		4.00%	5.11%	48	119	168	218
8	94025		5.40%	9.60%	121	693	974	1362
9	94043		7.70%	0.80%	14	88	247	317
10	94041		5.50%	0.40%	5	23	67	85
11	94040		4.90%	1.70%	19	124	238	319
12	94022		5.10%	12.50%	149	755	996	1397

Once the new data is on the screen, use the mouse or arrow keys to inspect the cells containing 1997 data. Notice that the formula in H6 uses the TREND function:

=TREND(E6:G6,E$4:G$4,H$4)

as do the rest of the formulas in column H. The TREND function is an alternative to the approach to trending described in the beginning of this section.

We also charted the data to turn the numbers into a visual representation:

Figure 10-7. Chart of 1997 Projections

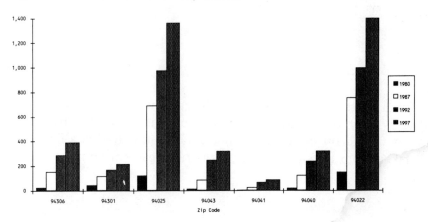

What would happen if the original data for which you were trying to determine a trend were very irregular, with each year's data quite different from the previous year's? The following example (Figure 10-8) was taken from the mean high average daily discharge of one of California's major rivers, over a period of 36 years.

Figure 10-8. Raw Data, River Outflow

	A	B	C	D	E
1	Sacramento River High Mean Daily Discharge				
2					
3					
4					
5		Cu. Feet			
6		per			
7	Year	Second			
8	1	77000			
9	2	68500			
10	3	77500			
11	4	67000			
12	5	48000			
13	6	56000			
14	7	63000			
15	8	49000			
16	9	57000			
17	10	56000			
18	11	60000			
19	12	65000			
20	13	62000			
21	14	67000			
22	15	62500			
23	16	37500			
24	17	71000			
25	18	66000			
26	19	69000			
27	20	63000			
28	21	65000			
29	22	48500			
30	23	63000			
31	24	71000			
32	25	49000			
33	26	74000			
34	27	48000			
35	28	68000			
36	29	59000			
37	30	70000			
38	31	78000			
39	32	64000			
40	33	30000			
41	34	66000			
42	35	76000			
43	36	64500			

If you plotted the real data, you'd get a widely varying line, and necessarily you'd have to be a bit suspicious of any linear trend computed on the basis of that data. Figure 10-9 is a line chart taken from the above data, showing these variations.

Figure 10-9. Line Graph, Raw Data

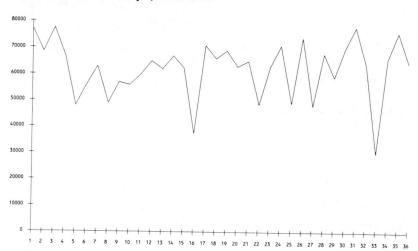

The chart is a little hard to follow. It's hard to generalize anything from it because the volume jumps all over the scale, but there are ways to smooth data statistically. The technique involved is called Moving Averages. This technique averages the raw data over a period of time (in this case 10 years) and produces data that more nearly reflects real trends, rather than simply annual variations, which might be caused by unusual events.

Figure 10-10 uses the same data, this time trended with 10-year moving averages. Note that the first and last five years of raw data don't have comparable averaged figures. That's because the formula needs data spanning 10 years to calculate the moving average.

Figure 10-10. Same Data as Figure 10-8, with 10-Year Moving Average

	A	B	C	D	E
1	Sacramento River High Mean Daily Discharge				
2					
3	Moving Averages				
4					
5		Cu. Feet	10 Year		
6		per	Moving		
7	Year	Second	Average		
8	1	77000			
9	2	68500			
10	3	77500			
11	4	67000			
12	5	48000			
13	6	56000	61900		
14	7	63000	60200		
15	8	49000	59850		
16	9	57000	58300		
17	10	56000	58300		
18	11	60000	59750		
19	12	65000	57900		
20	13	62000	58700		
21	14	67000	60400		
22	15	62500	61600		
23	.16	37500	62300		
24	17	71000	62800		
25	18	66000	61150		
26	19	69000	61250		
27	20	63000	61650		
28	21	65000	60300		
29	22	48500	63950		
30	23	63000	61650		
31	24	71000	61850		
32	25	49000	60850		
33	26	74000	61550		
34	27	48000	62850		
35	28	68000	64400		
36	29	59000	61100		
37	30	70000	60600		
38	31	78000	63300		
39	32	64000	62350		
40	33	30000			
41	34	66000			
42	35	76000			
43	36	64500			

Figure 10-11 shows what happens when this information is plotted on a line graph.

Figure 10-11. Chart of Data, with 10-Year Moving Average

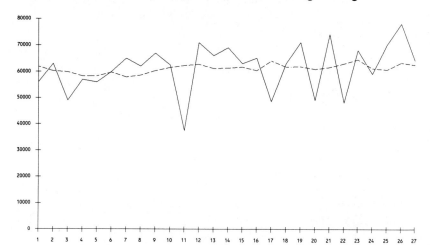

Other Statistical Functions

There are a number of other functions built into *Excel* that help you work with statistical data. Earlier you saw how to do a trend analysis, using the TREND function.

The LINEST function works with arrays to produce the parameters of a projected linear estimate. It works with the least squares method for determining the projection. As a return value you get the slope and intercept, as described at the beginning of the chapter as the basic linear regression formula.

The TREND function produces values on a projected linear trend. It returns values along that line.

The LOGEST function also works with arrays, but produces parameters for a projected exponential curve. As with LINEST, it returns the slope and intercept values.

The GROWTH function produces values along the projected exponential trendline and returns values along that line.

285

Index